Birnbaum's
New O...

A BIRNBAUM TRAVEL GUIDE

Alexandra Mayes Birnbaum
EDITORIAL CONSULTANT

Lois Spritzer
Editorial Director

Laura L. Brengelman
Managing Editor

Mary Callahan
Senior Editor

David Appell
Patricia Canole
Gene Gold
Jill Kadetsky
Susan McClung
Associate Editors

HarperPerennial
A Division of **HarperCollins***Publishers*

To Stephen, who merely made all this possible.

FIRST EDITION

ISSN 0749-2561 (Birnbaum Travel Guides)
ISSN 1061-5431 (New Orleans)
ISBN 0-06-278180-4 (pbk.)

95 96 97 ❖/RRD 5 4 3

Cover design © Drenttel Doyle Partners
Cover photograph © W. Cody/WestLight
Creole cottage, French Quarter, New Orleans

BIRNBAUM TRAVEL GUIDES

Contributing Editors

Gene Bourg
Sharon Donovan
Anita Peltonen

Maps

Mark Carlson
Susan Carlson

Contents

Diversions

A selective guide to a variety of unexpected pleasures, pinpointing the best places to pursue them.

Exceptional Pleasures and Treasures

Directions

Nine of the best tours in and around New Orleans.

Foreword

I made my first visit way down yonder in the early 1960s, and even my first view through a hot and humid August night could not dampen my anticipation about the city that jazz musicians dubbed "The Big Easy." And the nickname tells you a lot about this unique metropolis. It's a city that understands its roots better than most other cities, a place whose leisurely past is at least as important as its very vital present.

Over the years, my husband, Steve Birnbaum, and I would begin a New Orleans morning with fresh-from-the-frying pan *beignets* (no, they *don't* come from the oven), accompanied by the world's best cup of chicory coffee. We agreed that even if the tourist trade had taken away some of the authenticity of Bourbon Street, the bleat of a trumpet or the syncopated sound of jazz emanating from the doors of hot spots along this street that saw the birth of the blues was (and is) guaranteed to quicken your step. For fans of grillwork, the façades of the Vieux Carré continue to attract, and the cadence of a true native accent—most especially if someone addresses you as *chère* (or *cher*) and suggests sharing a bucket of fresh-from-the-Gulf crayfish—is impossible to resist.

The fact that there no longer is a streetcar named *Desire* in no way lessens a visitor's desire to see this Southern-cum-Cajun-cum-Creole city. Big it isn't. But it is easy to love. No doubt about it, the Louisiana Purchase was one of the best buys we ever made.

We have tried to create a guide to New Orleans that's specifically organized, written, and edited for today's demanding traveler, one for whom qualitative information is infinitely more desirable than mere quantities of unappraised data. We realize that it's impossible for any single travel writer to visit thousands of restaurants (and nearly as many hotels) in any given year and provide accurate appraisals of each. And even if it were physically possible for one human being to survive such an itinerary, it would of necessity have to be done at a dead sprint, and the perceptions derived therefrom would probably be less valid than those of any other intelligent individual visiting the same establishments. It is, therefore, both impractical and undesirable (especially in a large, annually revised and updated guidebook *series* such as we offer) to have only one person provide all the data on the entire world. Instead we have chosen what we like to describe as the "thee and me" approach to restaurant and hotel evaluation and, to a somewhat more limited degree, to the sites and sights we have included in the other sections of our text. What this really reflects is a personal sampling tempered by intelligent counsel from informed local sources.

This guidebook is directed to the "visitor," and such elements as restaurants have been specifically picked to provide the visitor with a representative, enlightening, and, above all, pleasant experience. Since so many extraneous considerations can affect the reception and service accorded a regular restaurant patron, our choices can in no way be construed as an exhaustive guide to resident dining. We think we've listed all the best places, in various price ranges, but they were chosen with a visitor's enjoyment in mind.

Other evidence of how we've tried to tailor our text to reflect modern travel habits is apparent in the section we call DIVERSIONS. Where once it was common for travelers to spend an urban visit seeing only the obvious sights, today's traveler is more likely to want to pursue a special interest or to venture off the beaten path. In response to this trend, we have collected a series of special experiences so that it is no longer necessary to wade through a pound or two of superfluous prose just to find exceptional pleasures and treasures.

Finally, I also should point out that every good travel guide is a living enterprise; that is, no part of this text is carved in stone. In our annual revisions, we refine, expand, and further hone all our material to serve your travel needs better. To this end, no contribution is of greater value to us than your personal reaction to what we have written, as well as information reflecting your own experiences while using the book. Please write to us at 10 E. 53rd St., New York, NY 10022.

We sincerely hope to hear from you.

Alexandra Mayes Birnbaum

ALEXANDRA MAYES BIRNBAUM, editorial consultant to the *Birnbaum Travel Guides*, worked with her late husband, Stephen Birnbaum, as co-editor of the series. She has been a world traveler since childhood and is known for her travel reports on radio on what's hot and what's not.

New Orleans

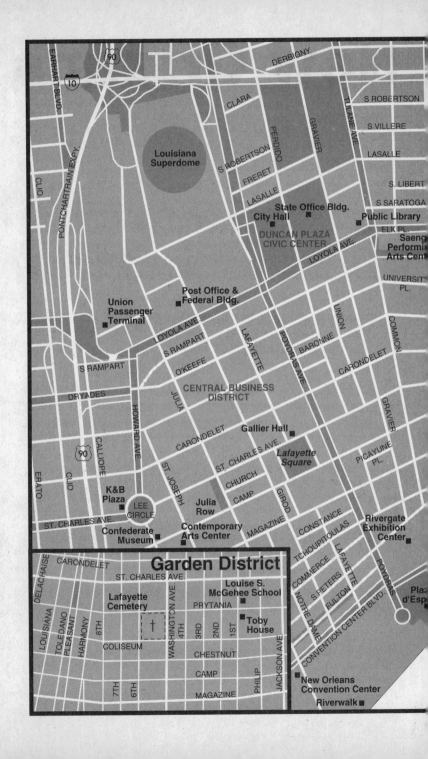

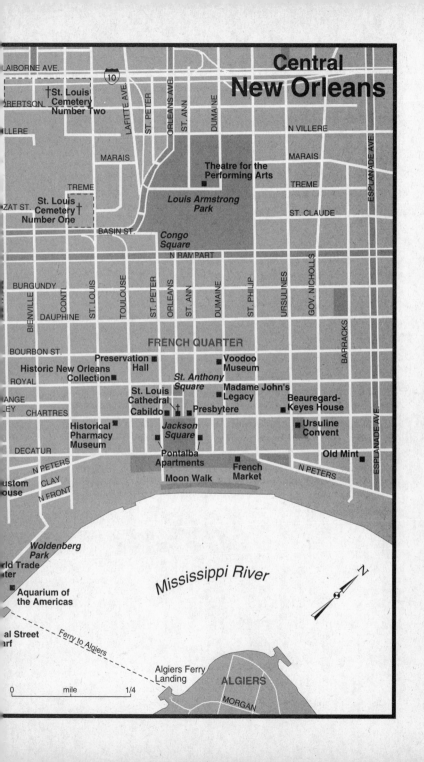

Central
New Orleans

CLAIBORNE AVE.

10

†St. Louis
Cemetery
Number Two

ROBERTSON

VILLERE

LAFITTE AVE.

ST. PETER

ORLEANS AVE.

ST. ANN

DUMAINE

N VILLERE

MARAIS

MARAIS

TREME

ESPLANADE AVE.

TREME

St. Louis
Cemetery †
Number One

ZAT ST.

Louis Armstrong
Park

ST. CLAUDE

BASIN ST.

Congo
Square

Theatre for the
Performing Arts

N RAMPART

BURGUNDY

CONTI

ST. LOUIS

TOULOUSE

ST. PETER

ORLEANS

ST. ANN

DUMAINE

ST. PHILIP

URSULINES

GOV. NICHOLLS

BIENVILLE

DAUPHINE

BARRACKS

BOURBON ST.

FRENCH QUARTER

Preservation
Hall

Voodoo
Museum

Historic New Orleans
Collection

ROYAL

St. Anthony
Square

Madame John's
Legacy

ORANGE

VLEY

CHARTRES

St. Louis
Cathedral
Cabildo

†

Presbytere

Beauregard-
Keyes House

Historical
Pharmacy
Museum

Jackson
Square

Ursuline
Convent

DECATUR

Pontalba
Apartments

Old Mint

N PETERS

CLAY

Moon Walk

French
Market

N PETERS

Custom
House

N FRONT

Woldenberg
Park

World Trade
Center

Aquarium of
the Americas

Mississippi River

N

Canal Street
Wharf

Ferry to Algiers

Algiers Ferry
Landing

ALGIERS

MORGAN

0   mile   1/4

How to Use This Guide

A great deal of care has gone into the special organization of this guide-book, and we believe it represents a real breakthrough in the presentation of travel material.

Our text is divided into four basic sections in order to present information in the best way on every possible aspect of a vacation to New Orleans. Our aim is to highlight what's where and to provide basic information—how, when, where, how much, and what's best—to assist you in making the most intelligent choices possible.

Here is a brief summary of what you can expect to find in each section. We believe that you will find both your travel planning and en route enjoyment enhanced by having this book at your side.

GETTING READY TO GO

A mini-encyclopedia of practical travel facts with all the precise data necessary to create a successful trip to New Orleans. Here you will find how to get where you're going, plus selected resources—including useful publications, and companies and organizations specializing in discount and special-interest travel—providing a wealth of information and assistance useful both before and during your trip.

THE CITY

Our individual report on New Orleans offers a short-stay guide, including an essay introducing the city as a historic entity and as a contemporary place to visit; an *At-a-Glance* section that's a site-by-site survey of the most important, interesting, and unique sights to see and things to do; *Sources and Resources,* a concise listing of pertinent tourism information, such as the address of the local tourist office, which sightseeing tours to take, where to find the best nightspot or hail a taxi, which are the shops that have the finest merchandise and/or the most irresistible bargains, and where the jazz clubs and theaters are to be found; and *Best in Town,* which lists our collection of cost-and-quality choices of the best places to eat and sleep on a variety of budgets.

DIVERSIONS

This section is designed to help travelers find the best places in which to engage in a variety of exceptional experiences, without having to wade through endless pages of unrelated text. In every case, our particular suggestions are intended to guide you to that special place where the quality of experience is likely to be highest.

DIRECTIONS

Here are six walks, two drives, and a streetcar ride that cover New Orleans, its main thoroughfares and side streets, its most charming neighborhoods and historic quarters, and its most compelling outlying communities.

To use this book to full advantage, take a few minutes to read the table of contents and random entries in each section to get a firsthand feel for how it all fits together. You will find that the sections of this book are building blocks designed to help you put together the best possible trip. Use them selectively as a tool, a source of ideas, a reference work for accurate facts, and a guidebook to the best buys, the most exciting sights, the most pleasant accommodations, and the tastiest foods—*the best travel experience* that you can possibly have.

Getting Ready to Go

Getting Ready to Go

When to Go

New Orleans has a subtropical climate. Winters are mild and summers are hot and humid, with frequent showers. From the standpoint of weather, the best time to visit may be in the fall, which offers the most sunshine and somewhat lower humidity. On the other hand, the most popular festivals are scheduled in winter and spring. And even the summer has its attractions—accommodations are less expensive and the city is less crowded.

When planning your visit, note that *Mardi Gras* week is from February 17 to February 28 this year. During this time, hotels are packed, bargains disappear, and reservations are required months in advance.

If you have a touch-tone phone, you can call *The Weather Channel Connection* (phone: 900-WEATHER) for current weather forecasts. This service, available from *The Weather Channel* (2600 Cumberland Pkwy., Atlanta, GA 30339; phone: 404-434-6800), costs 95¢ per minute; the charge will appear on your phone bill.

Traveling by Plane

SCHEDULED FLIGHTS

Leading airlines offering flights to *New Orleans International Airport* include *American, Continental, Continental Express, Delta, Northwest, Southwest, TWA, United, USAir,* and *USAir Express.*

FARES The great variety of airfares can be reduced to the following basic categories: first class, business class, coach (also called economy or tourist class), excursion or discount, and standby, as well as various promotional fares. For information on applicable fares and restrictions, contact the airlines listed above or ask your travel agent. Most airfares are offered for a limited time. Once you've found the lowest fare for which you can qualify, purchase your ticket as soon as possible.

RESERVATIONS Reconfirmation is not generally required on domestic flights, although it is wise to call ahead to make sure that the airline has your reservation and any special requests in its computer.

SEATING Airline seats usually are assigned on a first-come, first-served basis at check-in, although you may be able to reserve a seat when purchasing your ticket. Seating charts sometimes are available from airlines and also are included in the *Airline Seating Guide* (Carlson Publishing Co., 11132 Los Alamitos Blvd., Los Alamitos, CA 90720; phone: 310-493-4877).

SMOKING US law prohibits smoking on flights scheduled for six hours or less within the US and its territories on both domestic and international carriers. A free wallet-size guide that describes the rights of nonsmokers under current regulations is available from *ASH* (*Action on Smoking and Health;* DOT Card, 2013 H St. NW, Washington, DC 20006; phone: 202-659-4310).

SPECIAL MEALS When making your reservation, you can request one of the airline's alternate menu choices for no additional charge. Though not always required, it's a good idea to reconfirm your request the day before departure.

BAGGAGE On major carriers, passengers usually are allowed to carry on board one bag that will fit under a seat or in an overhead bin and to check two bags in the cargo hold. Specific regulations regarding dimensions and weight restrictions vary among airlines, but a checked bag usually cannot exceed 62 inches in combined dimensions (length, width, and depth), or weigh more than 70 pounds. There may be charges for additional, oversize, or overweight luggage, and for special equipment or sporting gear. Check that the tags the airline attaches are correctly coded for your destination.

CHARTER FLIGHTS

By booking a block of seats on a specially arranged flight, charter operators frequently can offer travelers bargain airfares. If you do fly on a charter, however, read the contract's fine print carefully. Federal regulations permit charter operators to cancel a flight or assess surcharges of as much as 10% of the airfare up to 10 days before departure. You usually must book in advance, and once booked, no changes are permitted, so buy trip cancellation insurance. Also, make your check out to the company's escrow account, which provides some protection for your investment in the event that the charter operator fails. For further information, consult the publication *Jax Fax* (397 Post Rd., Darien, CT 06820; phone: 203-655-8746; fax: 203-655-6257).

DISCOUNTS ON SCHEDULED FLIGHTS

COURIER TRAVEL In return for arranging to accompany some kind of freight, a traveler pays only a portion of the total airfare (and sometimes a small registration fee). One agency that matches up would-be couriers with courier companies is *Now Voyager* (74 Varick St., Suite 307, New York, NY 10013; phone: 212-431-1616; fax: 212-334-5243).

Courier Companies

Discount Travel International (169 W. 81st St., New York, NY 10024; phone: 212-362-3636; fax: 212-362-3236; and 801 Alton Rd., Suite 1, Miami Beach, FL 33139; phone: 305-538-1616; fax: 305-673-9376).

F.B. On Board Courier Club (10225 Ryan Ave., Suite 103, Dorval, Quebec H9P 1A2, Canada; phone: 514-633-0740; fax: 514-633-0735).

Halbart Express (147-05 176th St., Jamaica, NY 11434; phone: 718-656-8279; fax: 718-244-0559).

Midnite Express (925 W. Hyde Park Blvd., Inglewood, CA 90302; phone: 310-672-1100; fax: 310-671-0107).

Way to Go Travel (6679 Sunset Blvd., Hollywood, CA 90028; phone: 213-466-1126; fax: 213-466-8994).

Publications

Insiders Guide to Air Courier Bargains, by Kelly Monaghan (The Intrepid Traveler, PO Box 438, New York, NY 10034; phone: 212-569-1081 for information; 800-356-9315 for orders; fax: 212-942-6687).

Travel Unlimited (PO Box 1058, Allston, MA 02134-1058; no phone).

CONSOLIDATORS AND BUCKET SHOPS These companies buy blocks of tickets from airlines and sell them at a discount to travel agents or directly to consumers. Since many bucket shops operate on a thin margin, be sure to check a company's record with the *Better Business Bureau*—before parting with any money.

Council Charter (205 E. 42nd St., New York, NY 10017; phone: 800-800-8222 or 212-661-0311; fax: 212-972-0194).

International Adventures (60 E. 42nd St., Room 763, New York, NY 10165; phone: 212-599-0577; fax: 212-599-3288).

Travac Tours and Charters (989 Ave. of the Americas, New York, NY 10018; phone: 800-872-8800 or 212-563-3303; fax: 212-563-3631).

Unitravel (1177 N. Warson Rd., St. Louis, MO 63132; phone: 800-325-2222 or 314-569-0900; fax: 314-569-2503).

LAST-MINUTE TRAVEL CLUBS Members of such clubs receive information on imminent trips and other bargain travel opportunities. There usually is an annual fee, although a few clubs offer free membership. Despite the names of some of the clubs listed below, you don't have to wait until literally the last minute to make travel plans.

Discount Travel International (114 Forrest Ave., Suite 203, Narberth, PA 19072; phone: 215-668-7184; fax: 215-668-9182).

FLY ASAP (PO Box 9808, Scottsdale, AZ 85252-3808; phone: 800-FLY-ASAP or 602-956-1987; fax: 602-956-6414).

Last Minute Travel (1249 Boylston St., Boston, MA 02215; phone: 800-LAST-MIN or 617-267-9800; fax: 617-424-1943).

Moment's Notice (425 Madison Ave., New York, NY 10017; phone: 212-486-0500/1/2/3; fax: 212-486-0783).

Spur of the Moment Cruises (411 N. Harbor Blvd., Suite 302, San Pedro, CA 90731; phone: 800-4-CRUISES or 310-521-1070 in California; 800-343-1991 elsewhere in the US; 24-hour hotline: 310-521-1060; fax: 310-521-1061).

> *Traveler's Advantage* (3033 S. Parker Rd., Suite 900, Aurora, CO 80014; phone: 800-548-1116 or 800-835-8747; fax: 303-368-3985).
>
> *Vacations to Go* (1502 Augusta Dr., Suite 415, Houston, TX 77057; phone: 713-974-2121 in Texas; 800-338-4962 elsewhere in the US; fax: 713-974-0445).
>
> *Worldwide Discount Travel Club* (1674 Meridian Ave., Miami Beach, FL 33139; phone: 305-534-2082; fax: 305-534-2070).

GENERIC AIR TRAVEL These organizations operate much like an ordinary airline standby service, except that they offer seats on not one but several scheduled and charter airlines. One pioneer of generic flights is *Airhitch* (2790 Broadway, Suite 100, New York, NY 10025; phone: 212-864-2000).

BARTERED TRAVEL SOURCES Barter—the exchange of commodities or services in lieu of cash payment—is a common practice among travel suppliers. Companies that have obtained travel services through barter may sell these services at substantial discounts to travel clubs, who pass along the savings to members. One organization offering bartered travel opportunities is *Travel World Leisure Club* (225 W. 34th St., Suite 909, New York, NY 10122; phone: 800-444-TWLC or 212-239-4855; fax: 212-564-5158).

CONSUMER PROTECTION

Passengers whose complaints have not been satisfactorily addressed by the airline can contact the *US Department of Transportation* (*DOT;* Consumer Affairs Division, 400 Seventh St. SW, Room 10405, Washington, DC 20590; phone: 202-366-2220). Also see *Fly Rights* (Publication #050-000-00513-5; *US Government Printing Office,* PO Box 371954, Pittsburgh, PA 15250-7954; phone: 202-783-3238; fax: 202-512-2250). If you have safety-related questions or concerns, write to the *Federal Aviation Administration* (*FAA;* 800 Independence Ave. SW, Washington, DC 20591) or call the *FAA Consumer Hotline* (phone: 800-322-7873).

On Arrival

FROM THE AIRPORT TO THE CITY

New Orleans International Airport is located 12 miles west of the city center. The ride from the airport to downtown takes from 30 to 45 minutes, depending on the traffic. The taxi fare is set at $21 for up to two passengers, $8 per person for three or more. *Airport Shuttle* (phone: 504-522-3500) provides van service between the airport and downtown and French Quarter hotels for $10 per person for adults (children six and under ride for free).

The *Louisiana Transit Company* (phone: 504-737-9611) runs an *Airport-Downtown Express* bus from downtown at the corner of Elks Place and Tulane Avenue for $1.10 (children three and under ride for free). Note that the *Regional Transit Authority* (phone: 504-569-2700) offers a *VisiTour*

Pass good for one day ($4) or three days ($8) of unlimited travel on all streetcar and bus lines (free for children under three).

RENTING A CAR

You can rent a car through a travel agent or national rental firm before leaving home, or from a regional or local company once in New Orleans. Reserve in advance.

Most car rental companies require a credit card, although some will accept a substantial cash deposit. The minimum age to rent a car is set by the company; some also may impose special conditions on drivers above a certain age. Electing to pay for collision damage waiver (CDW) protection will add to the cost of renting a car, but releases you from financial liability for the vehicle. Additional costs include drop-off charges or one-way service fees.

Car Rental Companies

Agency Rent-A-Car (phone: 800-321-1972 or 504-866-0177).
Alamo (phone: 800-327-9633).
Auto Rent International (phone: 504-524-4645).
Avis (phone: 800-331-1212).
Budget (phone: 800-527-0700).
Dollar Rent A Car (phone: 800-800-4000).
Enterprise Rent-A-Car (phone: 800-325-8007).
Hertz (phone: 800-654-3131).
National (phone: 800-CAR-RENT).
Payless (phone: 800-PAYLESS).
Rainbow Rent-A-Car (phone: 504-468-2990 or 504-821-2248).
Sears (phone: 800-527-0770).
Spinato Car Rental (phone: 504-822-4400).
Thrifty (phone: 800-367-2277).
Value Rent-A-Car (phone: 800-327-2501).

Package Tours

A package is a collection of travel services that can be purchased in a single transaction. Its principal advantages are convenience and economy—the cost usually is lower than that of the same services purchased separately. Tour programs generally can be divided into two categories: escorted or locally hosted (with a set itinerary) and independent (usually more flexible).

When considering a package tour, read the brochure *carefully* to determine exactly what is included and any conditions that may apply, and check the company's record with the *Better Business Bureau*. The *United States Tour Operators Association* (*USTOA;* 211 E. 51st St., Suite 12B, New York, NY 10022; phone: 212-750-7371; fax: 212-421-1285) also can be helpful in determining a package tour operator's reliability. As with charter flights, to safeguard your funds, always make your check out to the company's escrow account.

Many tour operators offer packages focused on special interests such as the arts, local history, sports, and other recreations. *All Adventure Travel* (5589 Arapahoe St., Suite 208, Boulder, CO 80303; phone: 800-537-4025 or 303-440-7924; fax: 303-440-4160) represents such specialized packagers. Many also are listed in the *Specialty Travel Index* (305 San Anselmo Ave., Suite 313, San Anselmo, CA 94960; phone: 415-459-4900 in California; 800-442-4922 elsewhere in the US; fax: 415-459-4974). In addition, a number of companies offer half- or full-day sightseeing tours in and around New Orleans.

Package Tour Operators

ABA Tours and Travel (444 Charles St., New Orleans, LA 70130; phone: 504-525-8585; fax: 504-525-8658).

Adventure Tours (10612 Beaver Dam Rd., Hunt Valley, MD 21030-2205; phone: 410-785-3500 in Baltimore; 800-638-9040 elsewhere in the US; fax: 410-584-2771).

American Airlines FlyAAway Vacations (offices throughout the US; phone: 800-321-2121).

American Express Vacations (offices throughout the US; phone: 800-YES-AMEX).

Capitol Tours (PO Box 4241, Springfield, IL 62708; phone: 217-529-8166 for information; 800-252-8924 for reservations; fax: 217-529-5831).

Certified Vacations (110 E. Broward Blvd., Ft. Lauderdale, FL 33302; phone: 800-233-7260 or 305-522-1440; fax: 305-357-4687).

Collette Tours (162 Middle St., Pawtucket, RI 02860; phone: 800-752-2655 in New England; 800-832-4656 elsewhere in the US; fax: 401-727-4745).

Contiki Holidays (300 Plaza Alicante, Suite 900, Garden Grove, CA 92640; phone: 800-266-8454 or 714-740-0808; fax: 714-740-0818).

Continental Grand Destinations (offices throughout the US; phone: 800-634-5555).

Corliss Tours (436 W. Foothill Blvd., Monrovia, CA 91016; phone: 800-456-5717 or 818-359-5358; fax: 818-359-0724).

Dan Dipert Tours (PO Box 580, Arlington, TX 76004-0580; phone: 800-433-5335 or 817-543-3710; fax: 817-543-3729).

Delta's Dream Vacations (PO Box 1525, Ft. Lauderdale, FL 33302; phone: 800-872-7786).

Domenico Tours (751 Broadway, Bayonne, NJ 07002; phone: 800-554-8687, 201-823-8687, or 212-757-8687; fax: 201-823-1527).

Globetrotters SuperCities (139 Main St., Cambridge, MA 02142; phone: 800-333-1234 or 617-621-0099; fax: 617-577-8380).

GOGO Tours (69 Spring St., Ramsey, NJ 07446-0507; phone: 201-934-3759).

Jefferson Tours (1206 Currie Ave., Minneapolis, MN 55403; phone: 800-767-7433 or 612-338-4174; fax: 612-332-5532).

Kerrville Tours (PO Box 79, Shreveport, LA 71161-0079; phone: 800-442- 8705 or 318-227-2882; fax: 318-227-2486).

Le Ob's Tours (4635 Touro St., New Orleans, LA 70122-3933; phone: 504-288-3478; fax: 504-288-8517).

Maupintour (PO Box 807, Lawrence, KS 66044; phone: 800-255-4266 or 913-843-1211; fax: 913-843-8351).

Mayflower (1225 Warren Ave., Downers Grove, IL 60515; phone: 800-323-7604 or 708-960-3430; fax: 708-960-3575).

MLT Vacations and Northwest World Vacations (c/o *MLT,* 5130 Hwy. 101, Minnetonka, MN 55345; phone: 800-328-0025 or 612-989-5000; fax: 612-474-0725).

New England Vacation Tours (PO Box 560, West Dover, VT 05356; phone: 800-742-7669 or 802-464-2076; fax: 802-464-2629).

New Orleans Tours (4220 Howard St., New Orleans, LA 70125; phone: 800-543-6332 or 504-592-1991; fax: 504-592-0549).

Prestige Programs (136 E. 56th St., New York, NY 10022; phone: 212-759-5821; fax: 212-754-5198).

Saga International Holidays (222 Berkeley St., Boston, MA 02116; phone: 800-343-0273 or 617-262-2262).

Smithsonian Study Tours and Seminars (1100 Jefferson Dr. SW, Room 3045, Washington, DC 20560; phone: 202-357-4700; fax: 202-786-2315).

Tauck Tours (PO Box 5027, Westport, CT 06881; phone: 800-468-2825 or 203-226-6911; fax: 203-221-6828).

Tours and Travel Odyssey (230 E. McClellan Ave., Livingston, NJ 07039; phone: 800-527-2989 or 201-992-5459; fax: 201-994-1618).

Tours by Andrea (2838 Touro St., New Orleans, LA 70122; phone: 800-535-2732 or 504-942-5708; fax: 504-942-5737).

TravelTours International (250 W. 49th St., Suite 600, New York, NY 10019; phone: 800-767-8777 or 212-262-0700; fax: 212-944-5854).

TWA Getaway Vacations (Getaway Vacation Center, 10 E. Stow Rd., Marlton, NJ 08053; phone: 800-GETAWAY; fax: 609-985-4125).

United Airlines Vacations (PO Box 24580, Milwaukee, WI 53224-0580; phone: 800-328-6877).

Companies Offering Day Tours

American-Acadian (2421 Mississippi Ave., Metairie, LA 70003; phone: 504-467-1734).

Gray Line Tours of New Orleans (World Trade Center, Suite 1300, New Orleans, LA 70130; phone: 800-535-7786 or 504-587-0861; fax: 504-587-0708).

Machu Picchu Tours (4450 General DeGaulle Dr., Suite 1117, New Orleans, LA 70114; phone: 504-392-5118; fax: 504-393-6404).

New Orleans Tours (address above).

Tours by Andrea (address above).

Tours by Isabelle (PO Box 740972, New Orleans, LA 70174; phone: 504-391-3544; fax: 504-391-3564).

Travel New Orleans (400 Magazine St., Suite 200, New Orleans, LA 70130; phone: 800-535-8747 or 504-561-8747; fax: 504-522-3790).

Insurance

The first person with whom you should discuss travel insurance is your own insurance broker. You may discover that the insurance you already carry protects you adequately while traveling and that you need little additional coverage. If you charge travel services, the credit card company also may provide some insurance coverage (and other safeguards).

Types of Travel Insurance

Automobile insurance: Provides collision, theft, property damage, and personal liability protection while driving.

Baggage and personal effects insurance: Protects your bags and their contents in case of damage or theft at any point during your travels.

Default and/or bankruptcy insurance: Provides coverage in the event of default and/or bankruptcy on the part of the tour operator, airline, or other travel supplier.

Flight insurance: Covers accidental injury or death while flying.

Personal accident and sickness insurance: Covers cases of illness, injury, or death in an accident while traveling.

Trip cancellation and interruption insurance: Guarantees a refund if you must cancel a trip; may reimburse you for additional travel costs incurred in catching up with a tour or traveling home early.

Combination policies: Include any or all of the above.

Disabled Travelers

Make travel arrangements well in advance. Specify to all services involved the nature of your disability to determine if there are accommodations and facilities that meet your needs. For information on accessibility, contact the *Easter Seal Society of New Orleans* (4937 Hearst Plaza, Suite 2L, Metairie, LA 70001; phone/TDD: 504-455-5533; fax: 504-455-5622), which publishes a booklet called *Access New Orleans.*

Organizations

ACCENT on Living (PO Box 700, Bloomington, IL 61702; phone: 800-787-8444 or 309-378-2961; fax: 309-378-4420).

Access: The Foundation for Accessibility by the Disabled (PO Box 356, Malverne, NY 11565; phone/fax: 516-887-5798).

American Foundation for the Blind (15 W. 16th St., New York, NY 10011; phone: 800-232-5463 or 212-620-2147; fax: 212-727-7418).

Information Center for Individuals with Disabilities (Ft. Point Pl., 27-43 Wormwood St., Boston, MA 02210; phone: 800-462-5015 in Massachusetts; 617-727-5540 elsewhere in the US; TDD: 617-345-9743; fax: 617-345-5318).

Mobility International (main office: 228 Borough High St., London SE1 1JX, England; phone: 44-171-403-5688; fax: 44-171-378-1292; US office: *MIUSA,* PO Box 10767, Eugene, OR 97440; phone/TDD: 503-343-1284; fax: 503-343-6812).

Moss Rehabilitation Hospital Travel Information Service (telephone referrals only; phone: 215-456-9600; TDD: 215-456-9602).

National Rehabilitation Information Center (8455 Colesville Rd., Suite 935, Silver Spring, MD 20910; phone: 301-588-9284; fax: 301-587-1967).

Paralyzed Veterans of America (*PVA;* PVA/ATTS Program, 801 18th St. NW, Washington, DC 20006; phone: 202-872-1300 in Washington, DC; 800-424-8200 elsewhere in the US; fax: 202-785-4452).

Royal Association for Disability and Rehabilitation (*RADAR;* 12 City Forum, 250 City Rd., London EC1V 8AF, England; phone: 44-171-250-3222; fax: 44-171-250-0212).

Society for the Advancement of Travel for the Handicapped (*SATH;* 347 Fifth Ave., Suite 610, New York, NY 10016; phone: 212-447-7284; fax: 212-725-8253).

Travel Industry and Disabled Exchange (*TIDE;* 5435 Donna Ave., Tarzana, CA 91356; phone: 818-368-5648).

Publications

Access Travel: A Guide to the Accessibility of Airport Terminals (Consumer Information Center, Dept. 578Z, Pueblo, CO 81009; phone: 719-948-3334).

Air Transportation of Handicapped Persons (Publication #AC-120-32; *US Department of Transportation,* Distribution Unit, Publications Section, M-443-2, 400 Seventh St. SW, Washington, DC 20590; phone: 202-366-0039).

The Diabetic Traveler (PO Box 8223 RW, Stamford, CT 06905; phone: 203-327-5832; fax: 203-975-1748).

Directory of Travel Agencies for the Disabled and **Travel for the Disabled,** both by Helen Hecker (Twin Peaks Press, PO Box 129, Vancouver, WA 98666; phone: 800-637-CALM or 206-694-2462; fax: 206-696-3210).

Guide to Traveling with Arthritis (Upjohn Company, PO Box 989, Dearborn, MI 48121; phone: 800-253-9860).

The Handicapped Driver's Mobility Guide (*American Automobile Association,* 1000 AAA Dr., Heathrow, FL 32746-5080; phone: 407-444-7000; fax: 407-444-7380).

Handicapped Travel Newsletter (PO Box 269, Athens, TX 75751; phone/fax: 903-677-1260).

Handi-Travel: A Resource Book for Disabled and Elderly Travellers, by Cinnie Noble (*Canadian Rehabilitation Council for the Disabled,* 45 Sheppard Ave. E., Suite 801, Toronto, Ontario M2N 5W9, Canada; phone/TDD: 416-250-7490; fax: 416-229-1371).

Incapacitated Passengers Air Travel Guide (*International Air Transport Association,* Publications Sales Department, 2000 Peel St., Montreal, Quebec H3A 2R4, Canada; phone: 514-844-6311; fax: 514-844-5286).

Ticket to Safe Travel (*American Diabetes Association,* 1660 Duke St., Alexandria, VA 22314; phone: 800-232-3472 or 703-549-1500; fax: 703-836-7439).

Travel for the Patient with Chronic Obstructive Pulmonary Disease (Dr. Harold Silver, 1601 18th St. NW, Washington, DC 20009; phone: 202-667-0134; fax: 202-667-0148).

Travel Tips for Hearing-Impaired People (*American Academy of Otolaryngology,* 1 Prince St., Alexandria, VA 22314; phone: 703-836-4444; fax: 703-683-5100).

Travel Tips for People with Arthritis (*Arthritis Foundation,* 1314 Spring St. NW, Atlanta, GA 30309; phone: 800-283-7800 or 404-872-7100; fax: 404-872-0457).

Traveling Like Everybody Else: A Practical Guide for Disabled Travelers, by Jacqueline Freedman and Susan Gersten (Modan Publishing, PO Box 1202, Bellmore, NY 11710; phone: 516-679-1380; fax: 516-679-1448).

The Wheelchair Traveler, by Douglass R. Annand (123 Ball Hill Rd., Milford, NH 03055; phone: 603-673-4539).

Package Tour Operators

Accessible Journeys (35 W. Sellers Ave., Ridley Park, PA 19078; phone: 800-846-4537 or 215-521-0339; fax: 215-521-6959).

Accessible Tours/Directions Unlimited (Attn.: Lois Bonnani, 720 N. Bedford Rd., Bedford Hills, NY 10507; phone: 800-533-5343 or 914-241-1700; fax: 914-241-0243).

Beehive Business and Leisure Travel (1130 W. Center St., N. Salt Lake, UT 84054; phone: 800-777-5727 or 801-292-4445; fax: 801-298-9460).

Classic Travel Service (8 W. 40th St., New York, NY 10018; phone: 212-869-2560 in New York State; 800-247-0909 elsewhere in the US; fax: 212-944-4493).

Evergreen Travel Service (4114 198th St. SW, Suite 13, Lynnwood, WA 98036-6742; phone: 800-435-2288 or 206-776-1184; fax: 206-775-0728).

Flying Wheels Travel (143 W. Bridge St., PO Box 382, Owatonna, MN 55060; phone: 800-535-6790 or 507-451-5005; fax: 507-451-1685).

Good Neighbor Travel Service (124 S. Main St., Viroqua, WI 54665; phone: 800-338-3245 or 608-637-2128; fax: 608-637-3030).

The Guided Tour (7900 Old York Rd., Suite 114B, Elkins Park, PA 19117-2339; phone: 800-783-5841 or 215-782-1370; fax: 215-635-2637).

Hinsdale Travel (201 E. Ogden Ave., Hinsdale, IL 60521; phone: 708-325-1335 or 708-469-7349; fax: 708-325-1342).

MedEscort International (*ABE International Airport,* PO Box 8766, Allentown, PA 18105-8766; phone: 800-255-7182 or 215-791-3111; fax: 215-791-9189).

Prestige World Travel (5710-X High Point Rd., Greensboro, NC 27407; phone: 800-476-7737 or 910-292-6690; fax: 910-632-9404).

Sprout (893 Amsterdam Ave., New York, NY 10025; phone: 212-222-9575; fax: 212-222-9768).

Weston Travel Agency (134 N. Cass Ave., Westmont, IL 60559; phone: 708-968-2513 in Illinois; 800-633-3725 elsewhere in the US; fax: 708-968-2539).

SPECIAL SERVICES

Wheelchair Getaways (3650 18th St., Metairie, LA 70002; phone: 800-962-9320 or 504-454-1178; fax: 504-455-7315) rents vans designed to accommodate wheelchairs.

Single Travelers

The travel industry is not very fair to people who vacation by themselves—they often end up paying more than those traveling in pairs. There are services catering to single travelers, however, that match travel companions, offer travel arrangements with shared accommodations, and provide information and discounts. Useful publications include *Going Solo* (Doerfer Communications, PO Box 123, Apalachicola, FL 32329; phone/fax: 904-653-8848) and *Traveling on Your Own,* by Eleanor Berman (Random House, Order Dept., 400 Hahn Rd., Westminster, MD 21157; phone: 800-733-3000; fax: 800-659-2436).

Organizations and Companies

Contiki Holidays (300 Plaza Alicante, Suite 900, Garden Grove, CA 92640; phone: 800-466-0610 or 714-740-0808; fax: 714-740-0818).

Gallivanting (515 E. 79th St., Suite 20F, New York, NY 10021; phone: 800-933-9699 or 212-988-0617; fax: 212-988-0144).

Globus/Cosmos (5301 S. Federal Circle, Littleton, CO 80123; phone: 800-221-0090, 800-556-5454, or 303-797-2800; fax: 303-347-2080).

Jane's International and Sophisticated Women Travelers (2603 Bath Ave., Brooklyn, NY 11214; phone: 718-266-2045; fax: 718-266-4062).

Marion Smith Singles (611 Prescott Pl., N. Woodmere, NY 11581; phone: 516-791-4852, 516-791-4865, or 212-944-2112; fax: 516-791-4879)

Partners-in-Travel (11660 Chenault St., Suite 119, Los Angeles, CA 90049; phone: 310-476-4869).

Singles in Motion (545 W. 236th St., Riverdale, NY 10463; phone/fax: 718-884-4464).

Singleworld (401 Theodore Fremd Ave., Rye, NY 10580; phone: 800-223-6490 or 914-967-3334; fax: 914-967-7395).

Solo Flights (63 High Noon Rd., Weston, CT 06883; phone: 800-266-1566 or 203-226-9993).

Suddenly Singles Tours (161 Dreiser Loop, Bronx, NY 10475; phone: 718-379-8800 in New York City; 800-859-8396 elsewhere in the US; fax: 718-379-8858).

Travel Companion Exchange (PO Box 833, Amityville, NY 11701; phone: 516-454-0880; fax: 516-454-0170).

Travel Companions (Atrium Financial Center, 1515 N. Federal Hwy., Suite 300, Boca Raton, FL 33432; phone: 800-383-7211 or 407-393-6448; fax: 407-451-8560).

Travel in Two's (239 N. Broadway, Suite 3, N. Tarrytown, NY 10591; phone: 914-631-8301 in New York State; 800-692-5252 elsewhere in the US).

Umbrella Singles (PO Box 157, Woodbourne, NY 12788; phone: 800-537-2797 or 914-434-6871; fax: 914-434-3532).

Older Travelers

Special discounts and more free time are just two factors that have given older travelers a chance to see the world at affordable prices. Many travel suppliers offer senior discounts—sometimes only to members of certain senior citizens organizations (which provide benefits of their own). When considering a particular package, make sure the facilities—and the pace of the tour—match your needs and physical condition.

Publications

Going Abroad: 101 Tips for Mature Travelers (*Grand Circle Travel,* 347 Congress St., Boston, MA 02210; phone: 800-221-2610 or 617-350-7500; fax: 617-423-0445).

The Mature Traveler (PO Box 50820, Reno, NV 89513-0820; phone: 702-786-7419).

The Senior Citizen's Guide to Budget Travel in the US and Canada, by Paige Palmer (Pilot Books, 103 Cooper St., Babylon, NY 11702; phone: 516-422-2225; fax: 516-422-2227).

Take a Camel to Lunch and Other Adventures for Mature Travelers, by Nancy O'Connell (Bristol Publishing Enterprises, PO Box 1737, San Leandro, CA 94577; phone: 510-895-4461 in California; 800-346-4889 elsewhere in the US; fax: 510-895-4459).

Unbelievably Good Deals & Great Adventures That You Absolutely Can't Get Unless You're Over 50, by Joan Rattner Heilman (Contemporary Books, 1200 Stetson Ave., Chicago, IL 60601; phone: 312-782-9181; fax: 312-540-4687).

Organizations

American Association of Retired Persons (*AARP;* 601 E St. NW, Washington, DC 20049; phone: 202-434-2277).

Golden Companions (PO Box 754, Pullman, WA 99163-0754; phone: 208-858-2183).

Mature Outlook (Customer Service Center, 6001 N. Clark St., Chicago, IL 60660; phone: 800-336-6330).

National Council of Senior Citizens (1331 F St. NW, Washington, DC 20004; phone: 202-347-8800; fax: 202-624-9595).

Package Tour Operators

Elderhostel (75 Federal St., Boston, MA 02110-1941; phone: 617-426-7788; fax: 617-426-8351).

Evergreen Travel Service (4114 198th St. SW, Suite 13, Lynnwood, WA 98036-6742; phone: 800-435-2288 or 206-776-1184; fax: 206-775-0728).

Gadabout Tours (700 E. Tahquitz Canyon Way, Palm Springs, CA 92262; phone: 800-952-5068 or 619-325-5556; fax: 619-325-5127).

Grand Circle Travel (347 Congress St., Boston, MA 02210; phone: 800-221-2610 or 617-350-7500; fax: 617-423-0445).

Grandtravel (6900 Wisconsin Ave., Suite 706, Chevy Chase, MD 20815; phone: 800-247-7651 or 301-986-0790; fax: 301-913-0166).

Interhostel (*University of New Hampshire,* Division of Continuing Education, 6 Garrison Ave., Durham, NH 03824; phone: 800-733-9753 or 603-862-1147; fax: 603-862-1113).

Mature Tours (c/o *Solo Flights,* 63 High Noon Rd., Weston, CT 06883; phone: 800-266-1566 or 203-226-9993).

OmniTours (104 Wilmot Rd., Deerfield, IL 60015; phone: 800-962-0060 or 708-374-0088; fax: 708-374-9515).

Saga International Holidays (222 Berkeley St., Boston, MA 02116; phone: 800-343-0273 or 617-262-2262; fax: 617-375-5950).

Money Matters

CREDIT CARDS AND TRAVELER'S CHECKS

Most major credit cards enjoy wide domestic and international acceptance; however, not every hotel, restaurant, or shop in New Orleans accepts all (or in some cases any) credit cards. It's also wise to carry traveler's checks while on the road, since they are widely accepted and replaceable if stolen or lost. You can buy traveler's checks at banks and some are available by mail or phone. Keep a separate list of all traveler's checks (noting those that you have cashed) and the names and numbers of your credit cards. Both traveler's check and credit card companies have international numbers to call for information or in the event of loss or theft.

CASH MACHINES

Automated teller machines (ATMs) are increasingly common worldwide, and most banks participate in international ATM networks such as *CIRRUS* (phone: 800-4-CIRRUS) and *PLUS* (phone: 800-THE-PLUS). Cardholders can withdraw cash from any machine in the same network using either a "bank" card or, in some cases, a credit card. Additional information on ATMs and networks can be obtained from your bank or credit card company.

SENDING MONEY

Should the need arise, you can have money sent to you in New Orleans via the services provided by *American Express MoneyGram* (phone: 800-926-9400 for information; 800-866-8800 for money transfers) or *Western Union Financial Services* (phone: 800-325-6000 or 800-325-4176).

Time Zone

New Orleans is in the US central time zone. Daylight saving time is observed from the first Sunday in April until the last Sunday in October.

Business and Shopping Hours

New Orleans maintains business hours that are fairly standard throughout the US: 9 AM to 5 PM, Mondays through Fridays. Although banks generally are open weekdays from 9 AM to 3 PM, some stay open later (usually until 5:30 or 6 PM) on Fridays or another day of the week. Some banks also are open on Saturdays from 9 AM to noon. Retail stores usually are open Mondays through Saturdays from 9:30 or 10 AM to 5:30 or 6 PM. Department stores may stay open at least one day a week—most often on Thursdays—until 9 PM. Many retail establishments also open on Sundays.

Mail

The main New Orleans post office, at 701 Loyola Ave., New Orleans, LA 70113 (phone: 504-589-1111), has a self-service section for weighing packages and buying stamps that is open 24 hours a day; counter service is available weekdays from 8 AM to 6 PM, and Saturdays from 8 AM until noon. In the French Quarter, the *Vieux Carré Station* post office, located at 1022 Iberville St., New Orleans, LA 70112 (phone: 504-524-0072), is open weekdays from 8:30 AM to 4:30 PM. Also in the French Quarter, a private firm called the *Postal Emporium* (940 Royal St., New Orleans, LA 70116; phone: 504-525-6651) offers regular mail, UPS, and other services, and is open weekdays from 9:30 AM to 6 PM, and Saturdays from 10 AM to 3 PM.

For additional post office branches, call the main post office or check the yellow pages. Stamps also are available at most hotel desks and from public vending machines. For rapid, overnight delivery to other cities, use *Express Mail* (available at post offices), *Federal Express* (phone: 800-238-5355), or *DHL Worldwide Express* (phone: 800-225-5345).

You can have mail sent to you in New Orleans care of your hotel (marked "Guest Mail, Hold for Arrival") or to the main New Orleans post office (sent "c/o General Delivery" to the address above, with a special zip code: 70172). *American Express* offices also will hold mail for customers ("c/o Client Letter Service"); information is provided in their pamphlet *Travelers' Companion.*

Telephone

The area code for New Orleans is 504. To make a long-distance call, dial 1 + the area code + the local number. The nationwide number for information is 555-1212; you also can dial 411 for local information. If you need a number in another area code, dial 1 + the area code + 555-1212. (If you don't know the area code, dial 555-1212 or 411 for information.) The nationwide number for emergency assistance is 911.

Although you can use a telephone company calling card number on any phone, pay phones that take major credit cards (*American Express, MasterCard, Visa,* and so on) are increasingly common. Also available are combined telephone calling/bank credit cards, such as the *AT&T Universal Card* (PO Box 44167, Jacksonville, FL 32231-4167; phone: 800-423-4343). Similarly, *Sprint* (8140 Ward Pkwy., Kansas City, MO 64114; phone: 800-THE-MOST or 800-800-USAA) offers the *VisaPhone* program, through which you can add phone card privileges to your existing *Visa* card. Companies offering long distance phone cards without additional credit card privileges include *AT&T* (phone: 800-CALL-ATT), *Executive Telecard International* (4260 E. Evans Ave., Suite 6, Denver, CO 80222; phone: 800-950-3800), *MCI* (323 Third St. SE, Cedar Rapids, IA 52401; phone: 800-444-4444; and 12790 Merit Dr., Dallas, TX 75251; phone: 800-444-3333),

Metromedia Communications (1 International Center, 100 NE Loop 410, San Antonio, TX 78216; phone: 800-275-0200), and *Sprint* (address above).

Hotels routinely add surcharges to the cost of phone calls made from their rooms. Long-distance telephone services that may help you avoid this added expense are provided by a number of companies, including *AT&T* (International Information Service, 635 Grant St., Pittsburgh, PA 15219; phone: 800-874-4000), *MCI* (address above), *Metromedia Communications* (address above), and *Sprint* (address above). Note that even when you use such long-distance services, some hotels still may charge a fee for line usage.

Useful resources for travelers include the *AT&T 800 Travel Directory* (phone: 800-426-8686 for orders), the *Toll-Free Travel & Vacation Information Directory* (Pilot Books, 103 Cooper St., Babylon, NY 11702; phone: 516-422-2225; fax: 516-422-2227), and *The Phone Booklet* (Scott American Corporation, PO Box 88, W. Redding, CT 06896; no phone).

Medical Aid

In an emergency: Dial 911 for assistance, 0 for an operator, or go directly to the emergency room of the nearest hospital.

Hospitals and Medical Centers

Charity Hospital/Medical Center of Louisiana (1532 Tulane Ave.; phone: 504-568-2311).

Mercy Hospital (301 N. Jefferson Davis Pkwy.; phone: 504-483-5777).

Touro Infirmary (1401 Foucher St., phone: 504-897-8250).

Tulane Medical Center (1415 Tulane Ave.; phone: 504-588-5711).

University Hospital (2021 Perdido St.; phone: 504-588-3000).

Pharmacies

Eckerd Drugs (3400 Canal St.; phone: 504-488-6661). Open 24 hours daily.

Walgreens (900 Canal St.; phone: 504-523-7201). Open from 7 AM to 9 PM weekdays, and from 9 AM to 7 PM on Sundays.

Walgreens (3311 Canal St.; phone: 504-822-8070). Open 24 hours daily.

Additional Resources

International SOS Assistance (PO Box 11568, Philadelphia, PA 19116; phone: 800-523-8930 or 215-244-1500; fax: 215-244-2227).

Medic Alert Foundation (2323 Colorado Ave., Turlock, CA 95382; phone: 800-ID-ALERT or 209-668-3333; fax: 209-669-2495).

Travel Care International (*Eagle River Airport,* PO Box 846, Eagle River, WI 54521; phone: 800-5-AIR-MED or 715-479-8881; fax: 715-479-8178).

Legal Aid

If you don't have, or cannot reach, your own attorney, most cities offer legal referral services maintained by county bar associations. These services ensure that anyone in need of legal representation gets it and can match you with a local attorney. In New Orleans, contact the *New Orleans Bar Association* (Attn.: *Lawyer Referral Service,* 228 St. Charles Ave., Suite 1223, New Orleans, LA 70130; phone: 504-561-8828; fax: 504-525-6549). If you must appear in court, you are entitled to court-appointed representation if you can't obtain a lawyer or can't afford one.

For Further Information

Tourist information is available from the *Greater New Orleans Tourist and Convention Commission* (1520 Sugar Bowl Dr., New Orleans, LA 70112; phone: 504-566-5011; fax: 504-566-5046), the *New Orleans Tourist Information Center* (529 St. Ann St., New Orleans, LA 70116; phone: 504-568-5661), and the *Louisiana State Office of Tourism* (PO Box 94291, Baton Rouge, LA 70804-9291; phone: 800-33-GUMBO or 504-342-8119; fax: 504-342-8390). For other sources of tourist information for New Orleans, see *Sources and Resources* in THE CITY.

The City

New Orleans

In New Orleans, food for both body and soul drives the urban psyche. And, to a large extent, the spirit of the city is conveyed through its cooks, who conjure up its soul-satisfying food, and through its jazz musicians, who syncopate its rhythms with soul-stirring hot licks or lyrical wails. Some of the city's renowned chefs never use a recipe and some of its best jazz players can't even read music. However, whether it's food, music, or a party that's being created here, intuition, improvisation, and passionate involvement are crucial ingredients; as the local saying goes: "If you ain't gonna shake it, what did you bring it for?"

Although New Orleans (with a metropolitan-area population of about 1.2 million) lacks manufacturing and heavy industry, throughout its long history it has been a center of trade and a source of great wealth for some. But not even the activity of its port on the Mississippi—once second only to New York City in cargo tonnage—has shaken the city out of a certain Old South torpor (which earned it the nickname "the Big Easy"). This languor has been both a blessing and a curse for New Orleans. It has helped to preserve the city's European, 18th-century charms, where in a different place they might have fallen before the trumpet of civic progress. Thus, for the wealthy the city remains a sophisticated, cultured haven. But for the poor, the city's stasis has offered little hope of improvement over the years. The poverty just seems to roll along like the river; and not much has appeared to change it.

Initially, New Orleans was something of a hot property, traded back and forth between governments. First, the French were attracted in the early 1700s by the area's deep, swift harbor. They named the city for Philippe, Duc d'Orléans, the Regent of France, and it served as the capital of the French territories in America from 1723 to 1763, when a Bourbon family pact transferred it to Spanish rule. It was subsequently ceded to France in 1800. Two important developments resulted from all this swapping and ceding: The creole culture, unique to North America, emerged, created by the influences of the French, Spanish, and Africans; and one of the greatest bargains of the century took place. In 1803 Napoleon sold New Orleans and the entire Louisiana Territory—extending from the Gulf of Mexico up the Mississippi Valley to the Canadian border—to the United States for $15 million, doubling the size of US territory. In 1815, to protect this wily investment, General Andrew Jackson and his Kentucky militiamen teamed with anyone and everyone—including the pirate Jean Lafitte, the Choctaw Indians, numerous Creoles, and some black slaves—and defeated the British in the Battle of New Orleans. The War of 1812, unfortunately, had ended about two weeks earlier, somewhat dampening the victors' spirits. (News of the peace treaty had not yet reached the combatants.) Jackson secured the Mississippi River for America, and New Orleans began to grow as a major port for the cotton, sugarcane, and indigo crops grown on the surrounding plantations, and as a kind of Old World cosmopolitan center in the midst of the deep South.

New Orleans sits on the flat plains of the river delta—a crescent of land with the Mississippi to the south, and the bay-size Lake Pontchartrain to the north. A city of 180 square miles, it's divided into several districts, the most famous of which is the Vieux Carré, or French Quarter. Although still the main area of touristic interest in New Orleans, the French Quarter is having some trouble hanging on to its historic charm—the T-shirt shops, fast food chains, and glitzy souvenir boutiques seem to multiply monthly. This is despite the fact that the powerful *Vieux Carré Commission*, a state-constituted agency, is supposed to regulate construction and modification of the district's buildings, as well as their commercial or residential usage. Meanwhile, boisterous crowds of partying tourists, college students, and conventioneers seem perpetually to be streaming through the Quarter even when *Mardi Gras* is nowhere near. For those seeking out more tranquil times here, the tawdry, circus aspect dies down a little during *Christmas* and at the height of summer (if you can stand the sodden heat); during the rest of the year, try weekdays from breakfast time to just after lunch.

Nonetheless, the French Quarter's interesting architectural history can still be traced through its many lovely, centuries-old buildings. Near the end of the 18th century, during the Spanish colonial period, two ferocious fires destroyed all but a handful of the district's French colonial structures; the Spaniards' renovation replaced the simple, classical French architecture with "iron lace" balconies and courtyards. The city's architects of the early 19th century borrowed from both cultures to create the creole hybrid found today on almost every block of the French Quarter. Fine examples of the mixture of cultures and styles are the *Cabildo*, once the headquarters of Spanish colonial rule, and the *Presbytère*. Both buildings (now museums) date to the 1790s and flank *St. Louis Cathedral* at Jackson Square. Each building features wide Spanish arches and a French mansard roof. Completing the Jackson Square quadrangle are the *Pontalba Apartments*, twin structures with French-inspired, red brick façades and elegant wrought-iron balconies.

The French Quarter has other attractions as well. The *French Market* dates from the pre-colonial era, when the site was used by the local Indians as a trading post. It still has a colorful atmosphere and some of the best café au lait on either side of the Atlantic. The best way to see the French Quarter is the old-fashioned way—simply by strolling down its pedestrian malls and sidewalks (preferably when the spring break crowds are nowhere near). Royal Street is closed to traffic from approximately late morning to late afternoon; Bourbon Street is car-free from 7 PM until the wee hours of the morning (although it's usually choked with revelers until sun-up); and Jackson Square never has any traffic.

The riverfront area is another must-see for visitors. At one time, a series of wharves formed a barrier between the Mississippi and the city. These have been removed, and the Mississippi is once more a vital part of New Orleans life—only this time the reason is tourism rather than shipping. The entire riverfront area has been completely renovated; on the riverbank, where Canal Street ends, are a number of noteworthy sites and attractions: the *Aquarium of the Americas;* beautiful Plaza d'España, with its spectacular central fountain and geometric tiles; *Riverwalk Mall,* filled with shops and casual restaurants; and the picturesque Warehouse District, where handsome turn-of-the-century brick structures have been converted into trendy apartment buildings, restaurants, and shops. Across Canal Street and parallel to the French Quarter is Poydras Street, whose high-rises now form the core of the city's business district.

The Garden District, about 30 blocks west of the heart of the French Quarter, is a quaint, beautifully preserved, late-19th-century neighborhood boasting graceful, pristine mansions that were built by prosperous American merchants and shippers to rival the creole townhouses found in the once more affluent French Quarter. Far from the bustle of the city center, the Uptown section, yet farther west, reveals another aspect of New Orleans's multifaceted personality. This leafy district is where you will find *Tulane University* as well as the *Audubon Park* and *Zoological Garden.* To the north, in the direction of Lake Pontchartrain, is *City Park*—which contains an enormous oak grove—the point where tranquil Bayou St. John begins, leading to the lake itself.

In New Orleans, however, you don't just see and feel the city, you must also taste what it has to offer. The indigenous cuisine is creole, which can be homey and hearty or elegant and subtle. Creole cookery is, like everything else from the city's polyglot past, a blend of the French, Spanish, African, American Indian, and Caribbean. The results are so good that in New Orleans they say that when a Creole goes to heaven, the first thing he asks St. Peter is where he can find the jambalaya (a rice dish that's a relative of Spain's paella) and filé gumbo (which falls somewhere between a stew and a soup and contains seemingly infinite combinations of seafood, poultry, game, and charcuterie—sausage). Other key dishes include remoulade, a thick, peppery vinaigrette usually ladled onto cool and spicy shrimp; and bread pudding, often drenched in a custard sauce spiked with rum or bourbon.

And then there is the *Carnival* season—an extravagant blowout that begins shortly after *Christmas* and builds up steam until *Mardi Gras* (Fat Tuesday), the day before *Ash Wednesday.* The tradition of *Mardi Gras* in New Orleans began in the mid-19th century with spontaneous street parades at the approach of the *Lenten* season. In 1857, a group of locals banded together to form the first *Carnival* parading organization, the *Mystick Krewe of Comus.* Other private clubs picked up the idea, which started the tradition of elaborate balls and parades that continues today. The balls are still major social events for all socioeconomic classes of New Orleans, and with rare exceptions are invitation-only affairs. "Kings" and "queens" are chosen from among the *krewe* (carnival club) membership, and in some *krewes,* the balls serve as formal "coming-out" parties for debutantes. But the parades are decidedly public; about 50 of them—they vary widely in size and complexity—are held in the city and its suburbs during the two weeks preceding *Mardi Gras* itself. In addition to the traditional parade floats, there are marching jazz bands and decorated flatbed trucks. Souvenir doubloons, cups, and beaded necklaces are tossed to onlookers. Beginning on the Friday before *Mardi Gras,* the parade routes along St. Charles Avenue and Canal Street are jammed with revelers, and the French Quarter is closed to vehicular traffic to accommodate the crowds. *Mardi Gras*'s royal personages are Rex, King of Carnival, and King Zulu, leader of the city's oldest parading black *krewe,* who shares some of the spotlight with the Big Shot of Africa. Zulu meanders through downtown New Orleans throwing painted coconuts, doubloons, and beads; in its 1909 debut, its antics were meant to satirize the conventions of white society. In the French Quarter, a colorful annual costume competition for transvestites jams the corner of Burgundy and St. Ann Streets, while less competitive maskers in all kinds of outrageous attire roam around. Suburban *krewes* also hold parades on *Mardi Gras;* the principal krewe is *Argus,* which conducts its own parade in Metairie.

Another special New Orleans event that's beginning to rival the *Carnival* season in popularity is the *Jazz and Heritage Festival,* usually held during the last two weeks of April at the *New Orleans Fair Grounds* racetrack. Dozens of top local and national performers—Fats Domino, Aaron Neville, and New Orleans native Harry Connick Jr., to name just a few—hold forth in the open air and in tents.

Mardi Gras and the *Jazz and Heritage Festival* are the best and the worst of times to visit New Orleans. The spontaneous fun reaches great heights, but so, too, do the hotel prices and the frenetic pace. Don't expect the more popular restaurants to operate at their best during these periods. There are other festivals that offer New Orleans in a different mood, without the huge crowds of the city's two biggest parties (see *Special Events*).

At any time of year, however, the place that launched such great jazzmen as Louis Armstrong, Buddy Bolden, Joe "King" Oliver, Kid Ory, and Jelly Roll Morton still swings. The *Old US Mint,* which has been renovated, is the permanent home of excellent exhibitions on how it all began with a merging of African-American and European rhythms. At *Preservation Hall,* Dixieland jazz is played every night; and in countless honky-tonks on Bourbon Street the beat goes on.

New Orleans's legendary jazz funerals still are held occasionally, but they're increasingly rare (once or twice a year at the most). In the traditional "celebration," a marching band accompanies the procession from the church to the cemetery, playing solemn marches and hymns. As soon as the burial takes place, however, the rhythm picks up and the theme changes to something like "Didn't He Ramble" or "I'll Be Glad When You're Dead, You Rascal You." The mourners begin prancing and cavorting behind the band, picking up others who join the "Second Line," though they probably don't even know the person who died. But it doesn't really matter, because when you leave the Big Easy, New Orleans folk act as if you are on your way to the Bigger Easy, and send you off easily. If you're lucky enough to see a jazz funeral be sure to join in; the only way to know one is happening is a mention in the local daily newspaper, *The Times-Picayune.*

Another New Orleans tradition that has become more mythical than real is the exotic cult known as voodoo. Based partly on African tribal rites and partly on Catholic ritual, voodoo is believed to have been brought to New Orleans by slaves from the West Indies—Santo Domingo, in particular—in the early 18th century. Voodoo as a functioning religion disappeared from the city long ago, and the occasional report of a "Black Mass" or other bizarre rite always turns out to be something other than the real thing. In *Fabulous New Orleans,* published in 1928, writer Lyle Saxon, a specialist in local color, recounted witnessing a voodoo ceremony. But even in the 1920s, such events were rare. In any case, no tangible evidence of voodoo seems to exist in present-day New Orleans, though most people you ask would know where to find the memento-draped tomb of 19th-century "voodoo queen" Marie Laveau in *St. Louis Cemetery Number One* (see *Special Places*). One spot in the city with tenuous voodoo connections is Congo Square, across North Rampart Street near the French Quarter, where slaves once gathered to socialize. It may at one time have been used for voodoo rites—there's no way of knowing—but it is now a lush public park.

But myth and folklore are part of this city's charm, as vital to its sense of itself as its carefully preserved creole architecture and the mighty Mississippi that rolls right by. New Orleans is a tasty gumbo of Old South elegance and rowdy rockin' and rollin' good times set to the beat of legendary musicians and fed by transcendent chefs. There is an inspired cross-fertilization of cultures and memories here, added to the simple desire just to have fun. The attitude toward life that visitors find in New Orleans can best be summed up in the phrase that has become a kind of axiom: *"Laissez les bon temps rouler!"*—"Let the good times roll!"

A WORD ABOUT CRIME

New Orleans, like all large US cities, has its share of crime, and the statistics have been steadily worsening in recent years. Visitors are seldom the actual targets of violent crime here, but nonetheless should be on their guard. Generally speaking, this means keeping to the following parts of town: the French Quarter, the Warehouse, Garden, and Central Business

Districts, as well as the Uptown and University areas. Avoid all parks at night, especially *Louis Armstrong Park;* do not enter any cemetery alone, day or night; and stay away from housing projects, where one-third of the city's murders take place.

New Orleans At-a-Glance

SEEING THE CITY

The best bird's-eye view of New Orleans is from the *Top of the Mart,* a revolving bar on the 33rd floor of the World Trade Center, where Canal Street meets the Mississippi River (phone: 522-9795). An observation deck is on the same floor (open daily; admission charge). There is a grand view of the French Quarter and the river from the 11th floor of the *Westin–Canal Place* hotel (see *Checking In*).

SPECIAL PLACES

Nestled between the Mississippi River and Lake Pontchartrain, New Orleans's natural crescent shape can be confusing. North, south, east, and west mean very little here. Residents keep life simple by using terms such as "lakeside" or "riverside" and "uptown" or "downtown" for directions; for more details on how to orient yourself, see the introduction to DIRECTIONS.

FRENCH QUARTER (VIEUX CARRÉ)

Many have wondered why French explorer Jean Baptiste le Moyne, Sieur de Bienville, chose this muggy, low-lying spot to establish a colony in 1718. But back then it was the obvious choice—the nearest habitable spot north of the mouth of the Mississippi River and one of the few places for miles around that lay above sea level. The terrain to the south was, at the time, little more than muck, subject to frequent flooding. To this day, when New Orleans and its environs are hit by one of its monsoon-like rains, the French Quarter sits high and dry, while several inches or more cover the lower sections of the area. The street plan of the Vieux Carré (a term that translates roughly from the French as "old squared area") has not changed since it was first laid out in the 1720s. Most of the streets retain their original names, too. (Also see *Walk 1: The French Quarter* in DIRECTIONS.)

BOURBON STREET Though named for the illustrious French royal family, some say this street now has more in common with the alcoholic beverage that also shares its name. The atmosphere here has been likened to one long, unbroken college spring break. It's legal to drink on the streets throughout New Orleans, as long you are not drinking from metal or glass containers; the legal vessel is the plastic "to-go" cup, offered everywhere. And New Orleans establishments have added many drinks to the bartender's list, with such wicked liquids as the Hurricane and the Absinthe Frappé.

Round-the-clock honky-tonks offer live jazz, which can get wild in the wee hours, and late-night booze, which often leads to morning-after regrets. The seven blocks of Bourbon Street extending from Iberville to Dumaine Streets are filled with a hodgepodge of creole restaurants of varying quality, T-shirt stores galore, tacky corn-dog stands and fast food joints, elegant hotels, sleazy strip joints, jazz clubs, porno shops, and every sort of carny attraction. Often rowdy and raunchy, Bourbon Street has been a hot strip since the postwar years; this is where everybody heads to let it all hang out during the *Carnival* season or after a game in the *Superdome.* The area has a lot of strip joints and peep shows; even if you stay outside, you'll get more of an eyeful than a peep as the hawkers swing the doors open to lure customers. Among the hot spots are Al Hirt's club *Jelly Roll's*—the one place left on Bourbon with any really good music, but just once a week— and the *Famous Door* (see *Nightclubs and Nightlife* for details on both).

PRESERVATION HALL What's recorded in the jazz collection at the *Old US Mint* (see below) still happens live before an audience every night at *Preservation Hall.* In this ramshackle old creole building at the French Quarter's heart, 60- and 70-year veterans of the city's jazz scene perform nightly for an audience sitting hip-to-haunch on backless benches in a ramshackle double parlor. The New Orleans jazz renaissance—begun in the 1960s—continues to this day here as the small Dixieland bands perform classic renditions of "St. James Infirmary Blues," "Rampart Street Parade," and "When the Saints Go Marchin' In." The surroundings are spartan at best, but this is the real thing. Open nightly. Admission charge. 726 St. Peter St. (phone: 522-2841).

ROYAL STREET There really was a streetcar named *Desire* that used to run along Royal Street to Canal from the late 19th century to the 1950s. Though the streetcar is gone, along this street the desire for the past continues, and a stroll down here will yield views of some of the Quarter's finest examples of cast- and wrought-iron balconies and some of New Orleans's most distinctive architecture. The city's finest antiques shops still dominate the blocks between Bienville and St. Peter Streets (see *Antiques: New Orleans's Best Hunting Grounds* in DIVERSIONS), although T-shirt and inexpensive souvenir outlets have proliferated in recent years. The street is a pedestrian mall closed to traffic from late morning to late afternoon every day. Also see *Walk 2: Royal Street* in DIRECTIONS.

HISTORIC NEW ORLEANS COLLECTION Maintained at the aristocratic 18th-century *Merieult House,* this is one of the South's most impressive historical and cultural research centers. All of the materials, dating from the pre-colonial era to the present, relate to the history of New Orleans and Louisiana. They include maps, books, documents, photographs, and artwork that reflect the culture, economy, and politics of the city and the region, all catalogued and available to scholars and researchers (who are advised to call in advance). Among its recent acquisitions are thousands of negatives purchased from the estate of the celebrated New Orleans photographer Clarence John Laughlin. The immediately adjacent *Williams Residence* was once the home of the *Historic New Orleans Collection*'s major benefactors, General and Mrs. L. Kemper Williams, who bought it in 1938 and lived here in the 1940s. They decorated their elegant French Quarter home with numerous valuable and historic furnishings. There are tours of the house and courtyard (inquire at *Merieult House*). Closed Sundays and Mondays. Admission charge for tours of the *Williams Residence* and entry to the *History Galleries* in *Merieult House;* no admission charge to the *Williams Gallery* exhibition space in *Merieult House.* 533 Royal St. (phone: 523-4662).

ST. LOUIS CATHEDRAL While it is the oldest cathedral in the United States, the present-day building is actually the third to occupy the site. The first was the parish church erected by Jean-Baptiste Le Moyne Bienville soon after he founded the colony in 1718. Demolished five years later by a hurricane, the church was rebuilt in 1727, only to be destroyed in the great fire of 1788. In 1793 the parish church was proclaimed a cathedral and the seat of a diocese; a year later, the basic structure existing today was erected, with rounded Spanish-style steeples at the front. The present façade, with its columned entablature and three conical steeples (which took the place of the older ones, which were dismantled) was constructed between 1849 and 1851 to the specifications of architect J. N. B. de Pouilly. This beautiful Spanish-style building also boasts painted ceilings, an altar imported from Belgium, and a bell and clock in the central spire that has marked the hours for the city's inhabitants for more than two centuries. Today it is the seat of the Roman Catholic Archdiocese of New Orleans, and masses, weddings, and other rites are still held here regularly. The interior was completely refurbished in the early 1980s. Markers in French, Spanish, Latin, and English identify those buried in the sanctuary. Tours given daily except Sundays. Donations requested. 700 Chartres St., on Jackson Square (phone: 525-9585).

THE CABILDO AND PRESBYTÈRE Together, the *Cabildo* and the *Presbytère,* the twin Spanish colonial buildings flanking *St. Louis Cathedral* on Jackson Square, form the hub of the *Louisiana State Museum* network. They are filled with exhibits—documents, artifacts, portraits, costumes, and furniture—pertaining to the culture and history of the region. The successor to earlier governmental headquarters on the same site, the *Cabildo* (the Spanish word for "council") was built by the Spaniards in 1795 and served as the seat of the colonial governments of both Spain and France. In a large room on the second floor, documents were signed in 1803 that transferred the entire Louisiana Territory—stretching from the Gulf of Mexico to the Canadian border—from France to the United States. The *Cabildo,* which suffered a fire in 1988, reopened last year with a fresh new look and extensive changes in its exhibits. They are arranged on three floors and cover subject matter from the arrival of the first Europeans in the 1500s to the Reconstruction era after the war. The bronze casting of Napoleon's death mask remains one of the museum's most popular artifacts. There are also some items believed to have been possessions of the pirate Jean Lafitte. The *Presbytère,* once the offices of colonial church officials, is now devoted to temporary exhibitions on the history of New Orleans and Louisiana. Much of the material is related to Louisiana-born President Zachary Taylor; the early days of the shipping industry in New Orleans; and the history of Lafayette City, which is now the Garden District. Closed Mondays. Admission charge. 751 Chartres St., Jackson Square (phone: 568-6968).

JACKSON SQUARE This stately plaza, originally the Place d'Armes, was the town square of the original French colonial settlement and the scene of most of New Orleans's history—from hangings to the transfer ceremony commemorating the Louisiana Purchase. It is also where early French settlers worshiped, peddled their wares, and conducted governmental and military ceremonies. It was rebuilt, and the equestrian statue of General Andrew Jackson, the hero of the Battle of New Orleans, was placed at its center in the 1850s. Today it's a pleasant place from which to watch the passing scene against a backdrop of charming cast-iron and brick buildings, or to browse through shops. Heads no longer roll here, but occasional open-air jazz concerts do, and the only hangings are on the iron fence bounding the area, where local artists display their work. Since the early 1970s, this area has been a pedestrian mall. 700 Chartres (pronounced *Chart*-ers) St., bordered by St. Ann, St. Peter, and Decatur Sts.

PONTALBA APARTMENTS Extending along the two sides of Jackson Square perpendicular to the Mississippi River are these twin, block-long, red brick buildings, said to be the first true apartment houses constructed in the United States. The buildings, each of which contains eight row houses, were designed by Henry Howard for the Spanish Baroness Micaela Almonester y Pontalba. (Her family names, Almonester and Pontalba, are preserved in the "AP" monogram set into the original cast-iron balcony railings. Today, the buildings' upper floors are still private apartments, while the arcades below are lined with ice cream parlors, boutiques, and cafés. The building at 523 St. Ann Street houses the *1850 House,* furnished as it would have been in the mid-19th century (see *Museums*). Jackson Square at St. Ann and St. Peter Sts.

MOON WALK The name of this promenade alongside the Mississippi River may be a bit misleading: It is politically rather than celestially motivated, since it was named for former Mayor Moon Landrieu, whose administration in the early 1970s oversaw numerous physical improvements to the French Quarter's public spaces, including this one. The steps along Decatur Street lead to a landscaped terrace that offers superb views of the river and Jackson Square. Go to the grass-lined walkway right near the river—to the left is the first of many bends the river takes on its way to the Gulf of Mexico; to the right are fine views of the New Orleans skyline and river bridges. Across the levee from Decatur St. at St. Ann and St. Peter Sts.

FRENCH MARKET This is the oldest established marketplace in the Mississippi Valley. Although the five main buildings were erected between 1813 and the end of the 19th century, even before the French explorers arrived in 1718, the site was a trading post used by the Choctaw and other local Indians. The *French Market* still has a colorful atmosphere, with stalls beneath large stone colonnades offering a variety of local produce—try the Louisiana oranges, creole tomatoes, mirlitons (the pale-green, pear-shape squash known in Mexico as *chayote*), sugarcane, and sweet midget bananas—as well as meat and seafood, including live crabs, turtles, shrimp, catfish, and trout. There also are boutiques, cafés, and a large flea market. At Jackson Square and St. Ann Street is the *Café du Monde* (813 Decatur; phone: 581-2914), a bustling New Orleans coffeehouse serving authentic café au lait (half coffee with chicory, half hot milk) and beignets (square, fried crullers dusted with powdered sugar). The café closes only on *Christmas Day,* and the market itself is open daily. On Decatur St. extending from St. Ann St. to Barracks St.

OLD US MINT Designed in the Federalist style by William Strickland, this stately building is the oldest federal mint building still standing. Built in 1835, it minted nearly $300 million in silver dollars and other coins (including Confederate currency) between 1838 and 1909. Later, the building was used as a prison and then as offices of the US Coast Guard. In 1982, it became the home of the *New Orleans Jazz Collection* and *Mardi Gras Museum,* both part of the *Louisiana State Museum.* Fine exhibits trace the development of jazz from its origins in African-American rhythms and the European brass band tradition. Jazz lovers also will find souvenirs of the patron saints of jazz—Louis Armstrong's first horn, Bix Beiderbecke's cuff links, and instruments played by members of the *Original Dixieland Jazz Band.* In addition, there are resplendent costumes worn in the hundreds of *Carnival* parades and balls that precede New Orleans's world-famous *Mardi Gras* celebration. The *Historical Center* (phone: 568-8214), also located in the complex, contains a repository of historical documents from the French and Spanish Louisiana periods; it is open to the public Wednesdays through Fridays by appointment only for on-site research. The *New Orleans Jazz Collection* and *Mardi Gras Museum* are closed Mondays. Admission charge. 400 Esplanade Ave. (phone: 568-6968).

URSULINE CONVENT Constructed in 1734 in French Provincial style, this is the oldest building in Louisiana, and the only one to survive the two devastating fires that swept through New Orleans during the 18th century. Originally the home of the city's Ursuline nuns—who came from France in 1727 to care for the sick and orphaned and to teach the slaves, Indians, and the colonists' children—it later served as a Catholic school for boys, the Louisiana

Legislature, and the official residence of the Archbishop of New Orleans. Today the structure, topped by a mansard roof and surrounded by a brick stucco wall, contains archives of the Archdiocese of New Orleans. Open to the public for tours only on Tuesdays through Fridays at 10 and 11 AM and 1, 2, and 3 PM; weekends at 11:15 AM and 1 and 2 PM; closed Mondays. Admission charge. 1100 Chartres St. (phone: 529-3040).

BEAUREGARD-KEYES HOUSE Although George Washington never slept here, almost everyone else lived in this neoclassical residence, including the legendary chess champion Paul Morphy, Confederate General Pierre G. T. Beauregard, and, in the 1940s, novelist Frances Parkinson Keyes, whose will designated it for use as a museum. It was also here that a local wine maker was shot by a member of the Sicilian Black Hand, a secret organization that operated in the Quarter during the 1920s. Its rooms today are handsomely furnished, with a cozy, un-museum-like atmosphere, and Mrs. Keyes's antique-doll collection is on view. The adjoining formal garden, enclosed by a brick wall and lined with boxwoods, jasmine, and tropical flora, is one of the French Quarter's prettiest. Closed Sundays. Admission charge. It's across the street from the *Ursuline Convent.* 1113 Chartres St. (phone: 523-7257).

MADAME JOHN'S LEGACY This ancient frame cottage is believed to be one of the oldest buildings in the Mississippi Valley, constructed in 1726 by Jean Pascal, a sea captain from Provence who received the site from La Compagnie des Indes, which controlled the Louisiana colony for the King of France. The structure was one of the few to survive the two major fires that all but destroyed New Orleans during the late 1700s. A brick and stucco building, with a sloping roof and colonnaded gallery, it is an excellent example of the West Indies plantation architectural style. The ground floor is enclosed by thick brick walls and has an uneven rough brick floor; the upper floor is made of wood. The building's porch, steeply pitched roof, and depth of only one room were design features that maximized air circulation during the steamy summers. The house's name comes from *Tite Poulette,* a romance novel by 19th-century creole author George W. Cable that chronicles the lives of New Orleans Creoles in the late 1800s. The book's hero lives in the house and bequeaths it to his mistress, known as Madame John. Although it is one of the *Louisiana State Museum*'s properties and has major historical value, it is not open to the public. 632 Dumaine St.

ST. LOUIS CEMETERY NUMBER ONE About a block from North Rampart Street at the edge of the Vieux Carré, this old New Orleans cemetery, dating back to the early 18th century, is literally a diminutive necropolis. The tombs (the city's marshy ground dictated aboveground burial) are interesting for their structure, inscriptions, and number of remains inside (to solve overcrowding, they are opened and the remaining bones are moved deeper into the vault to accommodate new arrivals). Among the illustrious occupants here are Marie Laveau, who used her charms and spells as a voodoo queen in the 1900s; the two wives of Louisiana's first governor, W. C. C. Claiborne; Jean Etienne de Boré, father of the Louisiana sugar industry and first Mayor of New Orleans; and Louisiana historian Charles Gayarre. Many of the brick-and-stucco tombs have crumbled to near-ruin. The earliest decipherable epitaph is that of Nannette F. de Bailly, dated September 24, 1800. Because of the cemetery's isolation, visitors are strongly advised to visit only in daytime, and in large groups. Open daily. No admission charge to the cemetery, but there is a small charge for guided tours. 400 Basin St.

RIVERFRONT/WAREHOUSE DISTRICT

It has only been within the last two decades that the Mississippi River has been reunited with the city it spawned. During the rehabilitation of the waterfront area, huge wharves and sheds were torn down to make way for parks, bandstands, walkways, excursion-boat docks, plazas, hotels, a shopping mall, and public spaces. Stretching from the French Quarter to the Warehouse District, the riverfront has become a favorite spot to relax and stroll for locals and tourists alike. *Riverwalk,* a vast, two-level mall of trendy shops and eating spots, with exterior walkways and sweeping views of the Mississippi, is a remnant of the New Orleans *1984 World's Fair.* Another benefit of that otherwise ill-fated event was that it motivated city planners to rehabilitate many sturdy, handsome old warehouses, stores, and office buildings in the port area. Fashioned mostly of iron, brick, and wood beams, these highly practical, well-made—and often beautifully proportioned— buildings are getting a new lease on life. Their restoration revitalized the entire area, luring apartment dwellers, lawyers, architects, shop owners, and restaurateurs. The district is bounded by Canal and Poydras Streets and Convention Center Boulevard. Also see *Walk 4: The Riverfront (and Farmers' Market)* and *Walk 5: The Warehouse District* in DIRECTIONS.

AQUARIUM OF THE AMERICAS Opened in August 1990 on the bank of the Mississippi, this aquatic adventure has more than 6,000 specimens of marine life on view, including fish, reptiles, birds, and amphibians. The main attractions are the *Gulf of Mexico* exhibit, a two-story, 400,000-gallon tank holding hundreds of species found in the deep waters of the gulf; the walk-through *Amazon Rain Forest,* which re-creates the hot, humid environment of the subtropics with indigenous birds, butterflies, and flora; the *Caribbean Reef,* visible from a see-through, tunnel-shaped walkway; the *Mississippi River Delta Habitat,* featuring the freshwater reptiles and fish that inhabit inland Southern waters; and the sharks and penguins. There's a large and pleasant cafeteria on the second floor. Open daily. Admission charge. 1 Canal St. (phone: 861-2537).

WOLDENBERG PARK Fourteen acres of walkways and park areas bring an oasis-like serenity to the French Quarter riverfront area. Contemporary works by local sculptors are exhibited throughout the park, which also contains benches and a bandstand that is used primarily during festivals. Off Conti St. near the riverfront.

PLAZA D'ESPAÑA The dramatic fountain and intricately patterned tiles that form this huge pavilion along the Mississippi were a gift from the Spanish government in recognition of New Orleans's strong historical Hispanic ties. The pavilion has become a favorite spot for small festivals and band concerts. The *Plaza* is on the riverfront between the *Aquarium of the Americas* (see above) and the end of Poydras St.

ERNEST N. MORIAL CONVENTION CENTER This is the city's primary convention facility, and with more than 700,000 square feet of meeting and exhibition space, it is one of the largest facilities of its kind in the country. Completed in 1985, and later enlarged, it hosts numerous conventions and trade shows. The center's development has spurred a commercial renaissance in the Warehouse District, which each year sees the addition of new apartment and office complexes, restaurants, nightclubs, and shops. 900 Convention Center Blvd. (phone: 582-3000).

CONTEMPORARY ARTS CENTER This colorful, lively complex of exhibition and performance spaces is home to the avant-garde—local and regional artists, playwrights, dance groups, composers, and filmmakers. The strikingly contemporary spaces, refashioned from an early-20th-century drugstore and office building, contain no permanent collections, but the galleries are always filled with interesting new works, many by emerging artists. Closed Mondays and Tuesdays. Admission charge. 900 Camp St. (phone: 523-1216).

JULIA ROW Built in 1830–32 to accommodate newly arrived immigrants, this handsome set of 13 row houses is the Warehouse District's most important architectural setpiece. These elegant red brick buildings—once the homes of some of New Orleans's most well-to-do and socially prominent families—have graceful cast-iron balconies, ornamented entrances, fanlights, and sidelights, which were considered an architectural innovation at the time. After decades of neighborhood deterioration, the row houses were restored by local preservationists in the 1970s. Today, the street-level spaces hold offices and shops. *Julia Row* is along the 600 block of Julia St., west of Poydras and just south of St. Charles Ave. The nonprofit *Preservation Resource Center* (604 Julia St.; phone: 581-7032) offers information and interesting exhibitions concerning the district. The center also provides architectural tours of various neighborhoods; it's closed weekdays.

K&B PLAZA One of New Orleans's first examples of the sleek, modern "international style" of architecture, this creation of the Skidmore Owings Merrill architectural firm is now the headquarters of a regional drugstore chain. On the surrounding terrace are works by such noted late-20th-century sculptors as George Segal, George Rickey, Henry Moore, Jacques Lipschitz, and Isamu Noguchi. The ground-floor lobby also displays works from the K&B corporate art collection—one of the South's most important privately owned collections of contemporary paintings and sculpture. (By the way, if you're wondering why that woman sitting on a bench near the elevators is so immobile, it's because she's one of sculptor Duane Hanson's strikingly realistic creations.) Closed weekends. No admission charge. 1055 St. Charles Ave. at Lee Circle (phone: 586-1234).

CANAL STREET AND THE CENTRAL BUSINESS DISTRICT

Today's commercial hub of New Orleans, bounded roughly by Canal Street, the Mississippi River, Poydras Street, and South Claiborne Avenue, was where the city's English-speaking population first established roots in the mid-to-late 19th century. This is where cotton brokers traded, department stores flourished, and movie theaters first took hold. The blocks of Canal Street nearest to the French Quarter formed the city's primary shopping district for generations, and still contain many structures dating back 100 years or more. Poydras Street, about five blocks from Canal Street in the business district, is the densest concentration of financial, governmental, and legal offices in the city. Several major hotels and a dozen or more new office towers—including the city's tallest building, the 50-story One Shell Square—overlook the street's leafy median. At one end of Poydras is the *Louisiana Superdome,* and at the other end, the Mississippi Riverfront area.

CANAL STREET For most of the 19th century, this broad, tree-lined avenue formed the dividing line between the French sector of New Orleans and the newer, Anglo-Saxon part of town. The origin of its name is uncertain, since no canal ever existed here (although there were half-serious plans in the 19th century to dig one). In the 1800s, Canal Street boasted a couple of opera houses and a number of tony residences. Two private men's clubs—the *Pickwick Club* on the corner of St. Charles Avenue and the *Boston Club* at 824 Canal—are among the last vestiges of the street's aristocratic past. From the late-19th to the mid-20th century, Canal Street was New Orleans's shopping hub. While such long-established department stores as *Maison Blanche* and *Krauss* and a few other specialty merchants still operate, other buildings have either been boarded up or turned into office buildings. In recent decades, the river end of Canal has been the site of continuing development, with construction of the *Canal Place* office building and shopping mall, the *Rivergate* exhibition center (slated for possible renovation or demolition this year), major hotels, and the *Aquarium of the Americas.*

CUSTOM HOUSE Canal Street's most historic structure, the old US Custom House—which takes up the entire block bounded by Canal, Decatur, Iberville, and North Peters Streets—is the city's handsomest specimen of Federalist architecture. A fine example of Greek Revival style is the majestic *Marble Hall* (in the center of the building on the second floor), with its 14 columns of pure white marble that rise to a ceiling of huge iron and ground-glass plates. Begun in 1849, the building was still under construction in 1862, at the peak of the Civil War, and was never completed according to the original plans. The *Custom House* is still home to various offices of the *US Customs Service.* Closed weekends. No admission charge. 423 Canal St. (phone: 589-4532).

LOUISIANA SUPERDOME Completed in 1975, this awesome piece of architectural engineering has been described as the largest freestanding room in the world. Twenty-seven stories tall, with a seating capacity of 100,000 people, it is large enough to accommodate all of Rome's St. Peter's Basilica. The *1988 Republican National Convention,* several *Super Bowls,* and many rock concerts have taken place here. Primarily a football stadium, it is home to the *NFL*'s *New Orleans Saints* as well as to dozens of local high school and college sports teams. Daily tours, lasting 40 minutes, are offered when it's not in use. Admission charge. One Sugar Bowl Dr. at Poydras St. (phone: 587-3810).

GALLIER HALL Considered by many to be the best example of Greek Revival public architecture in New Orleans, the hall was designed by James Gallier Sr. and dedicated in 1853 as *City Hall;* it served in this capacity until the late 1950s. The granite and white-marble building has been restored over the years, and the classically proportioned rooms, separated by a 12-foot-wide central hall, are now used mostly for official receptions. It faces *Lafayette Square,* which contains a touching monument to John McDonogh, the 19th-century philanthropist who was the principal benefactor of the city's public school system. Closed weekends. No admission charge. 543 St. Charles Ave. (phone: 565-7457).

GARDEN DISTRICT

In the early 19th century, part of the 65 square blocks that now compose the Garden District formed a plantation. In the 1850s, the district became a residential community of newly arrived Anglo-Saxon entrepreneurs, and since the turn of the century, its image as an urban expression of Old Southern refinement has remained intact. The houses, in a seemingly riotous conglomeration of architectural styles, and the gardens, lush with tropical greenery and shaded by immense oak trees, blend to create a harmonious and unique neighborhood. Most of the Greek Revival mansions of the Lower Garden District, extending roughly from Lee Circle to Jackson Avenue, have succumbed to the demands of creeping commercialism; they have been converted to shops, restaurants, and galleries, although some are still private homes. Happily, the section beyond Jackson Avenue has retained its timeless air of grace and tranquillity. The best strolling is along and off Prytania Street, between First Street and Washington Avenue. Also see *Walk 6: The Garden District* in DIRECTIONS.

COLISEUM SQUARE When city planners laid out this rectangular park in the Lower Garden District in the 1830s, they designed it as the campus of a university to be called the Prytaneum. Appropriately, they named the nearby streets for seven of the nine Greek muses—Melpomene, Erato, Terpsichore, Clio, Euterpe, Thalia, and Calliope. The university was never built. Instead, the park became the catalyst for a tony neighborhood of Greek Revival residences, most of which remain today. While the square has lost its aristocratic veneer, many of the old homes have been restored. The Prytaneum survives only in the name of nearby Prytania Street.

TOBY-WESTFELDT HOUSE This imposing residence, a raised-frame cottage with a façade of square, white columns, dates from the 1830s. Typical of the period, it was built by Thomas Toby, a Philadelphian who established a large plantation on the site (it once dominated the area that was eventually to become the Garden District). Enclosed within the white picket fence is a garden filled with such typical New Orleans flora as palm and magnolia. Visible from the street is one of the city's finest oak trees, located at the rear of the house. Not open to the public. 2340 Prytania St.

LOUISE S. MCGEHEE SCHOOL "Free Renaissance" was the term used to describe the heavily decorative architectural style of this huge old residence, completed in 1870 and now a private school for girls. Pairs of fluted Corinthian columns define the wide porch at the front of the house. The building contains a fully finished basement, a rarity in New Orleans because of the city's watery substratum. The building is open by arrangement only for groups of 50 or more. 2343 Prytania St. (phone: 561-1224).

1300 BLOCK OF FIRST STREET Many a knowledgeable New Orleanian identifies this as the most beautiful residential block in the city, filled as it is with majestic examples of the Greek Revival style of the mid- to late-19th century. Two especially impressive houses are the residences at No. 1331, with its fancy stucco work, dental molding, and ironwork, and at No. 1315, a stately Greek Revival mansion that has been faithfully preserved in a condition close to the original.

LAFAYETTE CEMETERY Fans of New Orleans novelist Anne Rice will find this an especially interesting spot, since it figures prominently in her *Vampire Chronicles.* Before the Garden District became part of New Orleans, it was a suburban town called Lafayette. The community's cemetery, dating from the mid-1850s, was the first one in the area laid out on a grid of symmetrical lanes and driveways. Most of the aboveground tombs hold the remains of prosperous businessmen and traders who inhabited the fancy residences nearby. The gates are open weekdays from 7:30 AM to 2 PM and on Saturdays from 7:30 AM to noon. Visiting the cemetery alone at any time is not advised. For a fee, guided tours are given by *Save Our Cemeteries,* a preservationist organization, on Mondays, Wednesdays, and Fridays. Washington Ave. between Prytania and Coliseum Sts. (phone: 588-9357).

UPTOWN–UNIVERSITY SECTION

Encompassing some of the most genteel and some of the seediest precincts of the Crescent City, the Uptown–University neighborhoods are, alternatively, leafy, lively, rowdy, and downtrodden. There are high-society denizens and their regal homes near world-famous *Tulane University* (see *Major Colleges and Universities,* below) and *Audubon Park,* as well as middle- and lower-class neighborhoods; near the river are the dive bars and the loafers. The St. Charles streetcar almost perfectly bisects this sprawling area, which stretches from the western edge of the Garden District at Louisiana Avenue to just beyond the last street traveled on the streetcar's route, South Carrollton Avenue; also see *The St. Charles Streetcar* in DIRECTIONS, for further details of the history, architecture, and layout of the Uptown–University neighborhoods.

AUDUBON ZOOLOGICAL GARDEN Once a neglected, foul-smelling place, the *Audubon Zoo* has been transformed since the mid-1970s into one of the country's best. An exotic white tiger is just one of the 1,500 species housed here in habitats that approximate natural conditions. Some fascinating special exhibits re-create in-the-wild environments: Not to be missed is the *Louisiana Swamp,* with alligators and other indigenous creatures slithering and hopping through marshy terrain. Dozens of tropical and shore birds from Louisiana and around the world flit around the trees and shrubs of the huge, walk-through aviary. The *Asian Domain, Grasslands of the World,* and a large pool of frisky sea lions are other favorites. For children, there is a petting zoo, wildlife theater with live animals, and a hands-on natural history museum. Open daily. Admission charge. 6500 Magazine St. (phone: 861-2538).

AUDUBON PARK Under the leafy umbrella of *Audubon Park*'s immense oaks, joggers now tread ground that was, in the late 18th century, a sugarcane plantation. Occupying the 340 acres extending from St. Charles Avenue to the Mississippi River, the park was named for naturalist John James Audubon, who had lived briefly in New Orleans. In 1884–85, it was the site of the *World's Industrial and Cotton Exposition,* commemorating the 100th anniversary of the first shipment of Louisiana cotton to a foreign port. Today it's a haven, not only for joggers, but for picnickers, golfers, tennis players, and bicyclists. While the park's tranquil lagoons are no longer stocked with fish, they form, along with the graceful oaks, a pleasant backdrop for a morning stroll. Main entrances on the 6400 block of St. Charles Ave. and the 6500 block of Magazine St.

AUDUBON PLACE If New Orleans has a millionaire's row, it is this short, private parkway lined with 28 understated but sumptuous residences, which you can only glimpse from the arched gate on St. Charles Avenue; a security guard admits only residents and their visitors through the gate. It was developed early in the 20th century by a Texas real estate speculator, and all but a few of the homes flanking the elaborately landscaped median date from that period. The immense, white-columned manse to the left of the entry gate is the *Zemurray House,* the traditional residence of the President of *Tulane University.* 6900 St. Charles Ave.

ACADEMY OF THE SACRED HEART In 1889 the nuns of the Order of the Sacred Heart opened this school to educate the daughters of prominent creole families, and French conversation and grammar remain a major part of its curriculum to this day. Elementary and secondary students attend classes in the three buildings that overlook a large, pleasant garden near St. Charles Avenue. The red brick façade, with tiers of arched, shuttered windows, columns, and balconies, is one of the most graceful architectural spaces in the city's Uptown section. 4521 St. Charles Ave.

ORLEANS CLUB One of the few buildings on St. Charles Avenue inspired by the creole architecture of the French Quarter, the *Orleans Club* was built in 1868 as a private residence. Since 1925 it's been the headquarters of a local social-cultural women's group, which has carefully preserved the structure's elegant stucco façade, handsome iron lace balconies, and pleasantly man-icured gardens. Not open to the public. 5005 St. Charles Ave.

MILTON H. LATTER MEMORIAL LIBRARY None of St. Charles Avenue's mansions exceeds this one for lavishness. Built in 1907 in the Beaux Arts style and occupying an entire block, it was the home in the 1920s of silent-screen star Marguerite Clarke and her husband, aviator Harry Williams; their Jazz Age parties were the talk of the town. In 1948, the house was acquired by a couple who donated it to the *New Orleans Public Library* in memory of their son, a casualty of World War II. Many of the original mantels, murals, and ceiling paintings remain, making this branch of the city's library the most beautiful of all. Open daily. 5120 St. Charles Ave. (phone: 596-2625).

"TARA" As far as we know, Vivien Leigh and Clark Gable never set foot in this plantation-style residence, but Scarlett and Rhett would have felt right at home here. The house was constructed during the 1940s according to the antebellum descriptions of *Tara* in *Gone with the Wind.* Everything is here, from the lofty columns of partially exposed, whitewashed brick to the elegant arched doorway inset with a fan-shaped window. Not open to the public. 5705 St. Charles Ave.

THE LAKEFRONT

City Park extends almost to Lake Pontchartrain and, along with Bayou St. John, serves as a kind of gateway to the northern section of the city known as The Lakefront. Technically, Lake Pontchartrain, the body of water forming New Orleans's northern boundary, is a bay rather than a lake. In any case, this comparatively shallow, brackish basin has served the city in count-less ways: In winter, the chill of a north wind is warmed considerably as it skims southward; in fair weather, it becomes an ideal playground for picnickers and boaters (although pollution from sewage and industrial sources has made swimming a serious health hazard on the southern, New Orleans side). The northern area of the lake has always been a prime source of trout, crab, and shrimp almost any time of year. Named for Louis XIV's naval minister, Lake Pontchartrain connects with the Gulf of Mexico via narrow straits that have been fertile fishing grounds since before the Europeans arrived. Also see *Drive 1: Esplanade Avenue–City Park* in DIREC-TIONS.

CITY PARK Dozens of graceful ancient oaks and quiet lagoons make *City Park*'s 1,500 or so acres an ideal environment for jogging, tennis, fishing, biking and any number of participatory sports and games. Its occasional sculptures and formal gardens, especially the *Botanical Garden* and *Conservatory,* offer a pleasant respite from the city. From late November to early January each year, a large section near City Park Avenue is transformed into a magical place, with hundreds of thousands of lights and holiday decorations strung along the gigantic oaks. For children, there are all sorts of amusements, including pony and buggy rides, a puppet show, a vintage carousel, a miniature train, paddleboats, and the *Storyland* theme park. In the late 18th and early 19th centuries, when the park was part of the *Allard Plantation,* Creole gentlemen defended their honor here, dueling with swords or pistols under the lacy Spanish moss. Main entrance at Esplanade Ave. and Bayou St. John (phone: 482-4888).

NEW ORLEANS MUSEUM OF ART Built in 1912 by local philanthropist Isaac Delgado, *NOMA* has since become an important American museum. Set in pastoral *City Park,* its permanent exhibits include examples of the major European and American art movements as well as specialized collections, including Oriental porcelains and painting, late Gothic and early Renaissance painting from the *Samuel H. Kress Collection,* fine examples of French Impressionism and 20th-century European painting, a wide array of European and American decorative arts (including jewelry, ornamental pieces, exquisite *Easter* eggs, cigarette cases, and boxes created by Peter Carl Fabergé), contemporary photography, and pre-Columbian and African sculpture. Among the more unusual possessions is a portrait by French Impressionist Edgar Degas of his cousin, Estelle Musson; it was painted during the artist's extended 1873 visit to New Orleans, where his relatives were then residing. A major expansion in 1993 added two floors of exhibition space spotlighting African, Asian, Oceanic, and contemporary art. Lectures and other educational programs are presented frequently in the comfortable auditorium. A gift shop and a restaurant are on site. Closed Mondays. Admission charge. *City Park* (phone: 488-2631).

BAYOU ST. JOHN This gently flowing stream extending from *City Park* to Lake Pontchartrain once connected the heart of the Old City with the lake via canals that have long since been filled in or covered over. The local Indians and early settlers used the bayou to transport their wares into town. The bayou's banks have long been a favorite place for outings. A number of family-style resort hotels once dotted the area near the lake known as Old Spanish Fort; it is now the site of seafood restaurants, apartment buildings, and the city's largest marina. Along much of the bayou's length are some of the city's oldest residences, including the Caribbean-style *Pitot House* (see below), home of New Orleans's first mayor.

PITOT HOUSE Designed in the traditional West Indies style, featuring two stories topped by a high-pitched, gently tapering roof, this small plantation house was originally a country home for the aristocratic Ducayet family, who retreated to the cool edge of Bayou St. John on weekend getaways from their French Quarter cottage. Later, it was the home of the family of James Pitot, who served from 1804 to 1805 as the first mayor of the newly incorporated city. The outer wall construction is of *briquets-entre-poteaux* ("bricks between posts") covered with stucco; the interior has been furnished by the *Louisiana Landmarks Society* with Louisiana and American antique furniture, and fabrics and bibelots in the style of the early 1800s. Closed Sundays through Tuesdays. Admission charge. 1440 Moss St. (phone: 482-0312).

TAVERN ON THE PARK This handsome two-story structure—dating from 1860—faces two massive trees, known as the Dueling Oaks, across the avenue. Designed as a restaurant from the start, it was built 10 years after New Orleans's city government acquired the *City Park* tract for public use. The place gained considerable notoriety early in the century as a boxing arena, a speakeasy, and, at one point in its history, a bordello. In the late 1980s, the building was extensively restored to its present state. Currently, it is home to a steak and seafood restaurant, with an interesting but unpredictable menu. 900 City Park Ave. (phone: 486-3333).

LAKESHORE DRIVE The parkway that extends along much of Lake Pontchartrain's southern shore begins in the west with the *Orleans Marina,* where dozens of sailboats and pleasure craft are berthed when they're not plying the lake's gentle waters. Farther along the breezy landscaped roadway are the old *Southern Yacht Club,* and just past Marconi Drive, the *Mardi Gras Fountains* (memorializing the *krewes* who make the tradition of the pre-Lenten *Carnival* possible), the campus of the *University of New Orleans,* and the *New Orleans Municipal Airport,* now used mostly for private aircraft. On holiday weekends, the miles of grassy strips between Lakeshore Drive and the lake seawall are often filled with picnickers.

LAKE PONTCHARTRAIN CAUSEWAY Stretching more than 24 miles from the Jefferson Parish shoreline to Mandeville, the roadbed—sitting just a few yards above the lake—is advertised as the world's longest bridge. At midpoint, neither shore is visible, but the occasional spectacular sunset or thunderstorm offers respite from the rather monotonous drive. Entrance at the north end of Causeway Blvd. in Metairie. There's a $1 toll each way for passenger cars.

JEAN LAFITTE NATIONAL HISTORICAL PARK, BARATARIA UNIT If a trip to the Cajun country of southwest Louisiana is not practical, this beautiful slice of Louisiana wetlands, maintained by the *National Park Service,* is an excellent alternative. Less than an hour's drive from the French Quarter via the Crescent City Connection bridge to the West Bank, the park contains most of the marshy flora that flourish on the Louisiana coastline. There are a couple of pretty bayous surrounded by moss-draped cypress; one of the bayous is carpeted with beautiful water lilies. Wooden walkways lead from the parking area through rows of palmetto, oak, and cypress. Guided walking tours conducted by park rangers reveal some interesting archaeological and historic sites, and are available daily. No admission charge. 7400 La. Hwy. 45, in Marrero (phone: 589-2330).

METAIRIE CEMETERY This aboveground underworld of towering tombs and memorials pays tribute to some of New Orleans's most illustrious dead, mostly successful business and professional figures of the late 19th and early 20th centuries. The styles of the elaborate stone tombs range from Egyptian to rococo; much of the statuary is monumental. Bizarre examples of funerary art await at almost every turn along the alleys and walkways through the manicured grounds. The cemetery is on Pontchartrain Boulevard at Metairie Road, near the 17th Street Canal. Although the easiest way to get here is via bus tour or car, there is a Metairie Road bus that connects every 45 to 60 minutes to the northbound Canal Street bus from downtown. Although it's a journey of just a few miles, allow at least 45 minutes for travel by public transport. Note: This cemetery is in New Orleans, not in Metairie. A free tape-recorded tour is available at the *Lake Lawn Metairie Funeral Home* (5100 Pontchartrain Blvd.; phone: 486-6331), adjacent to the cemetery.

LONGUE VUE HOUSE AND GARDENS Although built in the mid-20th century, this handsome estate in the elegant, old suburb of Metairie evokes the grandeur of Edwardian England. It was the residence of the late philanthropists Edith and Edgar B. Stern Jr. Beyond the imposing neoclassical entrance, exquisitely decorated rooms contain a trove of treasures—from rare English furniture and porcelain to paintings by major contemporary artists. Inspiration for the design of the fountains and eight acres of gardens came from Mrs. Stern's frequent trips to Europe. Each of the meticulously maintained flower beds, shrubs, and trees is labeled. Closed Sunday mornings. Admission charge. The house is across from *Metairie Cemetery* at the intersection of Bamboo and Metairie Roads and can be most easily reached by tour bus. 7 Bamboo Rd., near Metairie Rd. (phone: 488-5488).

FREEPORT-MCMORAN AUDUBON SPECIES SURVIVAL CENTER Opened last year, this institute is dedicated to the breeding and preservation of such endangered species as the Louisiana black bear and the milky stork. Although the center itself is not open to the public, there is a 130-acre *Wilderness*

Park with nature trails, an education center, and a picnic site at English Turn, Algiers (Algiers is the section of New Orleans that lies across the Mississippi River). Open daily until dark. No admission charge. The center can be reached in 20 minutes by car from downtown; cross the river via the Crescent City Connection bridge (enter from the Warehouse District), then turn north toward Algiers Point, where Patterson Road begins. Call the center for precise directions. 10004 Patterson Rd., English Turn (phone: 861-2537).

EXTRA SPECIAL

Somewhere out there in Louisiana country, the heart of the Old South still beats faintly along the banks of the Mississippi. As late as the end of the 19th century, sugarcane was king in Louisiana, and large plantations established commercial empires, as well as an entire social system, around it. A few of these plantations have been restored and are open to visitors who want to see what the period was like, at least for the people on top. And the life that the Southern gentry created for themselves really is something to see. Just a short drive north of New Orleans, these elegant relics have survived not only the Civil War but countless hurricanes, humidity, and other perils. Among the most impressive are *Oak Alley* (on the west bank of the river at Vacherie), fronted by twin rows of 28 gnarled oaks that form a vast, majestic umbrella; *San Francisco Plantation* (on the river's east bank, north of LaPlace), with a combination of mid-Victorian and Steamboat Gothic ornamentation second to none in the state; *Houmas House* (on the east bank near Burnside), which boasts a magnificent setting and charming auxiliary buildings; and *Destrehan Plantation* (on the east bank in Destrehan), said to be the oldest building left intact in the Mississippi Valley. Detailed maps and brochures are available at hotels and the *New Orleans Tourist Information Center* in the French Quarter (see *Tourist Information,* below). Most of the city's tour companies offer bus tours of the plantation houses. (Also see *Drive 2: New Orleans Plantations* in DIRECTIONS.)

Sources and Resources

TOURIST INFORMATION

The *New Orleans Tourist Information Center,* in the French Quarter (529 St. Ann St., New Orleans, LA 70116; phone: 568-5661), provides a wealth of information on the city's attractions, including maps, brochures, and personal help. It's open daily. The *Greater New Orleans Tourist and Convention Commission* (1520 Sugar Bowl Dr., New Orleans, LA 70112; phone: 566-5011) has information about the outlying areas. It's also open daily. Contact the Louisiana state hotline (phone: 800-33-GUMBO) for maps, calendars of events, health updates, and travel advisories.

Frenchmen, Desire, Goodchildren, by John C. Chase (Robert L. Crager, $12.95), is an entertaining and informative guide to New Orleans's geography and history. Other recommended reading: *The French Quarter,* by Herbert Asbury (Mockingbird Books; $3.50), and *Voodoo in New Orleans,* by Robert Tallant (Pelican; $3.95).

LOCAL COVERAGE The city's daily, *The Times-Picayune,* has a special Friday edition that includes "Lagniappe," an arts-and-entertainment section with a comprehensive list of musical, art, theatrical, film, cultural, historical, and recreational activities. Other useful local publications include *Gambit,* a free arts-oriented weekly found in local shops and restaurants, and *New Orleans,* a general-interest monthly. Two other monthlies, *Tourist News* and *Where,* distributed free in hotels, list restaurants, shops, and hotels.

TELEVISION STATIONS WWL Channel 4–CBS; WDSU Channel 6–NBC; WVUE Channel 8–ABC; WNOL Channel 38–Fox; and WYES Channel 12 and WLAE Channel 32–both PBS.

RADIO STATIONS AM: WWL 870 (CBS, ABC Information, talk/news); WNOE 1060 (talk, news). FM: WWNO 89.9 (classical, National Public Radio); WWOZ 90.7 (jazz and folk); WRNO 99.5 (rock); and WLTS 106.3 (pop and light rock).

FOOD Check *The New Orleans Eat Book* by Tom Fitzmorris (New Orleans Big Band and Pacific Co.; $6.95); and the "Eating Out" column in the "Lagniappe" section of the Friday edition of *The Times-Picayune.*

TELEPHONE The area code for New Orleans is 504.

SALES TAX State and city sales taxes total 9.5%.

GETTING AROUND

BUS TOURS A variety of itineraries is offered by numerous companies operating bus tours of the French Quarter, Garden District, Lakefront, and major points of interest outside the city proper. Among the companies are *American-Acadian* (phone: 467-1734); *Gray Line* (phone: 587-0861); *Machu Picchu Tours* (phone: 392-5118); *New Orleans Tours* (phone: 592-1991); *Tours by Andrea* (phone: 942-5708); *Travel New Orleans* (phone: 561-8747); and *Tours by Isabelle* (phone: 391-3544). All tour companies pick people up, by arrangement, from their hotels.

BUSES AND STREETCARS The city's *Regional Transit Authority* operates buses throughout the city. The St. Charles Avenue streetcar (see *The St. Charles Streetcar* in DIRECTIONS) offers a scenic ride through the Central Business District and Uptown. Board at Canal and Carondelet Streets, or at St. Charles Avenue and Common Street. Special lines include the *Easy Rider,* which circuits the Central Business District and the riverfront; the French Quarter Minibus, operating between Elysian Fields Avenue and Poydras Street; and the Riverfront Streetcar, which runs along the Mississippi River from Esplanade Avenue to Julia Street. Detailed information is available from *RideLine* (phone: 569-2700). Carfare ranges from $1 to $1.25 (express routes are $1.25).

CAR RENTAL If you're planning a visit for *Carnival* or the *Jazz and Heritage Festival*, be sure to reserve wheels well in advance. All of the major national car rental companies have offices in New Orleans. For more information, see GETTING READY TO GO.

CARRIAGE RIDES Mule-drawn carriages, most with fringed tops and holding as many as 10 passengers, may be hired by the hour from early morning to nighttime on the Decatur Street side of Jackson Square. The carriages roll around the streets of the French Quarter as drivers comment on points of interest. Be aware that while carriages are supposedly licensed by the city, they are de facto unregulated, and practices—and prices—can vary. Many of the drivers have been known to deliver "historical" commentary that is more fancy than fact. Do not believe, for instance, that Napoleon died in the *Napoleon House Bar* (the house was offered to the exiled emperor, but he died before he could take up residence) or that Elvis Presley once lived at the *Cornstalk* hotel. Also, some drivers may attempt to give you a subtle sales pitch for some shops or restaurants along the way. Fact or fancy, sit back and enjoy the ride. Two of the companies offering carriage rides are *Charbonnet Transportation* (1615 St. Philip St.; phone: 581-4411), which rents carriages that hold eight to 10 passengers by the hour; and *Gay Nineties Carriage Tours* (1824 N. Rampart St.; phone: 943-8820), which offers a half-hour tour.

FERRY The Canal Street ferry, operating daily from 6 AM to 9 PM, provides free rides back and forth across the river to Algiers (phone: 362-2981).

RIVER TOURS The very best of the river excursions are those aboard the *Natchez,* one of the five remaining steamboats on the Mississippi. The large stern-wheeler departs the Toulouse Street Wharf (behind *Jax Brewery*) twice a day on two-hour runs up and down the river. The scenic tour includes a narrated history of such landmarks as Jackson Square and the Chalmette Battlefield and, for an extra fee, a luncheon buffet of creole specialties. A dinner cruise with live music by the *Crescent City Jazz Band* is also available. For information contact the *New Orleans Steamboat Company* (World Trade Center; phone: 586-8777; 800-233-BOAT for reservations).

In addition, the *Bayou Jean Lafitte* excursion boat departs the Toulouse Street Wharf for the bayou country, to Bayou Barataria, home of the famous pirate; a small paddle wheeler, the *Cotton Blossom,* makes three runs daily from the Canal Street docks to the *Audubon Zoo;* and a high-speed catamaran, the *Audubon Express,* makes six trips daily between the *Aquarium of the Americas* and the *Audubon Zoo* (for information on these excursions, call 586-8777). The motorized, three-decker *Cajun Queen* and the stern-wheeler *Creole Queen* offer both daytime and dinner cruises, which depart from behind the *Riverwalk Mall* and the *Aquarium of the Americas* (phone: 524-0814). *Gray Line* (phone: 587-0861) offers river or combined water and land tours of the city aboard the steamboat *Natchez* and coach bus, as well as swamp and bayou cruises and other combination tours.

TAXIS Cabs can be ordered by telephone, hailed in the streets, or picked up at stands in front of hotels, restaurants, and transportation terminals. Major taxi companies are *United* (phone: 522-9771); *White Fleet* (phone: 948-6605); and *Yellow-Checker* (phone: 525-3311).

VOODOO TOURS Voodoo, the ancient African religion once practiced here, first filtered into Louisiana in the early 1700s. When the government refused to recognize it as a religion and suppressed voodoo rites, believers went underground and voodoo became a cult. Although there are no credible signs that voodoo is seriously practiced in present-day New Orleans, several voodoo-oriented tours are available: a voodoo walking tour of the French Quarter, with a stop at the *Voodoo Museum* (see *Museums*), part of the same outfit that runs these tours; a tour that features a voodoo ceremony; a "Voodoo Ritual Swamp Tour"; and other excursions that wind through mysterious bayous, historic plantations, gardens, villages, Indian burial grounds, and fascinating swamp scenery and wildlife. Tours range from two and a half to 10 hours; for information, contact the *Voodoo Museum* (phone: 523-7685).

WALKING TOURS The *Friends of the Cabildo* (phone: 523-3939) lead walking tours of the French Quarter that begin at Jackson Square; the price includes admission to two of the four following sites: the *Cabildo,* the *Presbytère,* the *Old US Mint* (see *Special Places*), and *1850 House* (see *Museums and Historic Houses*). The *National Park Service* (phone: 589-2636) conducts free walking tours of the French Quarter, *St. Louis Cemetery Number One,* and the Garden District, and occasionally offers specialized tours on subjects that range from the story of pirate Jean Lafitte to the history of the Louisiana legal system. *Magic Walking Tours* (phone: 593-9693) offers on-foot explorations of the French Quarter, the port, and other points relating to such special interests as African history, the Civil War, Storyville, and jazz. The walks offered by *Heritage Tours* (phone: 949-9805) focus on the French Quarter's literary history, with commentary on the places where such writers as Tennessee Williams and William Faulkner lived and worked. *Gray Line* (phone: 587-0861), known for its bus tours, also gives walking tours of the French Quarter that begin at the *Old Ursuline Convent.*

LOCAL SERVICES

For additional information about services not listed below, call the *Chamber of Commerce of New Orleans and the River Region* (phone: 527-6900).

AUDIOVISUAL EQUIPMENT *AV Communications* (210 Decatur St.; phone: 522-9769) and *Jasper Ewing & Sons Inc.* (1904 Poydras St.; phone: 525-5257).

COMPUTER RENTAL *Audubon Computer Rentals* (1036 Annunciation St.; phone: 522-0348) and *New Orleans Computer Rental* (58 Westbank Expwy., Gretna; phone: 394-1324).

DRY CLEANERS/TAILORS *Alessi Cleaners* (837 Gravier St.; phone: 586-9632) and *Gonzales Tailoring* (1015 Common St.; phone: 524-2802).

LIMOUSINES *A Confidential Limousine* (phone: 833-9999); *London Livery Ltd.* (phone: 944-1984); and *A Touch of Class Limousine Service Inc.* (phone: 522-7565).

MECHANICS *MasterCare Car Service* (800 Camp St.; phone: 525-2241) and *Western Battery and Electric Co.* (524 S. Claiborne Ave.; phone: 523-8225).

MEDICAL EMERGENCY For information on area hospitals and pharmacies, see GETTING READY TO GO.

MESSENGER SERVICES *Controlled Business Deliveries* (401 Carondelet St.; phone: 525-9917) and *United Cabs* (1627 Polymnia St.; phone: 524-9606), which offers 24-hour service.

PHOTOCOPIES *Kinko's Copies* (762 St. Charles Ave.; phone: 581-2541; and many other locations).

POST OFFICES For information on local branch offices, see GETTING READY TO GO.

PROFESSIONAL PHOTOGRAPHERS *Mitchell L. Osborne Photography* (920 Frenchmen St.; phone: 949-1366) and *Commercial and Industrial Photographers* (613 Fielding Ave., Gretna; phone: 368-6089), which is on call 24 hours daily.

SECRETARIES/STENOGRAPHERS *Dictation Inc.* (phone: 895-8637), which offers 24-hour service, and *Workload Inc.* (225 Baronne St.; phone: 522-7171).

TELECONFERENCE FACILITIES The *Inter-Continental, Le Meridien, New Orleans Hilton, Omni Royal Orleans,* and *Westin–Canal Place* hotels have teleconferencing facilities (see *Checking In*).

TRANSLATOR *Professional Translators and Interpreters Inc.* (World Trade Center; phone: 581-3122).

TYPEWRITER RENTAL *Office Machine Rental* (605 S. Jefferson Davis Pkwy.; phone: 482-4408).

WESTERN UNION/TELEX *Western Union* (phone: 800-325-6000) has a number of offices, including one downtown (334 Carondelet St.; phone: 529-5971). For information on money transfers, see GETTING READY TO GO.

OTHER *H.Q. Headquarters Company* (1 Canal Pl.; phone: 525-1175) has word processing, telex and fax machines, and conference rooms.

SPECIAL EVENTS

The city kicks off the new year with the annual *Sugar Bowl Classic,* one of football's oldest college bowl games, held *New Year's Day* in the *Louisiana Superdome* (phone: 522-2600). The next celebration of the year is one of the biggest—New Orlean's famous pre-Lenten *Carnival* during the two weeks or so preceding the final blowout on *Mardi Gras* (Fat Tuesday). Since *Mardi Gras* is 47 days before *Easter,* the date varies from year to year; this year *Mardi Gras* is February 28. A score or more of street parades and dozens of costume balls (mostly private) are held, and the French Quarter, especially Bourbon Street, fills with revelers (also see *Mardi Gras Madness* in DIVERSIONS).

The first of this culturally diverse city's many annual ethnic celebrations is the *Black Heritage Festival* in early March; it features food booths, jazz and church music, and art exhibits (phone: 861-2537). The city's Irish Americans celebrate *St. Patrick's Day* (March 17) with a huge street party Uptown in the old Irish Channel and parades in several parts of the city and suburbs. A tradition that dates back to the turn of the century is the *St. Joseph's Day* parade, held on the weekend night nearest the March 19 feast day of the patron saint of Sicily. Italian-American men of all ages, dressed in tuxedos and carrying canes festooned with red, white, and green carnations, file through the French Quarter's streets amid floats, marching bands, and statues of the saint and the Virgin Mary.

One weekend in early April, the *French Quarter Festival* fills the Vieux Carré with parades, food vendors, artists, musical groups, and other performers (phone: 522-5730). Also in early April is the *Spring Fiesta,* highlighted by tours of private French Quarter patios by daylight or candlelight and a nighttime parade (phone: 581-1367).

The city's other huge annual outdoor event takes place in late April and early May. The two-week *New Orleans Jazz and Heritage Festival* features dozens of bands, vocalists, and gospel groups from nearby and around the world, as well as food and crafts stalls. Performances are held in the mornings to late afternoons on the grassy expanse inside the racetrack at the *New Orleans Fair Grounds;* nighttime concerts take place on riverboats and in nightclubs and concert halls. For festival information call 522-4786.

The Greek residents of the city have their day in late May, when traditional foods, crafts, and music fill the *Hellenic Cultural Center* near Bayou St. John for a *Greek Festival* (phone: 282-0259). Food is the focus of the *Great French Market Tomato Festival,* held inside the colonnades of the *French Market*'s complex of food and gift shops in the French Quarter, usually the first full weekend in June (phone: 522-2621 on weekdays only). In July the city celebrates *Carnaval Latino* (phone: 522-9927) and August brings the *Latino Festival* to Canal Street (phone: 524-0427). A few weeks later, in early September, the *Fiesta Latina* takes place at the *Audubon Zoo* (phone: 861-2537). On an early fall weekend, the *Patio Planters* organization conducts afternoon tours of private French Quarter gardens (phone:

566-5068). Italian-Americans are in the spotlight again in October, when the *Festa d'Italia* takes over the downtown Piazza d'Italia with traditional food, music, and exhibits (phone: 891-1904). The *Gumbo Festival* is another of October's special events; it's held in Bridge City, across the Huey P. Long Bridge from New Orleans (phone: 436-4712).

The *Christmas* season is observed in *City Park* with the *Celebration in the Oaks*. From late November to early January, several acres of the park's shrubbery and huge oaks are festooned with spectacular electrical ornaments. During December, the French Quarter celebrates *Creole Christmas*— the historic homes are decorated in 19th-century creole style and restaurants offer special menus replicating the traditional French-creole *reveillon* holiday meal.

MUSEUMS AND HISTORIC HOUSES

In addition to those described in *Special Places,* other notable New Orleans museums include the following:

CONFEDERATE MUSEUM Louisiana's oldest, this small, red stone museum, just off Lee Circle, dates from 1891. Civil War buffs will find a trove of weapons, uniforms, maps, records, flags, and other memorabilia. Closed Sundays. Admission charge. 929 Camp St. (phone: 523-4522).

1850 HOUSE This townhouse, one of the row houses that comprise the *Pontalba Apartments* flanking Jackson Square, has been furnished and decorated as a typical home of prosperous Creoles in the mid-19th century, when the Baroness Pontalba had the twin apartment buildings constructed. A lack of ostentation is the principal asset of the furnishings. Closed Mondays and Tuesdays. Admission charge. 523 St. Ann St. (phone: 524-9118).

GALLIER HOUSE MUSEUM Upper class New Orleans in the Victorian era is mirrored in the elaborate appointments of this meticulously restored mansion in a quiet section of the French Quarter. Designed by architect James Gallier Jr. as his family's residence, the house now features wall coverings, fabrics, rugs, and fixtures that authentically re-create the lifestyle of 1857. The small, simple garden contains a facsimile of the house's cistern, and a carriage sits ready in the carriageway separating the residence from the gift shop. After each tour, coffee is served on the balcony overlooking an especially picturesque block of Royal Street. Closed Sundays. Admission charge. 1118-1132 Royal St. (phone: 523-6722).

HERMANN-GRIMA HOUSE A small army of historians, botanists, and social scientists took part in the restoration of this aristocratic, red brick residence to its original state. Built in 1831 by a wealthy merchant at the outset of New Orleans's "golden age" (1830 to 1860), the house, with rooms flanking a central hall, was a departure from the typical creole floor plan of the era. The details are remarkably authentic, from the harnesses in the stables and the aromatic plants in the garden, to the cast-iron pots and beehive ovens of the kitchen, where creole cooking demonstrations take place each Thursday from October through May (there's also an annual cooking workshop in the spring). The appointments in the living quarters also are true to the period. Closed Sundays. Admission charge. 820 St. Louis St. (phone: 525-5661).

HISTORICAL PHARMACY MUSEUM In the 1820s, this little shop was the apothecary of Louis J. Dufilho, said to have been the first licensed pharmacist in the US. Its displays of 19th-century jars and equipment may not be as interesting as the quaint old rooms and the charming interior herbal and botanical garden. Closed Mondays. Admission charge. 514 Chartres St. (phone: 524-9077).

LOUISIANA CHILDREN'S MUSEUM More play-school than museum, this cleverly designed spot features all kinds of hands-on fun for kids under 12. It contains a little coffee factory, a "Safety City" driving exhibit, and miniature versions of a supermarket, TV studio, and hospital. Closed Mondays. Admission charge. 428 Julia St. (phone: 523-1357).

LOUISIANA NATURE AND SCIENCE CENTER Several of the natural sciences are spotlighted in this small museum, which is connected to nature trails on the city's eastern edge. The planetarium offers a number of astronomical programs (usually on weekends) as well as laser rock shows. Raised wooden walkways winding through the surrounding woods afford visitors a short, pleasant hike, and the center's staff also plans hiking and backpacking excursions into areas outside the city proper. Closed Mondays. Admission charge. *Joe Brown Park;* enter at Read Blvd. and Nature Center Dr. (phone: 246-5672; 246-9381 for recorded information).

MUSÉE CONTI WAX MUSEUM Voodoo, *Mardi Gras,* and the pirate Jean Lafitte are represented in the numerous tableaux here, featuring life-size wax mannequins in elaborate stage settings. Major events and personages of New Orleans's colorful history are the focus. There's printed and tape-recorded commentary. Open daily. Admission charge. 917 Conti St. (phone: 525-2605).

RIVERTOWN There are several small museums contained in these nostalgically designed buildings situated on the Mississippi River in the New Orleans suburb of Kenner. The *Freeport-McMoRan Daily Living Science Center* has a planetarium and observatory (409 Williams Blvd.; phone: 582-4000). Six working layouts of toy trains, trolleys, and a toy carousel are on display in the *Louisiana Toy Train Museum* (519 Williams Blvd.; phone: 468-7223). The *Louisiana Wildlife and Fisheries Museum* (303 Williams Blvd.; phone: 468-7232) features an aquarium and preserved wildlife specimens and displays. And the *Saints Hall of Fame Museum* (409 Williams Blvd.; phone: 468-6617) contains memorabilia of New Orleans's pro football team. All are closed Sunday mornings and Mondays; admission charge for each, but discount passes also are sold for those intending to visit more than one museum. The *Mardi Gras Museum* (see *Old US Mint,* above, in *Special Places*) is also included in this discount pass.

VOODOO MUSEUM Despite its name, this tiny outfit is really more a tourist shop than a museum. It displays African masks and voodoo dolls, and sells souvenirs inspired by the voodoo practices that once flourished in the city. Open daily. Admission charge. 724 Dumaine St. (phone: 523-7685).

MAJOR COLLEGES AND UNIVERSITIES

Tulane University (6400 St. Charles Ave.; phone: 865-5000) is one of the South's leading private universities. A bequest by philanthropist Paul Tulane in 1883 allowed an expansion that resulted in today's 93-acre campus. *Gibson Hall,* the Romanesque stone building facing St. Charles Avenue, was built in 1894, and now contains the *College of Arts and Sciences* and major administrative offices. *Tulane*'s sister institution, the *Sophie H. Newcomb College for Women,* adjoins *Tulane*'s central campus but has a separate dean and faculty. The university's *School of Medicine* and teaching hospital are in the Central Business District (6823 St. Charles Ave.; phone: 588-5187). Adjacent to the *Tulane University* campus is *Loyola University* (6363 St. Charles Ave.; phone: 865-2011), New Orleans's largest Catholic university, founded by the Society of Jesus in 1911. The open quadrangle facing St. Charles Avenue contains red brick buildings in the Tudor-Gothic style, which also inspired the design of the richly furnished *Holy Name of Jesus Church,* to the left of the quadrangle. *Loyola* maintains a *College of Music,* a *School of Law,* and departments of philosophy, theater, and English. The *University of New Orleans* (Elysian Fields near Lakeshore Dr.; phone: 286-6000) was once a branch campus of *Louisiana State University* in Baton Rouge; it became an independent institution in the 1960s.

SHOPPING

Although the largest shopping centers are found in the surrounding suburbs, downtown New Orleans also contains several major malls offering an immense variety of merchandise, as well as hundreds of specialty shops. The principal malls are the *New Orleans Centre* (just steps away from the *Louisiana Superdome* on Poydras St.), where *Macy's* and *Lord & Taylor* are the main tenants; *Canal Place* (at 333 Canal St. near the Mississippi River), with a three-level branch of *Saks Fifth Avenue* and a large *Brooks Brothers;* and *Riverwalk* (extending along the riverfront near Canal St.), with two levels of restaurants and shops that include *Banana Republic* (casual clothing), *Abercrombie & Fitch* (sportswear and gifts), and *Sharper Image* (electronic gadgets). Canal Street itself still contains a few department stores harking back to its years as the city's shopping artery; the two major ones are the upscale *Maison Blanche* (901 Canal St.; phone: 566-1000) and *Krauss* (1201 Canal St., phone: 523-3311). Each is a full-scale emporium. Antiques hunters should focus their attention on the French

Quarter, especially Royal and Chartres Streets, which contain all sorts of antiques shops and art galleries, and, farther out from the city center, Magazine Street, which contains dozens of stores offering moderate to expensive antique furniture, rugs, bric-a-brac, and artwork, from regional to European (also see *Antiques: New Orleans's Best Hunting Grounds* in DIVERSIONS). The following is a list of New Orleans's favorite shopping places.

Adler's A large selection of jewelry, porcelain, gifts, and bibelots fills the two floors of this plush establishment, now operated by the third generation of the Adler family. 723 Canal St. (phone: 523-5292).

Alfredo's Cameras Expert advice and a wide range of cameras and photographic equipment. 916 Gravier St. (phone: 523-2421).

Arthur Roger Gallery Top contemporary artists from New Orleans and other parts of the country show their paintings and sculpture in this spacious, elegantly designed gallery in the Warehouse District. 432 Julia St. (phone: 522-1990).

B. Dalton Bookseller A good place to seek out local guides, it also specializes in professional, technical, and other practical books. 714 Canal St. (phone: 529-2705).

Ballin's Women's and children's clothes, from the frilly to the very up-to-date, are the specialty here, with many well-known designer labels on the racks. 721 Dante St. (phone: 866-4367) and *New Orleans Centre,* 1400 Poydras St. (phone: 561-1100).

Bep's Antiques Modest treasures—you just might discover that indispensable objet d'art among the hundreds of old bottles, homey Victorian washstands, and charming little side tables. 2051 Magazine St. (phone: 525-7726).

Bergeron's Dozens of styles by top designers are the stock-in-trade at the city's preeminent source of fine-quality women's shoes. Unusual handbags are another specialty. *Canal Place,* 333 Canal St. (phone: 525-2195).

Bookstar Two very large floors filled with every type of publication. A good selection of audiotapes, magazines, and maps, too. 414 N. Peters St. (phone: 523-6411).

Brass Menagerie If it's brass, this place almost certainly stocks it—everything from faucets to coat hooks. 524 St. Louis St. (phone: 524-0921).

Central Grocery Co. Known for its muffuletta sandwiches and a huge array of Italian food specialties, this is also a good source for a wide variety of non-perishable groceries from around the world. 923 Decatur St. (phone: 523-1620).

Coghlan Gallery This shop features odds and ends to decorate your garden or terrace, including hand-crafted copper fountains and other ornaments. 710 Toulouse St. (phone: 525-8550).

Cuisine Classique You're more than likely to leave here with something for your kitchen that you didn't know you needed—an oversize stockpot, an apple corer, or a lemon zester. Along with the vast array of cooking tools offered, there is also a wide selection of local cookbooks. 439 Decatur St. (phone: 524-0068).

DeVille Books & Prints This is the place to check for hard-to-find authors and unusual literary works. The art, architecture, and photography sections are especially well stocked. Three locations: 1 Shell Sq., St. Charles Ave. at Poydras St. (phone: 525-1846); *Jax Brewery,* 620 Decatur (phone: 525-4508); and *Riverwalk Mall,* Poydras St. at the Mississippi River (phone: 595-8916).

Ditto 19th Century Antiques Specializes in clocks, cut-glass, and above-average bric-a-brac. 4838 Magazine St. (phone: 891-4845).

Esprit Moderate prices and chic casual styles for children and teens. 901 St. Charles Ave. (phone: 561-5050).

French Market This famous market sells a wide variety of items—souvenirs, sweets (including pralines), toys, candles, and funky clothes, just to name a few. Vendors' stalls set up along the street offer a cornucopia of fresh fruits and vegetables, as well as old books and records, tropical plants, and a hodgepodge of creole and Cajun spices. Decatur St., between St. Ann and Barracks Sts.

F. W. Woolworth The old five-and-dime is alive and well at two centrally located stores. 737 Canal St. (phone: 522-6426) and 1041 Canal St. (phone: 522-7461).

Galerie Simonne Stern Aficionados of abstract expressionism and other 20th-century schools of art should find this prestigious gallery worth a visit. Emerging local, regional, and national artists are featured in the ever-changing exhibitions. 518 Julia St. (phone: 529-1118) and 305 Royal St. (phone: 524-9757).

A Gallery for Fine Photography The work of the world's best-known photographers, from Matthew Brady to Irving Penn, are represented in this vast collection, shown on two floors. Also look for rare and unusual photographs relating to New Orleans, especially its musicians. 322 Royal (phone: 568-1313).

Gasperi Gallery Contemporary folk art and works that have strong ethnic connections. 320 Julia St. (phone: 524-9373).

Henry Stern Antiques A long-established dealer in fine English furniture and paintings from the late 18th and early 19th centuries. 329-331 Royal St. (phone: 522-8687).

Hové Parfumeur Perfumes, colognes, and soaps are produced on the premises of this charming, family-owned boutique, and dried aromatic herbs such as vetiver are also available. 824 Royal St. (phone: 525-7827).

The Idea Factory Hand-crafted wooden creations—whimsical creatures as well as marquetry boxes and other practical items—can be found here; all are made in a workshop out back. 838 Chartres St. (phone: 524-5195).

Jacqueline Vance Oriental Rugs The reliable quality of the merchandise and the expertise of the owner make this New Orleans's number one source of antique and modern oriental rugs. Appraisals and repairs are also offered. 3944 Magazine St. (phone: 891-3304).

Joan Vass New Orleans Fans of Ms. Vass, one of America's top designers of women's knitwear, will find this handsomely done shop a prime outlet for her creations, from the practical to the luxurious. *Martha and Me,* an affiliated shop in the same building, specializes in tailored wovens from other respected designers. 1100 Sixth St. (phone: 891-4502).

Jon Antiques Among the better purveyors of 18th- and 19th-century furniture, china, and objets d'art. 4605 Magazine St. (phone: 899-4482).

K&B Camera Center Whether you're a point-and-shooter or a professional, this is a handy source of camera equipment, film, and accessories; it also operates its own custom-processing laboratory. 227 Dauphine St. (phone: 524-2266).

Kaboom Books The number and selection of bookseller John Dillman's used volumes are excellent, and he's unusually knowledgeable about various editions. 901 Barracks St. (phone: 529-5780).

Kite Shop From the whimsical to the artistic, all kinds of kites crowd the ceiling and walls of this colorful and fascinating little store on Jackson Square. 542 St. Peter St. (phone: 524-0028).

Lucullus Crowded with antique French and English dining room furniture, crystal, porcelain, and decorative objects relating to food and wine. 610 Chartres St. (phone: 528-9620).

Maison Blanche The three floors of this fine regional department store at the heart of downtown are very well organized, with a multitude of nationally known brands, as well as designer clothing. 901 Canal St. (phone: 566-1000).

Maple Street Book Shop If New Orleans has a literary heart, it is this unpretentious uptown cottage crammed with a very selective collection of novels, anthologies, and biographies, from the latest best sellers to the most obscure Southern writers. A bookworm's paradise. 7523 Maple St. (phone: 866-4916). The branch at 2727 Prytania St. (phone: 895-2266) is interesting, too.

Merrill B. Domas American Indian Art The work of the best weavers, potters, and painters from the Southwest is sold here, as well as jewelry in silver and gemstones by some of Santa Fe's leading artisans. 824 Chartres St. (phone: 586-0479).

Mignon Faget Ltd. New Orleans's premier jewelry designer offers elegant pieces inspired by nature in precious metals and stones. Familiar regional icons, such as shellfish, are prominent motifs in the bracelets, brooches, necklaces, and cuff links. *Canal Place,* 333 Canal St. (phone: 524-2973); 710 Dublin St. (phone: 865-7361); and 8220 Maple St. (phone: 865-1107).

Morton M. Goldberg Auction Galleries A virtual warehouse filled with every sort of antique, it is worth a visit if only for browsing among the wealth of American, European, and Oriental objects. Estate auctions are a specialty, and good values are there for the cognoscenti. 547 Baronne St. (phone: 592-2300).

M. S. Rau Two large floors packed to the rafters with antiques—everything from art glass to music boxes, and more crystal and porcelain than you may have thought existed. 630 Royal St. (phone: 523-5660).

Old Town Praline Shop Charmingly old-fashioned, it turns out pecan-studded sugar patties with that traditional creole taste, wrapped in the same little waxed-paper bags they've used for decades. They'll pack and ship, as well. 627 Royal St. (phone: 525-1413).

Perlis Conservative men's clothing with a dash of élan. Fashion headquarters for many of the city's lawyers and stockbrokers, the styles range from Duck's Head khaki pants to Southwick and Ralph Lauren suits. Boy's and women's clothes are sold, too. 6070 Magazine St. (phone: 895-8661).

Le Petit Soldier Shoppe Collector or not, you're apt to be charmed by the hundreds of exquisitely crafted and painted lead soldiers sold in this museum-cum-shop. There are also all sorts of antique military memorabilia. 528 Royal St. (phone: 523-7741).

Progress Grocery Co. It's part delicatessen, part fancy grocery store, with a muffuletta sandwich take-out counter and a huge variety of exotic edibles on the shelves, including the proprietor's own herbed olive oils. Imported pasta and unusual dried legumes are also available. 915 Decatur St. (phone: 525-6627).

Rapp's Luggage and Gifts Whether you're looking for a plastic carry-on or a briefcase of fine leather, you'll probably find it here; also all sorts of handy travel gear. Minor luggage repairs, too. 604 Canal St. (phone: 568-1953).

Record Ron's Good & Plenty Records Everything from Bing Crosby to heavy metal to the baroque, with a specialty in rarities and the offbeat, fills the seemingly endless bins of LPs. 1129 Decatur St. (phone: 524-9444) and 239 Chartres St. (phone: 522-2239).

Rubenstein Bros. The fashion-conscious man looking for top American and European designers will find them here. So will the follower of the latest trends in casual wear. The choices, from haberdashery to topcoats, are many and varied. 102 St. Charles Ave. (phone: 581-6666).

Serendipitous A wide variety of brightly colored masks can be found here. 831 Decatur St. (phone: 522-9158).

Stan Levy Imports A good source not only of European pieces but also Southern armoires, 19th-century Louisiana furniture, and more recent objects from the region—affordable, too. 1028 Louisiana Ave., near Magazine St. (phone: 899-6384).

Still-Zinsel Contemporary Fine Art New painters and photographers working in a variety of styles are often introduced here. 328 Julia St. (phone: 588-9999).

Tower Records *The* place to find the CD or cassette you want. The classical section on the second floor is remarkably complete. 408 N. Peters St. (phone: 529-4411).

Victoria's Designer Discount Shoes From simple pumps to glittery evening shoes, much of the footwear is made by the leading names in fashion—and they're priced to sell. 532 Chartres St. (phone: 568-9990).

Waldhorn Co., Inc. An antiques dealer for connoisseurs of English and French furniture. 343 Royal St. (phone: 581-6379).

Wehmeier's Belt Shop The large inventory of men's and women's leather goods includes shoes and handbags; emergency repairs are made on the premises. 719 Toulouse (phone: 525-2758).

SPORTS AND FITNESS

BICYCLING While there are no designated bicycle paths in New Orleans, the tree-lined avenues that crisscross the city are unusually suitable for a bracing bike ride in almost any season. The flattened crest of the river levee in the Carrollton section is especially pleasant, offering a soothing view of the water; Wisner Boulevard along Bayou St. John, stretching from *City Park* to Lake Pontchartrain, is also a pleasant stretch. *Audubon* and *City* are two parks sought out in the summer for their cooling umbrellas of trees. Bicycles can be rented at *Bicycle Michael's* (618 Frenchmen St., a few blocks from the French Quarter; phone: 945-9505) and in *City Park* at Dreyfous Avenue (phone: 483-9371).

BOATING At *City Park,* you can rent canoes, paddleboats, and skiffs to cruise on the lagoons (phone: 483-9371).

CANOEING The swamps and marshes within an hour's drive from the center of town, teeming with vegetation and wildlife, provide an exotic backdrop for explorations by canoe. *Canoe and Trail Outings* (802 Chapelle St.; phone: 283-9400) specializes in "sunset paddling" excursions to the Manchac Swamp, west of the city, and the Honey Island Swamp to the east, among other places. The company rents all the necessary equipment.

FISHING New Orleans's location on the central Gulf Coast makes it ideal for freshwater and saltwater sport fishing year-round. The Gulf of Mexico, about

100 miles south of the city, teems with hundreds of species of sport and food fish, including tarpon, tuna, blue marlin, wahoo, ling, cobia, and dolphinfish. Full-day excursions from New Orleans to Venice, near the mouth of the Mississippi River, are easily arranged for groups of two to 20. Lakes, bays, inlets, and marshes less than an hour's drive from the center of town, are filled with redfish, largemouth bass, catfish, and freshwater drum. In the very heart of town, *City Park*'s lagoons are pleasant places to drop a line on a balmy afternoon. Temporary state licenses are required for non-state residents for all fishing, crabbing, and shrimping; they're available at the *Louisiana Department of Wildlife and Fisheries* office in the French Quarter (400 Chartres St.; phone: 568-5636), which is closed weekends. Be sure to inquire about seasonal regulations, too. The following are the area's most fertile fishing waters.

BEST BITES

City Park The tranquil lagoons inside *City Park* are where many local fisherfolk first discovered the joys of the sport. The ponds are regularly stocked, and acquiring a two-day permit is simply a matter of inquiring at the park's *Casino Building.* Contact *Boating and Fishing Department* (*City Park Administration Office,* 1 Dreyfous Ave.; phone: 483-9371).

Gulf of Mexico About a 90-minute drive from New Orleans are the *Venice Marina* (Venice; phone: 534-9357) and the *Empire-Delta Marina* (Empire; phone: 657-9726), the gateways to some of the best deep-sea fishing in the nation. All sorts of guided charter boats are available, for groups from two people to a dozen or more.

Mississippi River Many New Orleans residents don't know that it's still possible to fish the mighty river that courses through their city. But it can be done, once you've found a spot away from the wharves and flood walls. The most easily accessible one is Uptown, where St. Charles and Carrollton Avenues meet near the River Road. Climb the grassy levee and you'll reach the small strip of land (the local name for it is the "batture") separating the levee from the river. Drop your line and wait: That's what fishing is all about, isn't it?

Mississippi River Gulf Outlet This channel, about 20 miles from the city, was dug as an alternate commercial route from New Orleans to the Gulf of Mexico, bypassing the Mississippi. Locals also find it a fertile fishing ground. Fifteen-foot flat-bottomed skiffs with motors can be rented at the *Gulf Outlet Marina* (5353 Paris Rd., Chalmette; phone: 277-8229).

Pass Rigolets and Lake Borgne Less than an hour's drive from the French Quarter, this is one of the most prolific inshore saltwater fishing areas in America. Boats can be rented at the *Rigolets Marina* (US Hwy. 90 E.; phone: 662-5666).

FITNESS CENTERS The *New Orleans Athletic Club* (222 N. Rampart St.; phone: 525-2375) has a 60-foot indoor lap pool, exercise equipment and classes, a boxing ring, racquetball and basketball courts, and indoor and outdoor tracks. *Racquetball One Fitness Centers* (1 Shell Sq., 13th Floor, Poydras St. and St. Charles Ave.; phone: 522-2956; and *Canal Place,* Suite 380, 333 Canal St.; phone: 525-2956) offer five racquetball courts, aerobics programs, free weights, stair climbers, and exercise cycles. Several hotels also allow non-guests to use their centers for a fee. The *Rivercenter Racquet and Health Club* in the *New Orleans Hilton* (Poydras St. at the Mississippi River; phone: 587-7242) has a jogging track, weight training equipment, saunas, and basketball, racquetball, tennis, and squash courts. *Eurovita Spa* at the *Avenue Plaza Suite* hotel (2111 St. Charles Ave.; phone: 566-1212) offers a fitness room with weights, saunas, steamrooms, a whirlpool bath, and tanning rooms, as well as therapeutic massages. *Le Meridien Sports Center* (*Le Meridien Hotel*, 614 Canal St.; phone: 527-6750) has an outdoor heated pool, Nautilus equipment, Lifecycles, an aerobics program, yoga classes, a sauna, and massage therapists.

FOOTBALL The New Orleans *Saints* play in the *Louisiana Superdome* (Poydras St.; phone: 522-2600). The *Sugar Bowl Classic,* one of football's oldest college bowl games, takes place on *New Year's Day* in the *Superdome.*

GOLF Several public 18-hole courses, all open daily, are short distances from the city center. *City Park* has four courses (phone: 483-9396). *Audubon Park* (in the Uptown section; phone: 861-9511) has its own course. Also check out *Brechtel Park* (on the west bank of the Mississippi River; phone: 362-4761); *Joe Bartholomew Golf Course* (in eastern New Orleans's *Pontchartrain Park;* phone: 288-0928); and *Plantation Golf and Country Club* (1001 Behrman Hwy.; phone: 392-3363).

HORSEBACK RIDING The 2-mile trail at *Cascade Stables* is shaded by *Audubon Park*'s huge oaks. Horses and ponies are available for adults and youngsters daily (phone: 891-2246).

HORSE RACING The *Fair Grounds* (1751 Gentilly Blvd.; phone: 944-5515), one of the country's oldest thoroughbred-racing tracks, is a 15-minute taxi ride from the city center. It operates from *Thanksgiving* to mid-April. Although a fire in December 1993 destroyed the historic clubhouse and grandstand, as well as other major buildings, the track's owners resumed the races within weeks. At press time, plans for rebuilding were in the works.

JOGGING Good routes are in *City Park* at the end of Esplanade Avenue, *Audubon Park* in the Uptown section, *Woldenberg Park* on the French Quarter's edge, and along the Mississippi River levee on Leake Avenue in the Carrollton section.

SAILING Lake Pontchartrain's brisk breezes and typically calm waters make it ideal for Sunday sailors. The bayous and lagoons that ring New Orleans also provide relaxing excursions along the water. Even if you forgot to tow your boat, there are still ways to take advantage of New Orleans's favorite offshore activity. From March through October, recreational craft can be rented on the New Orleans lakefront from *Sailboats South* (300 Sapphire St.; phone: 288-7245). For lake boating, the choices include monohulls, catamarans, sailboats, and powerboats, ranging in size from nine to 36 feet. *Sailboats South* also rents rowing shells and skiffs for coasting along the nearby bayous and inlets.

TENNIS New Orleans has not escaped the tennis fever that still grips the country. The tropical (summer) and mild (winter) climate is, after all, tailor-made for virtually every outdoor sport that doesn't require snow, ice, or mountains (although the August humidity can definitely put a damper on your backhand). Visiting tennis players will find a good selection of public courts; if you belong to a club back home, it's worth checking to see if it enjoys reciprocity with one of New Orleans's private clubs. The following are among the city's top tennis spots.

CHOICE COURTS

Audubon Park In a place where summer can last up to ten months, tennis enthusiasts are grateful for any pocket of cooler air they can find. The park's courts, just yards away from the tempering waters of the Mississippi River, may be a few degrees less torrid than the others in town. Ten public courts with a clay-like surface are maintained in the rear of the park. They're not lighted, so don't plan on playing past sunset. Open daily. There is a court fee. 6320 Tchoupitoulas St. (phone: 895-1042).

Rivercenter Racquet and Health Club If the thought of game, set, and match on a rooftop court overlooking the Mississippi River appeals to you, this club, adjacent to the *New Orleans Hilton,* is the one for you. The eight indoor and three outdoor courts are beautifully maintained on top of the *Hilton*'s five-story garage, with great views of the river below. There's a matchmaker service if you need a partner, as well as a complete pro shop, racquet rentals, and instruction by the resident pro. Court reservations may be made three days in advance. Open daily. There's a court fee (reduced for *Hilton* guests). *New Orleans Hilton,* 2 Poydras St. (phone: 587-7242).

Wisner Tennis Center These well-maintained courts, nestled among the verdant spaces of *City Park,* are the most popular public venues in the city. There are 39 outdoor courts, some asphalt, some clay, and all with night lighting. Private or group instruction and complete pro shop services, including racquet and string repair, are offered. Open daily. There is a court fee. 1 Dreyfous Ave. (phone: 483-9383).

THEATER

National touring companies of Broadway shows perform regularly in the fall and spring at the *Saenger Performing Arts Center* (143 N. Rampart St. at Canal St.; phone: 524-2490). For those seeking something more daring, contemporary American plays, many of them by local writers and most of them avant-garde, are presented regularly in the arena theater of the *Contemporary Arts Center* (900 Camp St.; phone: 523-1216). In the French Quarter's community theater, the picturesque *Le Petit Théâtre du Vieux Carré* (616 St. Peter St.; phone: 522-2081) presents modern musical comedies and dramas from Broadway's past, and original plays for children. The several productions presented each year by the *Southern Repertory Theater* (1437 S. Carrollton Ave.; phone: 861-2254) stages a broad range of productions, but emphasizes works by Southern playwrights such as Tennessee Williams. Respectable amateur productions, from the spirited performances of the *Dashiki Theatre* group to original spoofs of old Hollywood musicals, are put on in the 100-seat *NORD Theater* space on the ground floor of *Gallier Hall* (543 St. Charles Ave.; phone: 565-7860). Original dramas, some experimental, are the forte of the little *Theater Marigny* (616 Frenchmen St.; phone: 944-2653), while campy satires and musical revues are the specialties of the *Toulouse Theatre* in the French Quarter (615 Toulouse St.; phone: 523-4207). Meatier works, from 19th-century classics to contemporary plays, are presented by *Tulane University* (*Dixon Performing Arts Center* on the *Newcomb College* campus; phone: 865-5106, the Drama Department, for theater productions during the year; phone: 865-5269, the Music Department, for summer stock musicals by the semi-professional *Summer Lyric Theater,* as well as opera and other music concerts); *Loyola University*'s *Lower Depths Theatre* (on the St. Charles Ave. campus; phone: 865-3824); and the *University of New Orleans Performing Arts Center* (near the Lakefront; phone: 834-9774). Lighter fare, in the form of contemporary Broadway comedies and revues, is the stock-in-trade at the city's numerous dinner-theaters. The main one is *Starcastle Dinner Theater* (2400 Belle Chasse Hwy., Gretna; phone: 366-0999).

CINEMA

If you want to see a particular first-run Hollywood production, you may have to head for a multi-screen theater in the suburbs (Metairie or the West Bank). But a couple of in-town cinemas also show current general-interest films. *Canal Place Cinema* (*Canal Place,* Fifth Floor, 333 Canal St.; phone: 581-5400) has four screens and shows top American and foreign films. Uptown near St. Charles Avenue, the *Prytania* (5339 Prytania St.; phone: 895-4513) focuses on more serious fare—art films and occasionally something from the underground.

MUSIC AND DANCE

The demise of the *New Orleans Symphony Orchestra* in early 1990 left the city without a major orchestra of its own for the first time since the 1930s. Later that year, however, a core group of musicians launched a grass-roots movement that resulted in the creation of the *Louisiana Philharmonic Orchestra,* with a limited season in the spring and fall and a roster of guest conductors. The group's concerts are given in the *Orpheum Theater* (129 University Pl., near Canal St.; phone: 523-6530). Aficionados of chamber music should check the schedule of the *Friends of Music* (phone: 895-0690), a group that sponsors several concerts each year by local and nationally known professionals; the performances are usually held at *Tulane University*'s *Dixon Performing Arts Center* on the *Newcomb College* campus. *Loyola University* and *Sophie Newcomb College* at *Tulane University* sponsor occasional recitals and concerts by students, faculty, and visiting performers at *Loyola*'s *Roussel Performance Hall* on the university campus (7214 St. Charles Ave.; phone: 865-2492) and at *Tulane/Newcomb*'s *Dixon Hall* or *Rogers Memorial Chapel* (information from *Tulane*'s Music Department; phone: 865-5269). New Orleans was the first American city to build an opera house, in the early 19th century. The musical tradition continues with several productions yearly by the *New Orleans Opera Association,* featuring internationally known performers offering classical European repertories. They're presented at the *Theatre for the Performing Arts* (N. Rampart St. near the corner of Dumaine St.; phone: 529-2278). Also, the music department of *Xavier University* occasionally stages student opera productions (7325 Palmetto St.; phone: 486-7411, university switchboard; phone: 483-7621, program director's office).

In the 1980s *The New Orleans City Ballet* merged with the *Cincinnati Ballet,* but kept its name and locale (phone: 522-0996); it stages several major productions annually in the *Theatre for the Performing Arts* (see above).

The biggest pop and rock stars regularly perform at the *Saenger Performing Arts Center* downtown (143 N. Rampart St.; phone: 524-2490); the *Kiefer UNO Lakefront Arena* (on the *University of New Orleans* campus; phone: 286-7222); the *Louisiana Superdome* (on Poydras St.; phone: 587-3800); and at private halls and clubs around town.

SOUNDS OF THE CITY

Jazz and Cajun musicians have brought the Big Easy its international reputation as a musical center. New Orleans is a port city, and nowhere is this more apparent than in the flamboyant overlapping of musical influences that have produced the distinctively syncopated swagger and improvisational fire of this city's music. The music is a rich gumbo created from the cross-fertilization of Caribbean music, African rhythms, the blues, zydeco, and traditional Cajun music. Today, New Orleans has exported its music around the globe and has garnered an enthusiastic international following. Some of the current stars of this musical seedbed include the *Neville Brothers,* Dr. John, the *Dirty Dozen Brass Band,* and such zydeco groups as *Buckwheat Zydeco* and *Rockin' Dopsie and the Zydeco Twisters.* At the same time, never forget that Louis Armstrong, Jelly Roll Morton, Sidney Bechet, and other jazz immortals were the New Orleans musicians who brought jazz to a new plateau of improvisational genius, making a major impact on the evolution of this quintessentially American sound. New Orleanians take quite justifiable pride in their unique musical heritage and no other city in the country has a beat quite like the Big Easy. Our favorite places to enjoy the sounds of New Orleans are listed in *Nightclubs and Nightlife,* below; for more information on the origins and the evolution of this very special American phenomenon, see *The Jazz Age* in DIVERSIONS.

NIGHTCLUBS AND NIGHTLIFE

No fan of classic New Orleans jazz should miss the authentic music and incomparable atmosphere of *Preservation Hall* (see *Special Places*). More comfortable, and just as much the real thing musically, is the *Palm Court Jazz Café* (1204 Decatur St.; phone: 525-0200), a spacious restaurant in an old French Quarter building where young and old traditionalists play nightly.

Two of the city's most celebrated Dixieland musicians, clarinetist Pete Fountain and trumpeter Al Hirt, have their own clubs, and the seats are always filled when the masters themselves are onstage. Fountain's headquarters is *Pete Fountain's* in the *New Orleans Hilton* (2 Poydras St.; phone: 523-4374), and Hirt holds forth from time to time at *Jelly Roll's* in the French Quarter (501 Bourbon St.; phone: 568-0501). Good-quality local bands perform in their absence; if you're interested only in the stars themselves, call ahead. Bourbon Street is lined with Dixieland clubs; one of the best is the *Famous Door* (339 Bourbon St.; phone: 522-7626); another is *Fritzel*'s (733 Bourbon St.; phone: 561-0432); or, off Bourbon, try *Maxwell's Toulouse Cabaret* (615 Toulouse St.; phone: 523-4207). A cushy spot to enjoy traditional New Orleans music is the *Louis Armstrong Foundation Jazz Club* in *Le Meridien* hotel's vast ground-floor lobby (see *Checking In*), where *Jacques Gauthé's Yerba Buena Creole Rice Jazz Band* regularly performs on weekends. Another especially compatible setting for Dixieland is *LeMoyne's Landing,* near the Plaza d'España and the *Riverwalk Mall* (Canal St. at the Mississippi River; phone: 524-4809).

The music of southwest Louisiana's bayous has an international following and it is certainly not neglected in New Orleans clubs. Authentic Cajun bands, including groups performing in the even earthier and folksier zydeco style, stomp and fiddle every night in the Warehouse District at *Mulate's* (201 Julia St.; phone: 522-1492), which also has a dance floor and a kitchen dispensing spicy Louisiana dishes. Another choice Cajun dance hall–restaurant is *Michaul's,* on the Warehouse District's fringe (701 Magazine St.; phone: 522-5517). Other clubs where Cajun groups often perform are the *Maple Leaf* (8316 Oak St.; phone: 866-9359), with its tiny dance floor, and *Tipitina's* (501 Napoleon Ave.; phone: 895-8477), an earthy spot deep in the heart of the Uptown waterfront. The "New Orleans Sound" and the blues are also featured at *Tipitina's,* where the music is down-and-dirty and the crowd never stops moving—on or off the dance floor.

The New Orleans sound and the blues also are in the spotlight at *Jimmy's* (8200 Willow St.; phone: 861-8200) and at the *New Orleans Entertainment Hall* in the Warehouse District (907 S. Peters St.; phone: 523-4311). Blues great Marva Wright can often be found at *Muddy Water's* in Carrollton (8301 Oak St.; phone: 866-7174). At *Benny's Bar,* a funky club featuring New Orleans rhythm and blues, the real action doesn't get going until after midnight (938 Valence St.; phone: 895-9405). A new but already premier blues spot in the Quarter is *House of Blues* (225 Decatur St.; phone: 529-2583), an immense music space and restaurant opened last year by comedian Dan Akroyd. The $7 million complex holds a vast collection of folk art in addition to its awesome sound system.

At *Snug Harbor* (626 Frenchmen St.; phone: 949-0696), a couple of blocks from the French Quarter, you can hear both the New Orleans Sound, performed by such masters as singers Charmaine Neville and Germaine Bazzle, and contemporary jazz; pianist Ellis Marsalis often plays here. At another contemporary jazz spot, the *Crescent City Brewhouse* (527 Decatur St.; phone: 522-0571), Marsalis's son, Delfeayo, holds forth with his quintet nightly.

Other nightspots worth visiting include *The Mint* (504 Esplanade Ave.; phone: 525-2000), a large, laid-back gay bar with a floor show in which homegrown talent performs Friday through Sunday nights. The humor usually has lots of local connotations, but out-of-towners seem to catch on quickly. At *Chris Owens* in the French Quarter (502 Bourbon St.; phone: 523-6400), the club's namesake is the sole performer, and if her maraca shaking and fancy footwork aren't the most advanced in town, her showmanship usually fills the place to the rafters. The *Napoleon House Bar* (500 Chartres St.; phone: 524-9752) is an unpolished, bohemian, yet authentically charming spot to sip the house's special Pimm's Cup Cocktail (Pimm's Cup Mix blended with rum) while soaking up the early 19th-century atmosphere; their hearty Italian-style sandwiches are excellent.

Visitors interested in games of chance should note that plans to open a *Harrah's Grand Palais Casino* on the site of the *Rivergate* exhibition center (Canal Street at the Mississippi River) were incomplete as we went to press, due to contractual tangles and continued debate over whether to renovate or demolish *Rivergate;* check with your hotel or any tourist information officer upon your arrival. Meanwhile, the only other options are riverboat-type casinos, including the *Star Casino,* on Lake Pontchartrain (10001 Lake Forest Blvd.; phone: 243-0400) near the *New Orleans Municipal Airport,* and the *Queen of New Orleans* (2 Poydras Pl.; phone: 587-7777) on the Mississippi River, docked at the *New Orleans Hilton* hotel (see *Checking In,* below). Both operate daily.

Best in Town

CHECKING IN ·

Hotels in New Orleans usually are more than just places to stay after spending a day (and half the night) seeing the city. Many of the hotels reflect the influence of French, Spanish, and/or Louisiana colonial architecture and often a full measure of charm. No matter where you stay or what you pay, make reservations well in advance, particularly during *Sugar Bowl Week* (approximately December 30 to January 2) preceding the annual football classic on *New Year's Day, Carnival* season (in February or early March), and the *New Orleans Jazz and Heritage Festival* (in late April or early May). Expect rates to increase by about 25% during these periods of high demand. (Many hotels have three- or four-day minimum stays during *Carnival.*) In general, however, the spate of hotel building that coincided with New Orleans's ill-fated *1984 World's Fair* has tended to keep the hotel business very competitive and rather reasonable—especially on weekends, when special promotional packages are frequently offered by the large chain hotels. Most of New Orleans's major hotels have complete facilities for the business traveler. Those listed below as having "business services" usually offer such conveniences as meeting rooms, photocopiers, computers, translation services, and express checkout, among others. Call the individual hotel for additional information. Expect to pay $110 to $160 a night for a double room—and much higher, especially for suites—at hotels in the expensive range; $75 to $95 at places in the moderate category; and $50 to $70 at establishments in the inexpensive category.

For bed and breakfast accommodations, contact *Bed & Breakfast Inc.* (1360 Moss St., Box 52257, New Orleans, LA 70152; phone: 525-4640; 800-228-9711); *Bed & Breakfast of New Orleans* (671 Rosa Ave., Metairie; phone: 838-0071); or the *Greater New Orleans Tourist and Convention Commission* (1520 Sugar Bowl Dr., New Orleans, LA 70112; phone: 566-5011). Unless we note otherwise, rooms in the hotels listed below have air conditioning, private baths, TV sets, and telephones, and all telephone and fax numbers are in the 504 area code.

For an unforgettable experience in the Big Easy, we begin with our favorites, followed by our recommendations of cost and quality choices listed by price category.

SPECIAL HAVENS

Inter-Continental Though this very modern and efficient establishment caters most specifically to business travelers, it draws all those who appreciate all-around quality. The lustrous wood-paneled mezzanine lobby is decorated with striking works by contemporary New Orleans artists, and is further brightened by the fresh flowers lining the escalator leading from the driveway to the registration desk. *Veranda,* a dramatic dining room with a lofty glass ceiling and lush greenery, serves continental fare created by celebrated New Orleans chef Willy Coln (see *Eating Out*). Among the 482 guestrooms are several suites luxuriously decorated in 19th-century Louisiana style with antique furniture, canopied beds, and prints and fabrics reflecting that bygone era. Even the standard rooms are equipped with mini-bars and dressing alcoves containing telephones and small TV sets. On the top floor are a health club and pool. Located at the corner of St. Charles Avenue and Poydras Street, the hotel is steps away from both the business district and the Mississippi Riverfront. During *Carnival,* guests are treated to an ideal glimpse of the pageantry as many parades pass by. There is butler service on the executive floor, and 24-hour room service is available, as are business services and a concierge desk. 444 St. Charles Ave. (phone: 525-5566; 800-327-0200).

LaMothe House Built in the early 1800s by a successful planter named Jean LaMothe, this exquisite early New Orleans townhouse, surrounded by moss-draped oaks, is a delightful place to call home while visiting the Big Easy. With its stately foyer, lushly planted courtyard, and antique furnishings, this elegant establishment transports visitors to the city's earlier, gentler days, without exposing them to the discomforts of the past. Continental breakfast, the only meal served, is always an event: Everyone sits at a long banquet table and lingers over chicory coffee. The inn is in the French Quarter, very close to the jazz, good food, and intriguing shops. 621 Esplanade Ave. (phone: 947-1161; 800-367-5858).

Maison de Ville This gem of a hotel in the heart of the French Quarter offers a choice of accommodations: In the *maison*—where

Tennessee Williams did his final draft of *Streetcar*—are 16 magnificent rooms and suites furnished with antiques and with balconies and street or courtyard views. Out back are the remodeled slave quarters (ca. 1742), and a stroll away on Dauphine Street are the seven delightful *Audubon Cottages,* where John James Audubon lived and worked in 1821. Built in the creole brick-and-post style (something like the old European half-timbered buildings), the cottages have perhaps the most elegant rooms of all, with luxuriously furnished bedrooms, kitchens with stocked refrigerators, private gardens, and patios with access to a small swimming pool. The entire *maison* stands out, however, for the service: Tables in restaurants and space on sightseeing tours are booked by an omniscient concierge; shoes left outside your door are shined; a classic French breakfast is served on a silver tray, along with copies of *USA Today* and the *Wall Street Journal*—and a rose. And when you return after a night on the town, you find a chocolate on your pillow. Enjoy casual dining and conversation at the *Bistro* (see *Eating Out*). Room service is available for lunch and dinner only. 727 Toulouse St. (phone: 561-5858; 800-634-1600).

Le Meridien This classy, sleek member of the French chain has become a major presence on Canal Street's hotel row. The plush, marble lobby is dominated by a spectacular, geometrically shaped chandelier that casts a soft glow on the muted tones of the carpeting, walls, and comfortable furniture. Beyond the lobby, *Jazz Meridien* is a marble-and-wood bar where traditional jazz bands play nightly, adding a sassy energy to the atmosphere. *La Gauloise,* a bistro-style restaurant, borrows the look of turn-of-the-century Paris and serves excellent buffets featuring creole and French dishes. Chic understatement and contemporary style characterizes the look of the 497 guestrooms and five bi-level suites. An entire floor is reserved for nonsmokers. To soothe travel-weary muscles, guests can order a massage in the fully equipped penthouse health club or take a swim in the pool. Amenities also include a concierge, 24-hour room service, and business services. 614 Canal St. (phone: 525-6500; 800-543-4300).

New Orleans Hilton The Mississippi River is almost at the doorstep of this immense and impressive link in the Hilton chain. The lavish multilevel lobby, which connects directly to the *Riverwalk* shopping mall, is luxuriously appointed, with lustrous marble floors and polished wood walls decorated with paintings by some of the country's most respected artists. Located here is *Pete Fountain's,* a nightclub where some of the city's top musicians perform, including Fountain himself. At *Kabby's* (see *Eating Out*), diners get not only a dramatic, close-up view of the Mississippi, but also the authentic creole-Cajun cookery of native chef Stanley Jackson. The state-of-the-art *Racquet and Health Club* has 11 tennis courts—eight indoor and three outdoor—as well as two squash courts and one basketball court. All of the 1,602 guestrooms are sound-proofed, and children occupying their parents' room stay free. Business services and a concierge are available. Room service delivers around the clock. 2 Poydras St. (phone: 561-0500; 800-HILTONS).

Soniat House No hostelry in New Orleans captures the city's romantic charm and Old Southern gentility quite like this one does. Proprietors Rodney and Frances Smith refurbished two balconied, early-19th-century creole townhouses in the tranquil lower French Quarter and furnished them with stunning period antiques and exquisite paintings and objets d'art. Each of the 16 elegant and comfortable rooms and eight suites in the main houses and rear slave quarters is unique, with canopied beds in the larger rooms. A breakfast of orange juice, biscuits with homemade strawberry preserves, and New Orleans chicory coffee is served (for a small additional charge) in the inner courtyard, shaded by aromatic tropical trees and plants. Service has a distinctly personal touch: In the downstairs sitting room a home-style bar operates on the honor system—guests who return after-hours can pour their own drinks and leave a check at the desk; umbrellas are available on request; and the Smiths, avid restaurant patrons, can recommend dining spots tailored to individual preferences. No wonder many guests feel as though they're visiting friends who happen to live in one of the city's most tasteful old residences. Reserve as far in advance as possible. 1133 Chartres St. (phone: 522-0570; 800-544-8808).

Westin–Canal Place Although the entrance may be unassuming, this hotel located near the French Quarter, Canal Street, and the Mississippi River is as modern and plush as they come. What makes it unique is the view from its 11th-floor lobby—a panorama that takes in the French Quarter and the river as it begins forming its famous crescent. The vast pale wood-and-marble lobby is richly decorated with cushy armchairs, antiques, and thick rugs. The glistening marble bar off the lobby—known simply as the *Bar*—is a wonderful place to stop for a drink. Beyond the lobby proper is *Le Jardin,* an elegant restaurant and bar, which offers contemporary creole cuisine; it's also an ideal setting for either coffee and croissants in the morning or a cognac after dinner. Most of the 438 spacious rooms and suites, decorated in pastels and accented with prints of the French Quarter, have views of the river. All contain mini-bars and such extras as Caswell & Massey soaps and toiletries.

Twenty-four-hour room service is available, as are business services. 100 Iberville St. (phone: 566-7006; 800-228-3000).

Windsor Court The handsome, secluded driveway is an indication of the pleasures that lie within, and indeed this impeccably furnished hotel doesn't disappoint. Delicate Oriental figurines rest in glistening antique cases, sprays of cymbidium orchids crown massive marble tables, and four centuries of art—oil paintings, sculpture, tapestries, and antique furniture—decorate the ground-floor lobby and public rooms. Of the 310 rooms, about 250 are suites with separate living rooms, dressing rooms, and kitchenettes or wet bars. All of the guestrooms have private balconies or bay windows, Italian marble bathrooms, and three telephones equipped with two incoming lines. The spacious rooms are decorated with luxurious fabrics in traditional prints, dark-stained traditional furniture, and thick carpeting. There are 55 two-bedroom suites and two spectacular penthouse suites on the 22nd floor, each of which includes a library and a large, landscaped terrace overlooking the Mississippi. In *Le Salon,* a string quartet plays as guests sit among the palms and munch on scones and cucumber sandwiches served at afternoon tea. The elegant *Grill Room* (see *Eating Out*) features regional and international delicacies. There is 24-hour room service, a multilingual staff, business services, an Olympic-size pool, a fully equipped health club, and a parking garage. The location, near Canal Street and the Mississippi Riverfront, is another plus. 300 Gravier St. (phone: 523-6000; 800-262-2662).

EXPENSIVE

Cornstalk This old Victorian home is surrounded by a New Orleans landmark—an elaborate wrought-iron fence with a cornstalk and pumpkin-vine motif. The interior is something of a landmark, too—a grand entrance hall and lobby with antique mirrors and crystal chandeliers. The 14 rooms feature four-poster beds, and you can take continental breakfast in the front gallery or on the patio; there's no restaurant. The staff can be less than friendly at times. 915 Royal St. (phone: 523-1515; fax: 525-6651).

Fairmont Successor to the legendary *Roosevelt,* which once occupied this same site, this hotel is a delightful blending of the best in San Francisco style and New Orleans charm. The 750 rooms are efficiently maintained (but ask for one in the newer wing). Its location, just a half block from Canal Street and a few blocks from the heart of the French Quarter, makes it convenient for shopping and dining. The *Sazerac,* a luxury restaurant, is frilly and romantic (see *Eating Out*), and the more casual *Bailey's,* open 24 hours, is a satisfactory place for everything from snacks to good creole fare. There's also a heated pool and two tennis courts. Other amenities include a concierge desk and business services. University Pl. (phone: 529-7111; 800-527-4727; fax: 522-2303).

Hyatt Regency A stone's throw from the *Superdome* and connected to the *New Orleans Centre* shopping mall, this locally-designed, 1,200-room link in the Hyatt chain is bunkerlike on the outside, but has an atrium-style lobby, an inner courtyard fountain, lots of greenery, and numerous multilevel public spaces. In 1993, the hotel underwent a $16-million renovation of its lobby, restaurants, and guestrooms. Some rooms have private patios and balconies, others overlook the heated outdoor swimming pool. The grand view of the city from the *Top of the Dome* restaurant is a plus, and *Hyttops,* the sports bar on the mezzanine level, is always lively, especially during big *Superdome* sports events. Room service and business services are available. 500 Poydras Plaza (phone: 561-1234; 800-233-1234).

Lafayette After undergoing a complete refurbishment in 1991, this stately hotel, just two blocks from Poydras Street, has reemerged as a handsome choice among the hotels of the Business District. The *Louisiana Superdome* and *Ernest N. Morial Convention Center* are a few minutes' walk away. Its 144 guestrooms and 20 suites, all with high ceilings, are elegantly decorated with handsome period-style furniture. Suites contain marble wet bars and refrigerators, and four are equipped with Jacuzzis. Just off the small ground-floor lobby is *Mike's on the Avenue,* a sleekly designed restaurant offering the eclectic cuisine of chef Mike Fennelly (see *Eating Out*). Business services are available. 600 St. Charles Ave. (phone: 524-4441; 800-733-4754; fax: 523-7327).

Melrose A lushly renovated Victorian house with polished wood floors and antiques, this luxury bed and breakfast establishment is cozy yet elegant. Fresh flowers and down pillows are found in each of the eight rooms. Convenient to the Faubourg Marigny neighborhood of New Orleans, a less famous and less touristic French section of town (see *Drive 1: Esplanade Avenue–City Park* in DIRECTIONS), it isn't within easy walking distance of the French Quarter's heart, but you can use taxis if you're without a car. A limo greets guests at the airport. Breakfast is served in the parlor or in guests' rooms. 937 Esplanade Ave. (phone: 944-2255).

New Orleans Marriott Unabashedly glitzy, this 1,290-room hotel is tailor-made for those in search of Las Vegas–style ambience. Its spacious but low-ceilinged lobby houses a warren of casual eateries and lounges; and guestrooms are done up in lots of bright colors. On the top floor, the *River View* restaurant offers a pleasant panorama of the Mississippi, the French Quarter, and Canal Street. There's also a health club with Nautilus equipment and a pool. Efficient, affable service is a plus. Business services are offered. Canal and Chartres Sts. (phone: 581-1000; 800-228-9290; fax: 523-6755).

Omni Royal Orleans Moderate in size and elegantly appointed, this was the first of the French Quarter's hotels to combine 19th-century atmosphere with modern, efficient facilities. Most of the 350 rooms are elegantly furnished, and the Tennessee Williams Suite is lined with photographs and other memorabilia relating to the writer's career. The *Esplanade Lounge* is popular with the late-night crowd, as is the three-level *Touché Bar*. The menu at the plush *Rib Room* includes meat and seafood prepared on a giant rotisserie, as well as typical New Orleans dishes. The outdoor rooftop *Riviera* restaurant, near the swimming pool, serves breakfast on balmy days. Amenities include a fitness center, shops, a garage, a concierge, 24-hour room service, and business services. 621 St. Louis St. (phone: 529-5333; 800-THE-OMNI; fax: 523-5076).

Pontchartrain With 100 tastefully decorated rooms, each furnished with provincial antiques, this is a favorite of celebrities and dignitaries. There are two restaurants, the casual *Coffee Shop* and the lavishly appointed *Caribbean Room* (see *Eating Out*), which offers creole specialties. A jazz pianist performs nightly in the intimate *Bayou Bar*. Around-the-clock room service is offered, as well as business services. 2031 St. Charles Ave. (phone: 524-0581; fax: 524-1165).

Royal Sonesta Somewhere between glitzy and elegant, this swank marble, crystal, and brocade-bedecked French Quarter establishment, with 500 rooms and 35 suites, is in the heart of brassy Bourbon Street. The lobby is surprisingly quiet, as are the rooms overlooking the lush interior patio. Then again, there are also rooms with balconies overlooking the frenetic Bourbon Street nighttime revelry. *Begue's,* the hotel's prestigious restaurant, offers creole-continental food with occasional lighter, contemporary dishes. Facilities include an outdoor pool, a concierge desk, business services, and a garage. 300 Bourbon St. (phone: 586-0300; 800-343-7170; fax: 586-0335).

St. Louis One of the many French Quarter hostelries designed to blend in with the surrounding 19th-century architecture, its modest size (69 rooms) and subtle elegance are proof that good things do come in small packages. The rather plain rooms may be a letdown after the classiness of the small, welcoming lobby, but they all open onto a lovely courtyard. The handsomely decorated *Louis XVI* restaurant flanking the courtyard is one of the city's better purveyors of French-creole cooking (see *Eating Out*). 730 Bienville St. (phone: 581-7300; 800-535-9111; fax: 524-8925).

Sheraton New Orleans Ideally located—right across from the French Quarter and a few blocks from the Mississippi—this 1,100-room, 49-story establishment has a comfortable multilevel lobby and offers the admirable service to its guests that the national chain is noted for. On the premises are the *Gazebo Lounge, Cafe Promenade,* and the *Creole Tomato* snack bar, a gift shop, a parking garage, and an outdoor pool with its own bar and grill. Business services are offered. 500 Canal St. (phone: 525-2500; 800-325-3535; fax: 561-0178).

Bourbon Orleans On a quiet block of the French Quarter, this 210-room hotel incorporates what was, from 1815 to the late 19th century, a ballroom for Creole ladies and gentlemen. Today it is certainly more luxurious, with its Queen Anne furniture, canopied king-size beds, marble baths, and crystal and brocade accents. An outdoor pool and secretarial services are other pluses. There is a small restaurant. 717 Orleans St. (phone: 523-2222; 800-521-5338; fax: 525-8166).

Dauphine Orleans Almost hidden along one of the French Quarter's more residential streets is this well-run, 109-room establishment that blends modern conveniences with a reasonable amount of creole charm. Across the street is *Dauphine Patios,* a small annex, with pleasant rooms opening onto a courtyard. Amenities include a complimentary newspaper, a fitness room, free parking, continental breakfast, and a lending library; there is no restaurant. A complimentary open-air jitney transports guests around the Quarter and Central Business District. 415 Dauphine St. (phone: 586-1800; 800-521-7111; fax: 586-1409).

Doubletree New Orleans When the small Doubletree chain took over this modern property in the late 1980s, it transformed the once glitzy lobby into a more intimate space and added French country accents to the 363 rooms and 15 suites. The *Chicory Rotisserie and Grill* serves continental fare, and the hotel's location—near the Mississippi River, the *Ernest N. Morial Convention Center,* and the French Quarter—adds to its appeal. 300 Canal St. (phone: 581-1300; 800-528-0444; fax: 522-4100).

Holiday Inn Château LeMoyne The fancier of the French Quarter's two Holiday Inns, it is decked out in traditional New Orleans fashion: period wallpaper, Baroque accents in the lobby, and a courtyard. The 175 rooms are comfortable, but have a run-of-the-mill look about them. There's a swimming pool and a serviceable restaurant. 301 Dauphine St. (phone: 581-1303; 800-HOLIDAY; fax: 523-5709).

Holiday Inn Crowne Plaza The image of this internationally known chain was elevated a notch or two when this sleek-looking member was added. Convenient to the *Ernest N. Morial Convention Center* and the office towers of Poydras Street, its 440 rooms are designed for comfort and efficiency. There's a restaurant, a swimming pool, and an exercise room on the premises. Business services and room service are available. 333 Poydras St. (phone: 525-9444; 800-522-6963; fax: 581-7179).

Holiday Inn Downtown-Superdome A convenient location and 300 guestrooms are the drawing cards here. The *John James Audubon Room* restaurant serves standard New Orleans fare, and the rooftop Olympic pool is a great perch for watching sunsets. Other amenities include room service until midnight, a concierge desk, and business services. 330 Loyola Ave. (phone: 581-1600; fax: 586-0833).

Maison Dupuy Off the French Quarter's beaten track is this modern, handsomely turned out four-story hostelry with a spectacular courtyard and meticulously maintained public spaces. The 195 rooms and suites are decorated in pastels and floral motifs; some suites have three bedrooms. *Le Bon Creole,* a colorful, casual restaurant and lounge, offers updated creole standards. 1001 Toulouse St. (phone: 586-8000; 800-535-9177; fax: 525-5334).

Monteleone At the gateway to the Vieux Carré, this 600-room property maintains a friendly atmosphere while offering the amenities of a large operation. Features include a rooftop pool and bar; a revolving lounge; formal dining at *Steaks Unlimited; Le Café,* a lobby-level coffee shop; an oyster bar; and a garage. Amenities include 24-hour room service, a concierge, and business services. 214 Royal St. (phone: 523-3341; fax: 561-5803).

Le Pavillon Eighteenth-century France was the obvious inspiration for this refurbished Poydras Street place, whose style is locally referred to as "barbecue Baroque." The lobby is filled with a profusion of crystal chandeliers, marble, and brocades. There are 200 rooms, a rooftop swimming pool, and a restaurant on the premises. Business services are available. 833 Poydras St. (phone: 581-3111; 800-535-9095; fax: 522-5543).

Place d'Armes A few steps from Jackson Square, this functional but tastefully decorated hostelry has a lovely courtyard with a pool, fountains, and outdoor tables. There are 79 rooms and eight suites in five renovated 18th-century buildings. The lobby is diminutive, but the place is comfortable and clean, and some rooms have balconies overlooking the Chartres Street corner of Jackson Square. Room service delivers a complimentary continental breakfast only (there is no restaurant on the premises), and business services are available. 625 St. Ann St. (phone: 524-4531).

De la Poste A comprehensive renovation completed in 1993 added sparkle to this sedate hotel on reasonably quiet Chartres Street. Built in 1973 in traditional French Quarter style, the property has 100 rooms and four carriage house suites with private patios; the drive-through, brick-paved carriageway leads to a spacious and simply landscaped courtyard with a swimming pool. Much of the ground floor is taken up by *Bacco* (see *Eating Out*), a large, beautifully decorated Italian restaurant. Coffee and fresh fruit in the lobby are complimentary, as is the weekday newspaper delivered to guests' doors. The courtyard, which has trees and a fountain, can be reserved for receptions; some conference and function rooms open onto the courtyard as well. 316 Chartres St. (phone: 581-1200; 800-448-4927).

Provincial A personal touch is evident throughout this well-designed establishment on lower Chartres Street. A French-country look characterizes the 106 guestrooms, many of which are furnished with canopied beds and old armoires. The small bar and moderately priced *Honfleur* restaurant are especially picturesque, decorated with unpretentious antiques and old prints. There is no charge for children sharing rooms with adults. Convenient to the *French Market,* Jackson Square, and Decatur Street. 1024 Chartres St. (phone: 581-4995; 800-535-7922; fax: 581-1018).

Quality Inn–Maison St. Charles A few blocks from Lee Circle, this pretty complex of renovated buildings with 121 rooms and 11 suites has a touch of old New Orleans charm combined with up-to-date efficiency. On the premises is the *J. Lillian* restaurant (see *Eating Out*), serving southern Louisiana dishes in handsome surroundings near the pool. The French Quarter and business district are a short ride away on the St. Charles streetcar. 1319 St. Charles Ave. (phone: 522-0187; 800-831-1783; fax: 525-2218).

Radisson While in a prime location for *Ernest N. Morial Convention Center* activities, it is otherwise rather isolated—unless you're planning to spend lots of time in the Warehouse District and on the riverfront. Made up of 253 one-, two-, and three-bedroom suites, this starkly modern hotel has an airy feeling, thanks to the large, glass atrium that forms the lobby. There also is a restaurant on the premises. 315 Julia St. (phone: 525-1993; fax: 515-1993, ext. 4109).

Le Richelieu This 69-room hostelry on the fringes of the French Quarter was the place where former *Beatle* Paul McCartney hung his hat when he came to town. Fans may be surprised at his rather modest taste. Still, the place does have its charms, such as kitchenettes in the 17 suites and, in many of the rooms, such old-fashioned touches as brass ceiling fans and pull-down ironing boards. Other pluses: a pleasant little restaurant overlooking the pool, and cheerful, efficient service. 1234 Chartres St. (phone: 529-2492; 800-535-9653; fax: 524-8179).

Ste. Helène A carefully preserved historic building, this guesthouse has a courtyard pool and three floors with 16 rooms, seven with balconies overlooking the pool or busy Chartres Street. The decor features reproductions of 19th-century antiques; room service is available for breakfast only; and continental breakfast is served near the lobby. There is no restaurant, but a complimentary Champagne Happy Hour is offered each day. Conveniently located two blocks from Jackson Square and near the historic *Napoleon House Bar* (see *Nightclubs and Nightlife* above). 508 Chartres St. (phone: 522-5014; fax: 523-7140).

INEXPENSIVE

Château Motor Hotel In a relatively quiet part of the French Quarter, this attractive, serviceable hotel is for the traveler seeking comfort and convenience with a minimum of frills. Access from the small lobby to the 37 rooms and five suites is through a carriageway and patio. While the rooms are not luxurious, they're well maintained and pleasantly decorated. There is also a small restaurant and bar. Jackson Square is a short walk away. 1001 Chartres St. (phone: 524-9636).

French Quarter Maisonettes A converted Vieux Carré townhouse in the French Quarter with a flagstone carriageway and spacious patio, this inn is a quaint and friendly place to stay, with no frills (there is no restaurant, for example). While the seven suites and one double room have no phones, all have private baths and TV sets. The two- or three-room suites are neat and comfortable. The neighborhood, almost entirely residential, is always serene. The proprietor is happy to offer touring suggestions. No credit cards accepted. Reservations must be made between 11 AM and 7 PM central time; be persistent, as they are somewhat erratic about answering their phone. 1130 Chartres St. (phone: 524-9918).

Prytania Inns This one's for budget-minded travelers who enjoy a homey atmosphere. Although it's located in the Lower Garden District, away from the urban hubbub, it's easily accessible to downtown. Made up of three former residences, the property is operated much like a bed and breakfast establishment. The 60 tastefully appointed bedrooms and sitting rooms reflect the turn-of-the-century architecture of the handsome old buildings; there are no TV sets. Traditional creole breakfasts are served, but there's no restaurant. Streetcars and buses are a short walk away. 1415 Prytania St. (phone: 566-1515; fax: 566-1518).

EATING OUT

The natives of this city have always looked on good food as a birthright, whether the matter at hand be a delicately composed cream sauce, a hearty dish of ham-flavored red beans and rice, or the newest variation on jambalaya to come out of a trendy bistro. Gastronomy is embedded in the New Orleans consciousness, and some of the more traditional dishes—like gumbo and jambalaya—date back almost two centuries. Creole cookery is a sophisticated, ever-evolving cross-fertilization of many cultural styles and tastes. The city's earliest French, Spanish, African, and Caribbean cooks created unique dishes by using their own techniques and spices to prepare regional seafood, game, and produce. Throw in Acadian (more commonly known outside the area as Cajun) cooking, the boldly flavored peasant-style dishes developed by people from backwater, southern Louisiana, and it's easy to see why the food in New Orleans is a passion and a constant source of inspiration to the scores of celebrated chefs who practice their art here today.

Choosing New Orleans's best restaurant is akin to choosing the most dazzling diamond from *Tiffany's*—there simply are too many gems. The city is in the midst of a restaurant revolution of sorts, thanks to a cadre of very creative chefs who are forging a bold new contemporary cuisine founded on the bedrock principles of creole and Cajun cooking. The more traditional places meanwhile continue to thrive, so the spectrum of cooking styles is wider than ever; for help in depicting some of the special food terminology, see *Big Easy Food Facts* at the end of the restaurant listings.

Expect to pay $80 or more for two at the places we've described as expensive; between $50 and $80 at restaurants listed as moderate; and $50 or less at places in the inexpensive category. Prices include tax and tips, but not drinks or wine. Except where noted, restaurants are open for lunch and dinner, and *reservations are advised;* it is best to call well in advance to reserve, and then confirm your reservation on the day of dining. Jackets for men are advised at the more expensive restaurants. All telephone numbers are in the 504 area code.

So, for an unforgettable taste of New Orleans, try our favorite culinary selections in the *Big Easy's Best Eats,* below, or any one of our other recommendations of cost and quality choices, listed by price category.

BIG EASY'S BEST EATS

Bayona Even though it is located in a quaint, 150-year-old cottage in the French Quarter, this restaurant is no shrine to New Orleans's past. Warm terra cotta colors, boldly striped chair cushions, flower-filled urns, and strikingly modern photographs define the decor, and chef and co-owner Susan Spicer's fertile imagination defines the menu. Calling her cooking "New World," she combines an innovative use of herbs with diverse inspirations—Mediterranean, Oriental, Californian, and, occasionally, creole. Try the tiny medallions of lamb tenderloin in a pinot noir sauce with fennel seed, rosemary, and three types of peppercorns; a gratinéed casserole of polenta and thin crescents of artichoke in an Italian cheese sauce of fontina, *grana padano,* and *crescenza;* or a tart of ricotta blended with cream cheese, lemon juice, molasses, and a tinge of vanilla. Wines are carefully selected to accompany the chef's earthy style, and service is informed and energetic. Dining in the lush, candlelit courtyard is a decidedly romantic experience, with the magnolia, banana, wax ligustrum, and ginger flora casting shadows on the white linen tablecloths. Closed Sundays. Major credit cards accepted. 430 Dauphine St. (phone: 525-4455).

Brigtsen's Homey curtains and simple mantels in a small and unpretentious cottage are the setting for chef Frank Brigtsen's dazzling food, which is rooted in southern Louisiana bayou country but is full of fresh approaches. Try the delicately flavored fish brushed with light butter sauces seasoned with roasted garlic, sun-dried tomatoes, and thyme; roast duck with pecan gravy and "dirty rice" (a traditional Cajun side dish of rice with ground giblets, beef, vegetables, and spices); or a creamy and rich oysters Rockefeller soup. The pecan pie and bread pudding are close to perfect, as are the banana ice cream and double-chocolate cake. The three dining rooms are small, and service is informal, but efficient. Though the wine list is short, the selections complement the deep, rich flavors of the dishes. Open for dinner only; closed Sundays and Mondays. Tables are hard to come by on Saturdays, so book early. Major credit cards accepted. In the Carrollton section, 723 Dante St. (phone: 861-7610).

Commander's Palace This big, festive—yet undeniably elegant—restaurant in a handsome late-19th-century Garden District mansion is cast in the rich, traditional creole mold. The menu ranges from familiar classics to creative innovations. You'll find what is arguably the world's best turtle soup here, as well as fresh fish such as trout or grouper prepared in a zesty horseradish crust with a saffron cream sauce. Among other winners are a thick, bracing creole bouillabaisse loaded with shellfish, fish, and seafood sausage, and fried oysters wrapped in bacon inside a crunchy batter and served on a piquant jelly of sweet and hot peppers. There's no better finale to all this than the renowned bread pudding soufflé. There are several dining rooms, two of them overlooking the oak-shaded courtyard (where meals are served in the spring and fall); the upper Garden Room, with its exposed view of the sinuous oak trees that makes you feel as if you are dining in an elegant treehouse, is the more celebrated. The wine cellar holds a bounty of premium California chardonnays and cabernets, and service is impeccable. Open daily. Reserve as early as possible, and wear your best duds; jackets are required for men. Major credit cards accepted. 1403 Washington Ave. (phone: 899-8221).

Emeril's This dining spot is a haven for serious eaters looking for modern New Orleans cooking. Owner-chef Emeril Lagasse uses creole, Acadian, and "New American" influences to create an array of unique dishes. The duck and mushroom *étouffée* has all the lustiness of the bayou gastronomy that inspired it; the pan-roasted salmon in herb crust is a new approach to a seafood dish often misunderstood by other New Orleans chefs. The culinary repertoire is impressive: On any given evening, as many as 15 desserts will be offered, including a luscious chocolate bread pudding and mouth-watering banana-cream and peanut-butter pies. The wines, primarily Californian, have been chosen for their novelty and quality. The lofty dining room has a geometric, post-modern look with its persimmon-pink textured walls, exposed brick, black metal bar stools, and modern furniture—which fits right into its trendy Warehouse District neighborhood. It's noisy, though—not the place for intimate conversation. Closed Sundays. Reservations necessary a week or more in advance. Major credit cards accepted. 800 Tchoupitoulas St. (phone: 528-9393).

Galatoire's A visit to this classic old French-creole bistro in the French Quarter is a necessity if you want to understand the foundations of New Orleans gastronomy. While it adheres to some unbending rules—no reservations, no pasta, and no obscure ingredients—it has retained a vitality untarnished since its founding in 1905. The mood is convivial, especially on weekend nights, when spiffily dressed locals squeeze into the deep, narrow dining room that's more functional than fussy. Mirrors run the length of the room, multiplying the images of the antique brass chandeliers, gleaming brass coat hooks, white linen–draped tables, and bentwood chairs. The menu reads like a museum catalogue, and it can lead to an exceptional meal. *Galatoire's* remains at heart an upscale seafood house, with dishes such as shrimp remoulade (the best in New Orleans) and fried oysters with bacon *en brochette.* Everything served here is seasonal, and if delicate, buttery pompano (a flounder-like gulf fish) is in the kitchen, order it grilled or broiled with a sprinkle of crabmeat sautéed in butter and green seasonings. Or dig into a simple cold appetizer of crab lumps tossed with mayonnaise and a bit of onion. Some regulars swear by the lamb or veal chops in a rich, herbal béarnaise sauce. Desserts are perfunctory. The best way to order is to discuss your preferences with one of the tuxedoed waiters and follow his advice. Wines are similarly dealt with, since the printed list is basically generic. Closed Mondays. Avoid the usual long lines outside by planning to dine early. Visa and MasterCard accepted. 209 Bourbon St. (phone: 525-2021).

Gautreau's Nestled among the oak trees in a quiet Uptown neighborhood, this is an elegant bistro where a single dish might contain shrimp from the Louisiana wetlands, greens grown in Southern California, herbs from the Orient, and a Mediterranean garlic mayonnaise. The creator of this polished, urban cooking style is Larkin Selman, a New Orleans native and an alumnus of New York City's *Gotham Bar & Grill.* There is a superb, light seafood gumbo on the menu, along with the moistest, most delicate crab cakes in town. The breast of guinea hen in a luscious sage sauce, accompanied by prune-flavored risotto, is another winner. Salads and soups are as imaginative as they are delicious, and desserts are good, especially the sweet, refreshing tequila Key lime pie with coconut whipped cream, the orange *crème brûlée,* and the dark-chocolate terrine spiked with Baileys Irish Cream. There is something on the eclectic wine list for both the connoisseur and the novice. The original downstairs dining room, with its handsome antique drugstore display case set against the deep burgundy walls, is charming but sometimes noisy. The pale yellow room upstairs is more tranquil most nights. Closed Sundays. The place is rather small, so book early. Major credit cards accepted. 1728 Soniat St. (phone: 899-7397).

Grill Room For its visual splendor alone, the *Windsor Court* hotel's dining room has few rivals. Turn-of-the-century oil portraits of members of the English aristocracy grace a sumptuous room rich in tufted damask banquettes and expensive crystal and porcelain; waiters tread unobtrusively from table to table; and the menu, choreographed by the executive chef, Kevin Graham, changes daily, depending on which fresh ingredients are available. One evening you might be tasting thick, pink slices of duck foie gras, the edges seared to a crisp brown, with shiitake mushrooms, reed-thin green beans, and a tarragon sauce. Another day might bring smoked blue marlin with zucchini ribbons. The creamy seafood bisque with a touch of saffron is excellent, vibrant with deep, rich creole flavors. Desserts are similarly rich: a crisp *tuile* of ginger-snap dough filled with fresh berries and sorbets, served atop a white-wine gelatin; and a little cup and saucer made of cookie dough and filled with espresso ice cream. The number and quality of wines are stunning, too—ask for the wine list and you'll get an inch-thick tome listing an eye-popping collection of some of the best Bordeaux vintages of the century, along with hundreds of other excellent choices. Service is stopwatch precise. Open daily. Major credit cards accepted. *Windsor Court Hotel,* 300 Gravier St. (phone: 522-1992).

Mr. B's Bistro The convivial atmosphere at this stylish bistro is underscored by a piano accompaniment during dinner; its informal, low-ceilinged dining room is made more intimate by wood-and-glass screens separating the tables. Chef Gerard Maras's handiwork includes appetizers of various types of fish cooked on a wood-fired grill and served with a number of herb and vegetable sauces. Louisiana oysters, hickory-smoked and blended with garlic, rosemary, and olive oil and served with little kernels of orzo, make an appealing entrée, as do the house-cured salmon and smoked sable in a dill-caper dressing. Shrimp remoulade, a creole staple, is done here with a twist—roasted sweet pepper is added to the thick and peppery vinaigrette and ladled onto cool, spicy shellfish. Desserts are heartily delicious: a fluffy lemon cassata; bread pudding with Irish whiskey sauce; and spice cake with apples and walnuts under a nutmeg double-cream. Forget the diet—you won't regret it. Open daily. Major credit cards accepted. 201 Royal St. (phone: 523-2078).

Upperline With three dining rooms located in an old frame building, this Uptown bistro has a smart decor with pale gray walls, colorful paintings and prints, bursts of flowers, Art Deco–style floor lamps, and a streamlined bar. The menu is just as sophisticated as the setting thanks to Chef Tom Cowman, who mixes the familiar and the innovative. The trout mousse, redolent of dill and lemon, is a grand way to begin a meal. What follows might be a knockout version of New Orleans–style barbecue shrimp, robust-tasting tamales with crawfish tails and andouille sausage, a glorious vichyssoise of roasted sweet pepper, or a well-prepared lamb curry. Cowman is that rare chef who can produce all of these, as well as four different gumbos faithful to the complex, distinctive flavors of true creole cuisine. Grilled fish is a specialty, and it's served with any of several salsas. For dessert, try the scrumptious coconut-banana cake. The small but selective wine list contains solid labels at easy-to-swallow prices, just as the menu offers several fixed-price bargains. Service is efficient, too. Closed Tuesdays. Major credit cards accepted. 1413 Upperline St. (phone: 891-9822).

Versailles This comfortable restaurant, with its body-hugging chairs, slightly Old World atmosphere, European service, and picturesque view of the St. Charles streetcars, is classy without being cloying. Although cast in the continental mode, the dishes are decidedly lavish, though not overwrought, just as the decor is plush without being intimidating. The Baroque accents and warm colors make a good setting for the food that owner/chef Gunter Preuss and his wife, Evelyn, serve—and it's the food that brings locals back time and again. They come for the salmon Argenteuil, perhaps the best preparation of this dish in the city, or the grill of scallops wrapped in filets of pompano—each little roulade adorned with a jumbo shrimp and set in a classic cream sauce tinged with mustard and capers. The elegant bouillabaisse and the superb mignonette of beef périgourdine in a truffled sauce with port are also favorites. Among the outstanding desserts are pears poached in red wine and stuffed with pecans, a fine *crème brûlée,* and a cookie tulip filled with hazelnut mousse. Closed Sundays. Major credit cards accepted. 2100 St. Charles Ave. (phone: 524-2535).

EXPENSIVE

Alex Patout's Part creole, part Cajun, this upscale eatery on upper Royal Street is a good place to get familiar with south Louisiana's mainstream cuisine.

You'll find rich gumbos, buttery seafood dishes, and robust duck and pork dishes on chef Alex Patout's bill of fare; an especially delectable dish is the duck with oyster stuffing. The ambience in the deep, narrow dining room is elegant but very welcoming. Open daily for dinner only. Major credit cards accepted. 221 Royal St. (phone: 525-7788).

Anacapri Italian regional cooking gets a classy continental veneer in this airy and colorful restaurant near the French Quarter riverfront. Ingredients, especially the seafoods and pasta, are first class. Favorites include fresh gulf fish baked in aromatic vegetables, and the quail, rabbit, and veal dishes, all done with chef Andrea Apuzzo's native Italian flair. Open daily. Major credit cards accepted. 320 Decatur St. (phone: 522-9056).

Antoine's With a menu that reaches back more than 100 years, and a maze of rooms filled with enough memorabilia for two or three small museums, this place defines the classical creole style in New Orleans. The recipe for oysters Rockefeller was invented here, and it is still excellent. Other good bets are the cool and spicy shrimp remoulade, crabmeat *ravigote* (in a cold, spicy mayonnaise), broiled pompano (a gulf fish similar to flounder) topped with sautéed lump crabmeat, and baked Alaska emblazoned with the date of the restaurant's founding—1840. Frances Parkinson Keyes wrote the best-selling romance novel *Dinner at Antoine's,* published in the 1940s, that used this restaurant as a setting. Closed Mondays. Major credit cards accepted. 713 St. Louis St. (phone: 581-4422).

Arnaud's Old-style creole elegance fairly oozes from this huge, glittery French Quarter establishment. An entire wall of the sparkling main dining room is made of antique glass, etched and leaded, reflecting the light from the delicate chandeliers hanging from the soaring ceiling. The reliable dishes include shrimp Arnaud (a superb version of remoulade), oysters in cream, sautéed fish in various seasoned butter sauces, the airiest soufflé potatoes, and bread pudding. Open daily. Major credit cards accepted. 813 Bienville St. (phone: 523-5433).

Bacco Italian cooking was late in coming to New Orleans. This bright, beautifully decorated restaurant, the brainchild of the owners of *Mr. B's Bistro* (see above), fills the bill. The menu is ambitious, with dozens of choices among antipasti, pizza, pasta, and entrées including *papardelle* with a rabbit ragout, roasted pork loin in a rosemary sauce, and hickory-smoked swordfish in a Mediterranean-style tomato sauce. Decorative accents in the four dining rooms and bar were inspired by several eras, from the Gothic to the contemporary. Open daily. Major credit cards accepted. *Hotel de la Poste,* 310 Chartres St. (phone: 522-2426).

Bella Luna With views of the lively Mississippi River, the dining room of this posh, second-floor establishment is inside the *French Market.* Soothing gray walls define the mood in the main dining room, while the second one, surrounded by French doors and fan windows, takes on the look of a Viennese ballroom. The osso buco is a standout, as are the pasta, creative salads, and luscious desserts. Open Mondays through Saturdays for dinner only, and for brunch on Sundays. Major credit cards accepted. In the *French Market* complex near the corner of Decatur and Dumaine Sts. (phone: 529-1583).

Brennan's Fancy and festive breakfasts and brunches with a creole lavishness are what put this picturesque French Quarter restaurant on the map. Many of the luxurious dining rooms, in a beautiful, early-19th-century building, are done up in the high style of the period. The bill of fare sticks fairly closely to classic creole with a fine gumbo, good fish dishes, and a profusion of butter and cream sauces. Poached eggs with elaborate and numerous embellishments can be ordered from morning to near midnight. *Brennan's* is not for the budget-minded at any hour, however. Open daily. Major credit cards accepted. 417 Royal St. (phone: 525-9711).

Caribbean Room The *Pontchartrain* hotel's exceptional dining room serves French and creole dishes. The menu is imaginative, and specialties are beautifully presented—red snapper Eugene (in lemon sauce with crab and shrimp), crabmeat Biarritz (lump crabmeat with whipped cream dressing and topped with caviar), and, if you can go the distance, Mile-High Ice Cream Pie for dessert. Open daily; closed at lunch weekends. Major credit cards accepted. 2031 St. Charles Ave. (phone: 524-0581).

Christian's The restaurant inhabits a church building, but there is nothing gimmicky about the food, which puts several new spins on the French-creole repertory. Seafood entrées, especially the bouillabaisse and sautéed fish, are standouts. Elbow room is at a minimum in the hyperactive dining room, designed with banquettes lining the walls, stained glass windows, and contemporary lighting fixtures hanging from the vaulted ceiling. Closed Sundays. Major credit cards accepted. 3835 Iberville St. (phone: 482-4924).

Kabby's For a big hotel dining room, it does an above-average job of putting out authentic creole-style food, ranging from such down-home fare as po-boys (hearty French-bread sandwiches made with a variety of local ingredients) to more elaborate and upscale dishes like oysters Rockefeller and sautéed shrimp in anisette liqueur. A big draw here is the close-up view of the Mississippi River; excursion boats and other craft often tie up in front of the place, just yards away from the window tables. Open daily. Major credit cards accepted. In the *New Orleans Hilton*'s *Riverside* complex, Poydras St. at the Mississippi River (phone: 584-3880).

K-Paul's Louisiana Kitchen Upstairs tables can be reserved, but chances are you'll have to cool your heels outside the door for an hour or more at dinnertime for a sampling of trailblazer Paul Prudhomme's creative Cajun dishes. Once inside the rather rudimentary first-floor dining room, you also may have to share a table with strangers. Still, legions of out-of-towners keep coming back for the Cajun guru's earthy gumbos, peppery *étouffées,* and fish dishes—the ones that started the blackening craze almost a decade ago. Wiser customers come at lunch, when the line is shorter, the prices are lower, and the food is much the same as it is at dinner. Closed weekends. American Express accepted. 416 Chartres St. (phone: 942-7500).

Louis XVI French classicism reigns in these soft, elegant spaces flanking the exceptionally pleasant courtyard of a French Quarter hotel. Typical creations are shellfish in puff pastry with cream sauce, beefsteak in wine sauce with mushrooms, Caesar salad, and baroque desserts. The cream soups are especially good. Banks of arched windows and a warm color scheme add to the appealing ambience. Open daily. Major credit cards accepted. *St. Louis Hotel,* 730 Bienville St. (phone: 581-7000).

Mike's on the Avenue "Fusion cooking" (dishes influenced by a blend of many different cultures) has been around for years now, but chef-owner Michael Fennelly takes the concept to its limits in his smartly minimal restaurant in a revitalized old hotel on the edge of the Warehouse District. Fennelly draws inspiration from Japan, Thailand, China, the American Southwest, New Orleans, and any other part of the culinary map that strikes his fancy. The results are such concoctions as spring rolls filled with crawfish, a black-bean dip spiked with Cajun seasonings, a casserole of shrimp, mussels, and Cajun sausage, and sautéed cakes of crab and scallops with three sauces zapped with chilies. Somehow, it all works deliciously in the spare, but beautiful, whitewashed dining rooms, bathed with light from wide glass walls and hung with the chef's own abstract expressionist paintings. Closed Sundays. Reservations necessary a week in advance for dinner. Major credit cards accepted. *Lafayette Hotel,* 628 St. Charles Ave. (phone: 523-1709).

Nola A spinoff of *Emeril's* in the Warehouse District, this big, modern eatery is chef Emeril Lagasse's tribute to the gutsy cuisine of the Louisiana bayous. The menu is filled with robust stews, sausages, earthy-tasting sweet potatoes, hogshead cheese, and novel treatments of regional seafoods. Typical are the creole "cassoulet" with blood sausage, beef brisket, and chicken in a ragout of red and white beans; a green salad with fried oysters and anisette dressing; and coconut cream pie. Downstairs is more casual than upstairs, and both are decidedly contemporary in design. Opens daily at 2:30 PM. Reservations advised, at least a week in advance for dinner. Major credit cards accepted. 534 St. Louis St. (phone: 522-6652).

Palace Café Canal Street's restaurant scene got a powerful shot in the arm when this sparkling two-level "grand café" opened in the early 1990s in a building that once served as New Orleans's biggest music store. The mezzanine, brightened with a large mural depicting the city's legendary musicians, is reached by a central staircase. Both levels are lively during peak hours, when the bar fills up and things start to sizzle in the open kitchen. "Clever creole" is the kitchen's style: rabbit ravioli in a Louisiana-style sauce piquante, a red-bean dip with the kitchen's own potato chips, a creamy "napoleon" of seafood, and a yummy white-chocolate bread pudding. Open daily. Major credit cards accepted. 605 Canal St. (phone: 523-1661).

Pascal's Manale While this Italian-creole eatery in the Uptown section is beginning to fray at the edges, it still pulls 'em in with a handful of signature dishes that first made its reputation. First among these is barbecued shrimp, baked in their shells with an herbal, spicy butter sauce. Pasta dishes are popular, too, especially those with seafood. The wait for a table is spent in a convivial oyster bar festooned with photos, posters, pennants, and memorabilia. Closed Sundays. Major credit cards accepted. 1838 Napoleon Ave. (phone: 895-4877).

Pelican Club Innovative New Orleans cooking is the trademark of this crisply stylish dining place located in a stately French Quarter townhouse. Proprietor/chef Richard Hughes's food combines New York sophistication with lots of Louisiana robustness. A popular appetizer is artichoke leaves topped with seared scallops in seasoned butter. A shellfish salad is refreshingly simple, and a seafood-and-rice creation is part Louisiana jambalaya and part Spanish paella. Each of the three dining rooms has its own mood, from the clubby, wood-paneled room in the back to the elegant space overlooking Bienville Street. Closed Sundays. Major credit cards accepted. 312 Exchange Alley at Bienville St. (phone: 523-1504).

Ruth's Chris Steak House What makes this comfortable no-nonsense restaurant the city's leading purveyor of steaks is the quality of the beef, the exemplary charbroiling, and a distinctive seasoned butter that arrives sizzling on the plate. The formula has paid off in a chain of *Ruth's Chris* branches from Honolulu to Manhattan. Politicians pack the place almost nightly, but the dark-wooded dining rooms, lined with soothing paintings, are spacious. Service is far above average. Open daily. Major credit cards accepted. 711 N. Broad St. (phone: 486-0810).

Sazerac With a dining room as frilly as a dozen wedding cakes, this very upscale hotel restaurant is just the place for a romantic—if expensive—evening. White lace covers the red tablecloths, and a dramatic burst of flowers crowns a central cluster of red-velvet banquettes. The menu, which seems to undergo a complete overhaul annually, is a combination of French, south Louisiana, and regional American cuisines. Foie gras, turtle soup, and fancied-up creole dishes are the mainstays, however. Open daily. Major credit cards accepted. *Fairmont Hotel,* University Pl. (phone: 529-4733).

Veranda On the second level of the *Inter-Continental* hotel, this meticulously maintained restaurant, decorated to resemble the dining room of an elegant antebellum mansion, has a lush tropical garden within a glass-canopied atrium. The braised veal shank and sautéed fish are especially good. Weekday lunches and fixed-priced Sunday brunch buffets are good buys for the quality and selection. Open daily. Major credit cards accepted. *Inter-Continental Hotel*, 444 St. Charles Ave. (phone: 525-5566).

MODERATE

Bacchi Somewhat off the beaten track, but worth the 15-minute taxi ride from the city's heart (and the 20-minute wait for a table), this upscale spot is a must for aficionados of "neo-Italian" restaurant fare. The headliners include imaginative pizza and salads and such seductive dishes as polenta stuffed with braised duck and fried leeks, fettuccine in a shrimp butter with mushrooms and scallions, and grilled fish with yellow tomatoes and basil-nut oil. The bar and split-level dining room, always aflutter with locals, are sleekly contemporary, informal, and bright. Open daily. No reservations. Major credit cards accepted. 900 Harrison Ave. (phone: 486-2500).

Bayou Ridge Cafe With more than a touch of the West Coast in its food, this sleekly handsome spot lures locals to the French Quarter's fringe with a combination of lightness and flavor: Pasta and pizza are creative without being silly. Succulent sautéed salmon, chicken moistened with zesty vegetable sauces, and *crème brûlée* are other winners. The decor of the angular dining rooms is minimal, with large framed photographs adding a cheerful note. Closed Mondays and Tuesdays. Major credit cards accepted. 5080 Pontchartrain Blvd. (phone: 486-0788).

Bistro at Maison de Ville While the menu at this French Quarter spot changes almost weekly, some things remain predictable—among them the light and herbal seafood soups, beef tournedos with boursin cheese in a subtle wine sauce, unusual pasta dishes, and first-rate *crème brûlée*. The tiny dining room, with lustrous wood paneling and a full-length maroon banquette, holds 40; the charming little courtyard out back is used in pleasant weather, too. Closed Sunday lunch. Major credit cards accepted. *Maison de Ville Hotel*, 733 Toulouse St. (phone: 528-9206).

Bon Ton Café A strong traditional streak runs through the menu in this rather old-fashioned, but always humming, creole-Cajun bistro at the Central Business District's core. Crawfish is perhaps the biggest seller; the crawfish *étouffée* bisque and the jambalaya are well seasoned. Space is at a premium in the brick-lined dining room, with checkered tablecloths and a cadre of energetic waitresses. Closed weekends. Major credit cards accepted. 401 Magazine St. (phone: 524-3386).

Charley G's "Casual and classy" sums up this large, efficiently run restaurant, a few yards from the boundary line between Orleans and Jefferson Parishes. Spicy south Louisiana cooking is the mainstay of the large menu of hearty appetizers and main courses. Among the better choices are the robustly seasoned crab cakes, the duck and andouille sausage gumbo, and fish grilled over mesquite. Desserts, such as the Bullwinkle chocolate mousse pie, are huge and delicious. The uncluttered, contemporary dining spaces are lined in stained woods and warm earth tones, with banquettes flanking the wraparound windows. Open daily. Major credit cards accepted. 111 Veterans Blvd., Metairie (phone: 837-6408).

Chez Daniel Add a dash of elegance to home-style French cooking and you have something akin to the menu offered at this lively and informal spot that's just a short drive across the city limits in Metairie. French-trained chef Daniel Bonnot has won over a small army of followers with his garlicky snails, endive salad, steak *au poivre,* grilled fish with fennel in *beurre blanc,* and *crème brûlée.* A large Belle Epoque–inspired mural adds to the gaiety. Closed Sundays and Mondays. Major credit cards accepted. 2037 Metairie Rd., Metairie (phone: 837-6900).

Clancy's If you're tired of the tourist track, consider this likable contemporary bistro deep within an Uptown residential section. It has tuxedoed waiters, very good food, and a decor so simple it's almost nonexistent. The crab bisque and shrimp remoulade are superb. Almost as good are the sautéed fish in cream sauce, sweetbreads with lemon and capers, lamb chops in béarnaise sauce, and home-style lemon icebox pie. Closed Sundays. Major credit cards accepted. 6100 Annunciation St. (phone: 895-1111).

Dooky Chase's The spirited cooking in this beautifully appointed establishment is traditional creole with a dash of Southern-style soul. Chef Leah Chase's okra with tomatoes is definitive, as are her veal grillades, pork chops smothered with onions, crab soup, and bread pudding. The weekday luncheon buffets are justifiably popular. Just minutes from the French Quarter by taxi, the restaurant is handsomely decorated with good-quality paintings and prints, mostly by local black artists. Open daily. Major credit cards accepted. 2301 Orleans Ave. (phone: 821-2294).

G & E Courtyard Grill This very pleasant place on bustling lower Decatur Street is always relaxed yet lively, thanks to the updated creole-Italian dishes and old-fashioned Italian atmosphere. Chef Michael Uddo's specialties include cream of oysters Rockefeller soup, zesty antipasto of crudités and cold cuts, grilled shrimp, and hearty pasta. In good weather, try for a table in the canopied courtyard. Closed Monday dinner. Major credit cards accepted. 1115 Decatur St. (phone: 528-9376).

J. Lillian Game and seafood dishes, aggressively seasoned and elaborately presented, are the focus of this large yet cozy Louisiana-style restaurant on St. Charles Avenue near Lee Circle. Pasta is tossed with bits of duck and smoked mushrooms; seared salmon is encrusted with herbs and escorted by a gratin of potato and poblano peppers; and gumbos and *étouffées* take on contemporary twists, too. A sweet tooth can be indulged with such desserts as a three-layer chocolate gâteau with praline sauce and roasted almonds. Open daily. Major credit cards accepted. *Quality Inn-Maison St. Charles,* 1319 St. Charles Ave. (phone: 529-4484).

Kelsey's Paul Prudhomme's kitchen has spawned any number of ambitious young chefs. One is Randy Barlow, who carves his own niche in this unassuming but attractive second-floor spot in Algiers, just across the Mississippi from central New Orleans. The menu's stars are the gumbos, a superb shrimp stew, and a terrific all-meat jambalaya. The orange-poppyseed cheesecake is addictive, as are the bread pudding and other desserts. Attractive paintings perk up the pleasant dining spaces. Closed Saturday lunch, Sundays, and Mondays. Major credit cards accepted. 3920 Gen. DeGaulle Dr., Algiers (phone: 366-6722).

Little Greek The deftly prepared traditional Greek food here is a real treat: The spreads and dips, especially the *taramasalata* (carp roe dip with olive oil, lemon juice, and garlic) and *skordalia* (a cold, garlicky sauce made either with mashed potatoes or bread crumbs, plus pine nuts or walnuts and olive oil), are deliciously authentic. Original creations include garlic sautéed fish in buttery phyllo dough and shrimp baked with olive oil, sherry, garlic, and lemon in a paprika sauce. The two colorful dining rooms and bar are hung with every sort of eastern Mediterranean artifact. Closed Mondays. Major credit cards accepted. 619 Pink St., Metairie (phone: 831-9470).

Mandich's What it lacks in chic it makes up for with an unusually good array of home-style classics such as white beans and rice, fried oysters with garlic butter, and buttery sautéed trout, augmented with such upscale dishes as filet mignon and oysters Rockefeller. It's located about a 15-minute drive from the downtown hotels, and its hours are quirky. Closed Mondays; open for lunch Tuesdays through Fridays, and dinner only on weekends. MasterCard accepted. 3200 St. Claude Ave. (phone: 947-9553).

Mosca's About a half hour's drive across the Mississippi River, via the Huey P. Long Bridge, this West Bank highway roadhouse in a rudimentary clapboard building serves the heartiest Italian-creole cuisine in the area. Everything on the moderate-size menu is a classic, but the most popular dishes are the baked oysters Mosca, Italian shrimp, roasted chicken with rosemary and garlic, and roasted sausage with potatoes. Closed Sundays and Mondays. No credit cards accepted. 4137 US Hwy. 90, Waggaman (phone: 436-9942).

La Provence Nestled in the piney woods of Lacombe, Louisiana, across Lake Pontchartrain, is the exceptionally comfortable establishment of Marseilles-born chef Chris Kerageogiu, who turns out exceptional, earthy Provençal dishes using local and regional ingredients. His quail gumbo, *jambalaya des gourmands,* rack of lamb, leg of rabbit, and fish dishes are among the best in the region. The atmosphere is reminiscent of a French country inn. Closed Mondays and Tuesdays. Major credit cards accepted. About 35 miles from central New Orleans, on the north shore of Lake Pontchartrain on US Hwy. 190, Lacombe (phone: 626-7662).

Ralph & Kacoo's Even with several locations in the French Quarter and in the suburbs, this casual and very popular Cajun eatery fills up fast. The Cajun theme is carried out with a full-size fishing boat in the bar and a jumble of nostalgic artifacts strewn everywhere. Highlights include a fine crab gumbo, trout meunière, fried shrimp or oysters, and good renderings of sautéed fish. Open daily. No reservations. Major credit cards accepted. 519 Toulouse St. (phone: 522-5226) and 601 Veterans Blvd., Metairie (phone: 831-3177).

INEXPENSIVE

Alberto's Slightly Bohemian and full of energetic pizzazz, this upstairs spot, a few blocks from the French Quarter, serves unusually good Italian food at reasonable prices. Any of the several cannelloni, especially the one with crawfish, is a good way to start. Shrimp with Pernod cream and fettuccine is fresh and flavorful, as are the sautéed soft-shell crab and the veal *panée,* a kind of breaded cutlet. Open for dinner only; closed Sundays. No reservations. No credit cards accepted. 611 Frenchmen St. (phone: 949-5952).

Casamento's Cleanliness is an obsession in this legendary oyster house on upper Magazine Street, its gleaming white tiles giving the two small dining spaces the look of a large bathroom. Oysters are the stars here, either fried and presented without a trace of grease, freshly shucked and served up on the half shell, or cooked in a homey stew with milk and scallions. The shrimp and oyster "loaves," made with scooped-out white bread, are delicious. The rest of the menu is unimpressive. Closed Mondays and June through August. No reservations. No credit cards accepted. 4330 Magazine St. (phone: 895-9761).

Central Grocery Company This grocery store has been here since 1906 and still stocks flour, beans, and other staples in barrels to sell by the pound. More popular, however, are the great take-out Italian sandwiches, cheeses, and salads. Open daily. No reservations. No credit cards accepted. 923 Decatur St. (phone: 523-1620).

China Blossom What may be the best Chinese-American restaurant in town is tucked away in a small shopping mall across the river. Chef Paul Fung does a great job with shrimp and oysters, grilling or sautéing them before adding marvelous piquant sauces. The pan-Chinese menu covers all the bases from egg rolls to fortune cookies, and it's all reliably good. Closed Mondays. Reservations advised on weekends. Major credit cards accepted. 1801 Stumpf Blvd., Gretna (phone: 361-4598).

Croissant d'Or This small nook makes an excellent morning stop. Ten varieties of croissants and more than 20 different French pastries are baked on the premises and are served with mugs of thick café au lait. Sandwiches, soups, and salads are also available. Open daily. No reservations. No credit cards accepted. 617 Ursulines St. (phone: 524-4663).

Kung's Dynasty A Greek Revival mansion in the Lower Garden District wouldn't be the first place you'd look for good Chinese food. But you'll find it here. The atmosphere inside the lofty double parlors is unusually nice. Open daily. Reservations unnecessary. Major credit cards accepted. 1912 St. Charles Ave. (phone: 525-6669).

Mandina's Once upon a time, every New Orleans neighborhood had its own purveyor of po-boys, red beans, and spaghetti, with a room out back for family gatherings. This place carries on the tradition faithfully. After a wait at the stand-up bar, sit at a Formica-topped table and dig into very good po-boys, garlicky cracked crab claws, butter-drenched trout meunière, or a creditable gumbo. Open daily. No reservations. No credit cards accepted. 3800 Canal St. (phone: 482-9179).

Praline Connection A couple of blocks beyond Esplanade Avenue near the Mississippi docks is this bright and bustling specialist in down-to-earth creole home cooking. Neat as a pin and always packed, it's a fun place to sample first-rate versions of fried chicken, meat-stuffed peppers, corn bread, sweet potato pie, beans and rice, succulent pork chops, or grand chicken stew. Top off your feast with some of the authentic and luscious pecan pralines. Open daily. No reservations. Major credit cards accepted. 542 Frenchmen St. (phone: 943-3934) and in the Warehouse District at 901 South Peters St. (phone: 523-3973).

Taqueria Corona Aficionados of tacos, nachos, and burritos will find exceptionally good renditions here. Try the "tacocado" salad, a fried tortilla filled with guacamole, meat, lettuce, olives, and cheese. Seating is at both the counter and tables. Service is make-do. Open daily. No reservations. No credit cards accepted. 857 Fulton St. and 5932 Magazine St. (phone: 897-3974 for both locations).

BIG EASY FOOD FACTS

Gumbo, a culinary essential of Louisiana life, is a thick, spicy soup based on seafood, poultry, sausage, duck, or any combination of these. No two cooks make it exactly alike. You'll find several especially good versions of it at three restaurants listed above: *K-Paul's Louisiana Kitchen; Mr. B's Bistro,* which features an extra-thick "gumbo ya ya," with chicken and sausage; and *Galatoire's,* which serves a seafood gumbo with okra in a light, well-seasoned broth. *Filé,* a powder made by grinding sassafras leaves, is often used in gumbos as a thickener. *Gumbo filé* is difficult to find in New Orleans, but *Eddie's at Krauss* on the second floor of *Krauss* department store (1201 Canal St.; phone: 523-3311) and *Dooky Chase's* (see above) both serve good versions of it.

A traditional Cajun-creole dish served all over town is *étouffée* ("smothered" in French), a thick stew that was once made exclusively with crawfish but now sometimes features shrimp or other seafood cooked in a covered black iron pot. Some good places to sample it are *Alex Patout's, K-Paul's Louisiana Kitchen,* and *Patout's* (see above for information on all three).

Po-boys, two-fisted sandwiches of thick French bread, slit open and filled with meat, seafood, and vegetables, are a New Orleans staple. Fried shrimp or oysters, ham, hot roast beef with gravy, and meatballs and tomato sauce are just some of the variations. Order your po-boy "dressed" and it'll come with lettuce, tomato, and mayonnaise. Best bets are the fried shrimp po-boy at *Acme Seafood and Oyster House* (724 Iberville St.; phone: 522-5973); roast beef or ham po-boy at *Mother's* (401 Poydras St.; phone: 523-9656); and the fried-oyster "loaf" at *Casamento's* (see above).

Another hearty sandwich is the muffuletta—round, crusty bread stuffed with ham, salami, mozzarrella, and a salad of pickled green olive and pimentoes. The best and most authentic are found at *Progress Grocery* (915 Decatur St.; phone: 525-6627) and *Central Grocery* (923 Decatur St.; phone: 523-1620).

And last, but far from least, are beignets, those sweet, square doughnuts, sprinkled with powdered sugar and the perfect complement to New Orleans–style chicory coffee. Get the best of both at *Café du Monde* (813 Decatur St.; phone: 581-2914) and *Café Beignet* (620 Decatur St.; phone: 566-1225).

If you want to see the preparation side of New Orleans dishes, check out the cooking workshops given each spring at the historic *Hermann-Grima House* (phone: 525-5661; see *Museums and Historic Houses*); the classes have themes such as "A Celebration of the Creole Table."

Diversions

Exceptional Pleasures and Treasures

Quintessential New Orleans

Romance, mystery, and an almost palpable sense of the past constantly converge in New Orleans. Peek through the wrought-iron gate of a French Quarter carriageway, beyond the cobblestones and into the verdant courtyard, and imagine what plots might have been hatched or what loves might have been consummated 100 years ago. From a table at *Antoine's,* watch a couple walk through the cavernous, neo-Gothic dining room into a labyrinth of inner sanctums. Who are they? What might they be up to? In New Orleans, the possibilities are endless. With such a beautiful and timeless setting, your imagination is stimulated at every turn, heightened by the sound of a jazz trumpet coming from who knows where, the perfume of blossoming sweet olive in the early spring, the pungent taste of a creole remoulade sauce, the arresting beauty of a black iron-lace balcony against tarnished stucco. If all of this seems unreal, that's as it should be—in New Orleans, reality is always put on hold until the final song is sung and the last drop of wine consumed.

MARDI GRAS When you think New Orleans, you think *Mardi Gras.* Choreographed parades and well-planned, fancy balls are the raison d'être of this celebration, but what makes *Mardi Gras* truly great happens spontaneously, unpredictably, and wildly—serendipitous moments that are the real magic of this more-than-a-century-old celebration. On one corner of the French Quarter, a high school linebacker and a primly dressed woman, probably old enough to be his grandmother, strangers only seconds ago, dance a makeshift jitterbug; down the block, a family of four dressed as clowns try to catch beaded necklaces being thrown from a balcony by some outrageously cross-dressed transvestites; on St. Charles Avenue, a senior partner in a Denver law firm finds himself scrambling on a curb in a good-humored contest with a 12-year-old kid for a 10¢ trinket tossed from a parade float. Meanwhile, on Canal Street, Pete Fountain's celebrated clarinet calls the tune as his *Half-Fast* (and half-sober) *Marching Club* wends its way through a wall-to-wall crowd without missing a beat. Multiply such vignettes by about 50,000 and the product is *Mardi Gras,* a magical day when reason sleeps and the real ties that bind are forged moment by moment. It's the day when an accountant from Akron can be Sir Lancelot, and a waitress from Seattle can fulfill her lifelong dream to be Marilyn Monroe, if only for a few hours. It's a day that reaffirms, finally, that underneath the costumes and greasepaint, all of us are the same. (For more information on the festivities, see *Mardi Gras Madness* in this section.)

JAZZFEST No single event captures the essence of New Orleans as vibrantly as the *New Orleans Jazz and Heritage Festival.* Held each year in late April and early May, *Jazzfest* celebrates the city's two great obsessions—music and food. Outdoors, indoors, on water and on land, more than 4,000 musicians and hundreds of cooks and artisans ply their musical, culinary, and artistic genius. Several concerts a night take place in music halls and nightclubs and on riverboats. The real blowout comes on the three-day weekends that begin and end the festival. Almost filling the huge inner greensward of the *New Orleans Fair Grounds* racetrack, on a dozen bandstands and in oversize tents, jazz and folk musicians from New Orleans and around the country and the world make music from morning to sunset. There are scores of booths offering soul-warming jambalaya, alligator sauce piquante, po-boy sandwiches, and other Big Easy specialties. Regional artisans display a colorful variety of carvings, pottery, textiles, and paintings. Festivalgoers sprawl on whatever slice of turf they can find and down spicy crawfish *étouffée* while taking in every note of a down-and-dirty blues band, an African folk troupe, or a group of Swedes delivering hot Dixieland licks. The huge *Gospel Tent* throbs nonstop with the wails and shouts of local church choirs. Happily, the sound of *Jazzfest* will linger with you long after you leave here. Just listen to a recording of Louis Armstrong playing "The Birth of the Blues"; you can recapture the experience—and perhaps make plans to return next year.

AND ALL THAT JAZZ Veteran banjoist Danny Barker claims that jazz sounds best in New Orleans because the city's pervasive high humidity endows the music with unique acoustical qualities. Sit for an hour or two in the *Palm Court Jazz Café* on Decatur Street listening to Barker play in his vintage style and you're not likely to argue the point. Or amble up a few blocks to the ramshackle *Preservation Hall,* take in a set by the *Olympia Brass Band,* and you might begin to wonder if mildewed old brick produces a similar effect on the quality of the music. Jazz has traveled the world many times over, but this is its hometown and remains its natural habitat. Where else but on the seedy edge of the New Orleans waterfront could a place like *Tipitina's* exist? Born many decades ago as a neighborhood restaurant and bar, its creaky wood frame now throbs every night till the wee hours with wailing, tooting, and plunking, priming the dance floor and urging the assembled crowd into a near-frenzy. Singer and percussionist Aaron Neville frequently appears here with his brothers, along with blues divas Irma Thomas and Marva Wright—not to mention any good band passing through town. Cooler heads prevail at *Snug Harbor,* in the Faubourg Marigny, a couple of blocks from the French Quarter. In a cramped, unadorned room out back, such masters of the "New Orleans Sound" as singers Charmaine Neville and Germaine Bazzle perform. Another regular is Ellis Marsalis, the most inventive contemporary jazz pianist the city has seen in decades and patriarch of the wondrous, musical Marsalis family (see *Nightclubs and Nightlife* in THE CITY for additional information about all of the above). While the special sound of New Orleans jazz may owe something to the city's incredibly high humidity—we think incredible talent has something to do with it, too.

BEIGNETS AND COFFEE AT CAFÉ DU MONDE Everybody comes to the *Café du Monde*—hard-core partygoers at dawn trying to sober up for the drive home; well-dressed matrons giving their feet a midday rest; a family from the Midwest, rosy-cheeked and sleepy-eyed at mid-morning, here to find out what a beignet is and how to pronounce it (ben-*yay*). A puffed-up square of rather chewy fried dough that you sprinkle with powdered sugar from the shaker on the table, a beignet is the ideal accompaniment to a steamy cup or two of café au lait New Orleans–style—half hot milk, half jet-black coffee brewed with a tad of ground, roasted chicory root. With stunning views of Jackson Square, Decatur Street, and the pavilion overlooking the Mississippi River framed by huge stucco arches, this is the best place to relax and watch the world go by. On cold days, the inside room fills up fast. The café is the gateway to the old *French Market,* made up of ancient colonnaded buildings extending several blocks along the river. Even though it is open 24 hours a day, every day except *Christmas,* getting a seat at one of the café's dozens of rudimentary tables usually involves a wait—but the unabashedly old-fashioned charm of the place is worth every minute.

PRALINES Pralines (pronounced *prah*-leens, not *pray*-leens) are almost as old as New Orleans itself. Aproned women once peddled them from huge baskets all over town. Today they're sold in more than a dozen shops in the French Quarter. As sweet confections go, the traditional creole praline is the soul of simplicity: Sugar is cooked down with butter, sometimes with a tad of milk and a sprinkle of the native pecan, to become a crisp candy wafer. Purists insist that they be eaten as soon as possible after cooling and disdain the recent additions of such things as vanilla, chocolate, coconut, and food coloring. For a taste of the real thing, begin at the *Old Town Praline Shop* (627 Royal St.; phone: 504-525-1413), where these down-home, super-sweet and slightly buttery candies have been sold for decades. Wrapped in old-fashioned waxed paper, they can be bought one at a time for a quick snack on the little patio just outside or packed in quaint little boxes, which can be shipped anywhere you wish. *Aunt Sally's Original Creole Pralines* in the *French Market* (810 Decatur St.; phone: 504-524-5107) adds a touch of vanilla to the pecan flavor of the basic praline. Just outside the Quarter, on the other side of Esplanade Avenue, is the *Praline Connection* (542 Frenchmen St.; phone: 504-943-3934), a restaurant and confectionery that specializes in all kinds of pralines, from the traditional sugar-and-pecan blend to chocolate and coconut varieties, as well as a delicious praline cookie. In the adjoining dining room, you can get a slice of cheesecake with praline sauce poured on top. Yum!

BOURBON STREET Synonymous with boisterous, bawdy exploits, it's eight blocks crammed with strip joints, naughty novelty shops, jazz clubs, and establishments offering transvestite shows and pornographic paraphernalia. The elegant buildings here, once inhabited by aristocratic creole families, now house raunchy activities that would make their ghosts blush. Bourbon Street began its evolution into the Bible Belt equivalent of Sodom and Gomorrah in 1917, not long after the federal government shut down the legendary bordellos of Storyville, just a few blocks away. Everything happens here—street performers dance to the music pouring from the nightclubs and hustle dollar bills; barkers hawk the feminine charms of the performers inside (sometimes failing to mention that the star's real name is Ralph). If you think Bourbon Street is just another Tenderloin district, check it out after a football game in the *Superdome,* when half the fans are indulging in some postgame high jinks. Since it's legal to drink on the streets of New Orleans if you use plastic containers, parties can pop up anywhere. Both sides of the block are crammed with places where you can get any kind of cocktail imaginable (don't forget that New Orleans's bartenders invented a couple themselves—the Hurricane and the Absinthe Frappé, all designed to put you in a merry mood as you stroll down one of the arteries of the fun-loving Big Easy). But with all the activity, real life does go on here—keep an eye out for couples pushing babies in perambulators, and don't forget to tip your hat at the house with the pale blue shutters in the 600 block, the full-time residence of retired Congresswoman Lindy Boggs, hardly the typical denizen of this naughty neighborhood.

JAZZ BRUNCH AT COMMANDER'S PALACE A late-morning feast on a Saturday or Sunday, accompanied by a small jazz ensemble playing favorite tunes as it weaves its way around the tables, has become a New Orleans ritual. Every major restaurant does it, but Ella and Dick Brennan, proprietors of *Commander's Palace* in the Garden District, do it better than anybody else. The several settings in the big frame mansion are ideal. In the understated main dining room, brightly colored balloons sprout from the tables like bouquets as waiters weave their way around table-hopping locals catching up on the latest gossip. Upstairs in the Garden Room, floor-to-ceiling windows on both sides look out over gigantic old oaks. The bright green and yellow walls and cushioned garden furniture give the sense of eternal spring. If the appropriate gods aren't angry, the day will be balmy enough to get a seat outside in the pavilion hung with lush tropical plants and shaded by giant oaks. Truth be known, the food suffers by comparison to the more sumptuous fare served at dinner (brunch prices are geared to filling the seats), but it's still good. The starter of sautéed shrimp with mushrooms is wonderful; the elaborate poached-egg dishes, drenched in buttery sauces, are nothing to be ashamed of. And the bread pudding soufflé is addictive. In any case, an icily invigorating milk punch or Bloody Mary can endow eggs with the flavor of nectar and transform a simple tune like "Do You Know What It Means to Miss New Orleans" into a piece worthy of Mozart. Don't be surprised if the waiters occasionally gather around a table and sing "Happy Birthday." Schmaltzy? Certainly. Cheering? You bet. The infectious conviviality of a *Commander's* jazz brunch just may convince you it's your birthday, too.

THE GARDEN DISTRICT This neighborhood, a sterling example of Protestant sobriety and tranquil beauty located within the same square mile as the wild, hedonistic Bourbon Street, presents yet another face of New Orleans. Unlike the French Quarter, the Garden District is not at all a "people place." You're not likely to encounter many other strollers as you walk in the cooling shade of its majestic oaks, the sidewalks buckling above the trees' unyielding roots. This is a place much more suited to contemplation than celebration, unless it's to revel in the incredible lushness of the vegetation and the 19th-century domestic architecture. The houses in this residential neighborhood come in a stunning array of styles—imposing Greek Revival, intricate neo-Gothic, and any other hybrid that struck the fancy of the local architects of the time. The neighborhood's integrity has remained remarkably intact. Take away the parked automobiles and the asphalt under them and you have an upper class town of the mid-19th century—which is precisely what the Garden District was. The original inhabitants were enterprising merchants, shippers, and lawyers, mostly of English and Scottish descent, whose wealth accumulated quickly in the glory days of New Orleans's river commerce. The air that lingers there today combines the seductive aromas of jasmine and magnolia with the faint scent of old money.

The area is especially beautiful in early spring, when the profusion of fuchsias and pink azaleas makes the stately white houses seem even more pristine, and the majestic trees and well-tended lawns even greener. The effect is much like strolling through an aristocratic old European colony on a Caribbean island—only better.

NEW ORLEANS NOËL Celebrating *Christmas* in the romantic, historic French Quarter is yet another of New Orleans's most delightful experiences. In early December, garlands of pine and holly tied with big red bows make their appearance on the iron-lace balconies along Royal and Chartres Streets, as this old historic district, with its elegant creole houses, gets ready to celebrate *Creole Christmas.* An annual event organized by the *French Quarter Festival,* it recaptures the holiday season as it was celebrated by the Creoles in the 19th century. For several weeks, historic homes like the *Hermann-Grima House* and *Gallier House* are decked out in heirloom decorations, and traditional creole delicacies are served in period porcelain and crystal serving dishes in elegant dining rooms. Carols are sung in Jackson Square, where an annual *Christmas* tree lighting takes place. More than a score of restaurants in the Quarter offer fixed-price menus replicating the *reveil-*

lons, the elaborate feasts held by the early French inhabitants when they returned from midnight mass at *St. Louis Cathedral.* Tours of private homes decorated in the style of the 19th century are another highlight of the season. *Joyeux Noël!*

A Few of Our Favorite Things

The Big Easy pulls people into its steamy embrace with an offer of pleasures not likely to be found elsewhere—or at least not in the combinations New Orleans provides them in. Below are some suggestions for the finest places to stay and savor the city and its fabulous fare. Follow our lead; we promise you won't be disappointed.

Each place listed below is described in greater detail in THE CITY chapter.

SPECIAL HAVENS

New Orleans hostelries can be heavenly; here are the best. Complete information about our choices can be found on pages 72 to 75 of THE CITY.

> *Inter-Continental*
> *LaMothe House*
> *Maison de Ville*
> *Le Meridien*
> *New Orleans Hilton*
> *Soniat House*
> *Westin–Canal Place*
> *Windsor Court*

BIG EASY'S BEST EATS

Some of the most daring and delectable dishes in the world are invented and served here. The restaurants below are the *crème de la crème.* Complete information about our choices can be found on pages 82 to 86 of THE CITY.

> *Bayona*
> *Brigtsen's*
> *Commander's Palace*
> *Emeril's*
> *Galatoire's*
> *Gautreau's*
> *Grill Room*
> *Mr. B's Bistro*
> *Upperline*
> *Versailles*

The Jazz Age

Musicologists still quibble over exactly how jazz, America's only truly original art form, actually evolved. There's no debate, however, about *where* it began—in the dance halls, bawdy houses, and back alleys of New Orleans, where black musicians took the hand-me-down rhythms of their African forebears and the vigorous hymns of their churches and created an entirely new musical species. To paraphrase Louis Armstrong, if you have to ask what jazz is, no explanation will suffice; you'll simply have to sample it for yourself. And New Orleans is the place to do that in style.

In New Orleans, escaping the sound of music is almost impossible. Gospel and blues singers hold forth in doorways along Royal Street; teenage horn players and impromptu bands play Jackson Square. At night, hardly a block of Bourbon Street is without a group of street musicians playing, an inverted hat or open instrument case ready to receive a tip. This is jazz in its purest form—spontaneous, sincere, and totally unpretentious. Visitors shouldn't be surprised if a marching band suddenly appears from nowhere, since New Orleanians will seize almost any excuse to grab their horns and drums and take to the streets.

The whole spectrum—from gospel and blues, through "moldy fig" traditionalism, Dixieland, rhythm and blues, the most cerebral modern styles, and the latest hybrid, "New Orleans Sound"—is heard every night of the week. Cajun and "zydeco," the music of southwestern Louisiana's fun-loving inhabitants, have gained a foothold in the city's clubs, too, joining the happy mix.

Every year, all of them come together in the *New Orleans Jazz and Heritage Festival,* two weeks of almost uninterrupted jazz, folk, Cajun, and gospel music in late April and early May. (For information, contact: *New Orleans Jazz and Heritage Festival,* 1205 N. Rampart St., New Orleans, LA 70116; phone: 504-522-4786; also see *Quintessential New Orleans.*) At other times, you may be lucky enough to catch a set by some native New Orleans musicians: pianist-singer Harry Connick Jr., or one of the horn-playing Marsalis brothers, Wynton and Branford. What follows is a basic rundown on jazz and its variations in its Big Easy birthplace. (For details on the clubs mentioned below, and other of New Orleans's hottest music spots, see *Nightclubs and Nightlife* in THE CITY.)

"MOLDY FIG" The jazz of the early 1900s is alive and well, and a surprisingly large number of musicians who helped shape the idiom are still active, passing on the ancient techniques to a whole new generation. Trumpeter Percy Humphrey is entering his 10th decade (his brother, clarinetist Willie Humphrey, died last year). Banjoist Danny Barker, not far behind in age, is showing no signs of slowing his strumming. The venerable *Olympia Brass*

Band, whose members' ages range from youth to extreme old age, is still hopping.

DIXIELAND Purists disdain the term, but "Dixieland" is as good a name as any for the brassy, syncopated jazz hybrid that emerged during the 1930s and 1940s. Its most celebrated present-day practitioners are clarinetist Pete Fountain and trumpeter Al Hirt, who have their own local nightclubs; Fountain plays regularly at his club, and Hirt occasionally appears at his. Many other hot Dixieland nightspots can be found along Bourbon Street.

BLUES The blues tradition, one of the lifelines of jazz, and rhythm and blues, the forerunner of rock 'n' roll, have an honorable lineage in New Orleans. Some of the great names in R&B and the basic blues—Professor Longhair, Dr. John, and Fats Domino—have their musical roots in the city. That tradition still continues, thanks to such knock-'em-dead wailers as Irma Thomas, Ernie K-Doe, and Marva Wright. The *House of Blues,* newly opened last year under the aegis of actor Dan Akroyd, not only holds performances, but also houses a massive, blues-connected memorabilia collection.

THE NEW ORLEANS SOUND While jazz continues to evolve, it also comes back to its roots in the newest form to emerge from the city's musical psyche. The "New Orleans Sound," as it's called, draws heavily on jazz's African roots, using unusual percussion instruments and a very basic rhythmic line. Its principal practitioners are the celebrated Aaron Neville and the *Neville Brothers,* singer Charmaine Neville (Aaron's niece), Allen Toussaint, George Porter and his band, singer Germaine Bazzle, and a duo of female singers going by the apt name of *Born Divas.*

CONTEMPORARY JAZZ As the Jacksons were to the Motown sound, the Marsalises are to contemporary New Orleans jazz. The first member of the family to make his mark was pianist Ellis Marsalis, and his sons Wynton, Branford, and Delfeayo have followed suit, carving out large niches of their own. Patriarch Ellis still plays frequently in New Orleans clubs; Wynton and Branford perform their music all over the world (though Branford usually can be seen leading his band on the "Tonight Show"), but they do make occasional appearances in the Big Easy.

CAJUN AND ZYDECO While Cajun music has only the most tenuous connections to the jazz idiom, both are rooted in the same raw spirit of southern Louisiana. Raucous but charming zydeco (the term derives from the Acadian pronunciation and corruption of the French *les haricots rouges,* or "red beans") is Cajun music with a distinctively black style. Fiddles and accordions are the essential instruments in a Cajun or zydeco band, producing a folksy sound that is beginning to rival Cajun cuisine in popularity. The most familiar names among performers in New Orleans are Allen Fontenot, *Beausoleil,* Bruce Daigrepont, the *Breaux Bridge Playboys,* and *Steve Cormier and the Cajun Sound.*

Mardi Gras Madness

Just as the medieval jousting of the *Palio* helps to define Siena, Italy, and *Fasching* annually reinvigorates Munich, Germany, the New Orleans *Carnival* is the ultimate reflection of the city's fun-loving communal spirit. The yearly celebration culminating on *Mardi Gras* (Fat Tuesday) is a reminder that New Orleans is, culturally speaking, much closer to Rio de Janeiro or Nice than it is to Atlanta or Houston.

Words don't do justice to the pleasures that *Carnival* can generate: the remarkable sense of camaraderie shared on the streets with thousands of strangers, the spectacle of glittery floats rumbling through masses of humanity screaming for trinkets, the incredible variety and ingenuity of the costumes. All of the usual traits we use to define (and often divide) us—age, income level, gender, and race—crumble in the face of the indefinable *Mardi Gras* spirit.

What we now call *Carnival* began more than a century and a half ago as a quaint, spontaneous celebration. The local descendants of French and Spanish settlers, picking up on a southern European tradition dating back several millennia, began carousing on the final day before the pre-*Easter Lenten* season. The first instance of an organized revelry dates to 1857, when six men formed the *Mystick Krewe of Comus,* which established the still-operative tradition of secret membership and elaborate parades and balls on specific days. Also in 1857, another group formed the *Rex* organization to entertain the visiting Grand Duke Alexis Romanoff of Russia and chose an ad hoc monarch who was anointed the *King of Carnival,* a title recognized to this day. Over the decades, the number of *krewes* multiplied, covering virtually every socioeconomic stratum of the population.

Carnival season traditionally begins on the twelfth night after *Christmas,* January 6. *Mardi Gras* itself is always 47 days before *Easter,* but the actual date changes from year to year because *Easter* is celebrated on a different date each year (this year *Mardi Gras* is February 28). Balls are held throughout the city and suburbs in the weeks preceding *Mardi Gras.* The first parade usually takes to the suburban streets about three weeks before *Mardi Gras;* the first in the city proper is held about 10 days before the big day, and the number accelerates toward the season's grand finale.

Although the balls are strictly private affairs (even the super-spectacular ones held in the *Louisiana Superdome* are by invitation only), the real fun of *Carnival* is available to everyone, as some 50 *krewes* parade day and night through the city and beyond. The number of floats per *krewe* varies from about 15 to 30, separated by marching bands and equestrians. The sizes and quality of the floats cover a wide range, too, the largest being more than 110 feet long, carrying a hundred-or-so masked riders, who energize the throng by tossing souvenir "doubloons" and cups, beaded necklaces, and other trinkets. The jostling for these trophies occasionally degenerates into a fracas, but, in fact, *Carnival* remains surprisingly crime-free, considering that more than a million people throng the city's thoroughfares. What follows is offered to help bring order out of the potential chaos of spending *Carnival* time in "The City That Care Forgot." Information: *Greater New Orleans Tourist and Convention Commission,* 1520 Sugar Bowl Dr., New Orleans, LA 70116 (phone: 504-566-5011).

A DRESS REHEARSAL

First, a cautionary note: Though visiting New Orleans at the height of *Carnival* season can mean a once-in-a-lifetime experience, it also means no-vacancy signs in hotels, often-mediocre meals in the top restaurants, chaotic nightclubs, traffic nightmares, and overbooked flights. Those who want to appreciate the year-round assets of the city are advised to visit during the other 50 weeks of the year. But for those who've come to see what *Carnival* is all about, here are a few tips.

WHAT TO BRING *Carnival* season is not the time for pearl necklaces and three-piece suits. The most practical clothes are jeans, a good pair of walking shoes, and rain gear. Thanks to the humidity, February can be a very cold month in New Orleans, with daytime temperatures in the low 30s F not uncommon.

HOTELS Most hotels and bed and breakfast establishments require a minimum stay of three, and sometimes four, nights up to *Fat Tuesday* itself. (The same policy applies during the April *Jazzfest.*) Room rates also rise by as much as 30%. Reservations should be made at least one month in advance for most accommodations. Understandably, the hotels and bed and breakfast places fill up quickly, so planning ahead can mean the difference between a comfortable room in a centrally located hotel or a makeshift one in a roadside motel a half hour's drive from New Orleans proper. Inside the city, festivalgoers can expect to pay premium rates for accommodations.

RESTAURANTS The size of the crowds at *Carnival* and *Jazzfest* place unusual pressures on fine dining places. Most of them try to accommodate their customers, but the reality is that food and service quality generally suffer.

TRANSPORTATION The French Quarter, Canal Street, and many central thoroughfares in and around New Orleans are frequently closed to vehicular traffic at *Carnival* time, making automobiles more of a burden than a convenience. Those who must come by car should arrange in advance for a place to park and take taxis during their stay.

CURTAIN UP

Parades and balls may form the framework for New Orleans's *Carnival,* but the nonstop partying in the streets is what really distinguishes it from other jamborees. Free-wheeling spontaneity is the order of the day—or night. In the French Quarter, the party begins about a week before *Mardi Gras* itself, as the crowds start arriving from virtually every state in the Union and from countries the world over. By Saturday night, a certain frenzy takes hold on Bourbon Street, spilling over to Jackson Square, Decatur Street, and the Mississippi Riverfront.

What's going on? Well, just about everything—most of it in good taste, some of it absolutely not. Inexorably, the momentum builds to Tuesday, when hardly a square foot of the French Quarter, Canal Street, and St. Charles Avenue isn't occupied by a masker, a marcher, or a gawker. Costume contests are always a good bet for entertainment. In the 600 block of Canal Street, in front of *Le Meridien* hotel, the line of contestants waiting to take the stage evokes images of the bar scene in *Star Wars*. The most famous competition, however, is the one in the French Quarter at Burgundy and St. Ann Streets. Known locally as the "He-She Contest," it puts the spotlight on some of the cleverest and funniest transvestite getups imaginable. Everybody from Bo-Peep to Bo Derek is represented. Like everything else about *Mardi Gras,* the contests never start at the advertised time, so play it by ear. If you miss one zany fashion show, another one is sure to pop up.

Until the 1970s, many *Carnival* parades filed through the French Quarter, but as they grew in size and complexity, and the crowds multiplied, this became, at best, impractical. Canal Street and St. Charles Avenue are the principal routes of the major *krewes.* The exact routes are published in the daily *Times-Picayune* on the day of the parade. Note: Many of the *krewes* grew out of private social clubs with restrictive membership policies, a practice challenged in late 1991 by a city antidiscrimination ordinance. As a result of the ensuing debate, three of the oldest organizations—*Comus, Momus,* and *Proteus*—no longer take to the streets. There may be additional alterations in some hallowed *Carnival* traditions, but no one doubts that its essential character will be retained.

THE PLAYERS

So now that you've made all the necessary arrangements and arrived at the festivities, what exactly can you expect to see? We'd like to introduce you to the cast of characters you'll find parading through the streets at *Carnival* time, as well as when they're likely to appear.

REX, KING OF CARNIVAL For many the personification of *Mardi Gras, Rex* reigns atop a glittery float draped in gold cloth edged with ermine, under a huge replica of a crown. True to tradition, the king's float leads the procession, followed by more than 25 others, all elaborately decorated according to the parade's theme, which might be taken from literature, history, mythology, nature, or the arts. The color-splashed carriages, many of them topped with gargantuan mobile figures, are always exceptionally imaginative. *Rex,* always a local businessman, begins his parade at 10 AM on *Mardi Gras,* starting uptown near St. Charles and Napoleon Avenues and reaching Canal Street around noon.

KING ZULU An hour or two before *Rex's* appearance, *King Zulu,* potentate of the fiercest African tribe, rolls along basically the same route with his 30-float entourage, tossing golden coconuts and other appropriate trinkets to the crowds. Humor is the strong suit here. In 1949, Louis Armstrong was the monarch. Other whimsical noblemen of this *krewe* are *Mr. Big Stuff,* the *Witch Doctor, Province Prince,* and *Big Shot.* The best marching bands in the city play in the parade, which usually reaches its climax on Canal Street about three hours after it starts.

THE KREWE OF BACCHUS Perhaps the most popular of all the *Carnival* parades, *Bacchus* takes to the streets on the Sunday night before *Mardi Gras* with 24 huge, elaborate, and animated floats. These riders are considered the most generous in all of *Carnival,* tossing thousands of doubloons, cups, and beads to the hundreds of thousands lining the curbs. *Bacchus* himself is invariably a show-biz celebrity. Among those chosen in years past were Bob Hope, Jackie Gleason, Charlton Heston, Kirk Douglas, and Dennis Quaid. After covering St. Charles Avenue and Canal Street, the *krewe* parades right into the vast *Ernest N. Morial Convention Center,* and its floats provide the backdrop for a spectacular ball featuring prominent entertainers.

THE KREWE OF ENDYMION *Bacchus's* only rival for unfettered spectacle, *Endymion* brings out 27 "super-floats" carrying 1,325 members on the Saturday night before *Mardi Gras.* Each member of the royal court, garbed in a stunningly intricate costume, is granted an individual float. The parade begins at *City Park,* then stretches along Canal Street, effectively cutting off one-half of the city from the other. Famous entertainers such as trumpeter Doc Severinsen and singer Kenny Rogers have played prominent roles in past parades.

THE KREWE OF HERMES The Friday night before *Fat Tuesday* belongs to *Hermes,* messenger of the gods. The *krewe* preserves a number of *Carnival* traditions—hand-held torches, for instance—and the 20 floats are usually designed with the traditional tinsel and painted in splashy colors. The float riders' costumes clearly fit the parade themes, an increasingly rare occurrence. After parading down St. Charles Avenue and Canal Street, the *krewe* files down North Rampart Street before disbanding at Armstrong Park.

The New Orleans Art Scene

In many ways, New Orleans is like the two-faced Roman god Janus, who looked to the past and the future at the same time. One of New Orleans's many ironies is this artful blend of reminiscence and anticipation. Nowhere is the contrast more striking than in the city's contemporary art galleries, where outrageously avant-garde paintings and sculpture often are housed in quaint, 150-year-old buildings. Below are some of the best.

CONTEMPORARY ARTS CENTER This early-20th-century former drugstore and office building on the edge of the Warehouse District is now the headquarters of New Orleans's artistic avant-garde. Three floors have been converted into gallery space that features the latest trends in painting, sculpture, film, theater, and photography. The nonprofit *CAC* often spotlights local artists and writers, but talent from other areas of the country and the world also is showcased. The range of exhibits and activities held here includes such diverse offerings as performance art by *Harlem's Urban Bush Women;* the big-band sound of Duke Ellington performed by local musicians; group shows by important up-and-coming regional artists such as George Dureau, George Dunbar, and Robert Tannen; and a multimedia event on the latest political crisis. The *CAC*'s annual *Sweet Arts Ball,* held in mid-February, is one of the top social events of the year, with music, food from local restaurants, and special exhibitions created around a central theme. Closed Mondays and Tuesdays. Admission charge. Information: *Contemporary Arts Center,* 900 Camp St. (phone: 504-523-1216).

JULIA STREET If the contemporary art scene has a nucleus, it is Julia Street in the Warehouse District, where a number of up-to-the-minute art galleries are located. Showcased are not only important regional artists, but emerging painters, sculptors, and photographers from around the country. Among the major galleries in this area are the *Galerie Simonne Stern* (518 Julia St.; phone: 504-529-1118), for abstract expressionist paintings and contemporary sculpture; *Arthur Roger Gallery* (432 Julia St.; phone: 504-522-1990), whose lavish exhibit spaces are given over to some of the more daring artists of the city and the region; *Gasperi Gallery* (320 Julia St.; phone: 504-524-9373), which specializes in contemporary folk art and works with strong ethnic connections; and *Still-Zinsel Contemporary Fine Art* (328 Julia St.; phone: 504-588-9999), which often introduces new painters and photographers who work in a variety of styles. Also see *Walk 5: The Warehouse District* in DIRECTIONS.

A GALLERY FOR FINE PHOTOGRAPHY Located in the French Quarter, this virtual treasure house of world class photographs is a must for photography buffs. The exhibits range from 19th-century daguerrotypes to original prints by such masters as Henri Cartier-Bresson, Margaret Cameron, Ansel Adams, Irving Penn, Helmut Newton, and Robert Doisneau. The collection contains dozens of excellent photographs relating to New Orleans's musical history as well. Open daily. No admission charge. Information: *A Gallery for Fine Photography,* 322 Royal St. (phone: 504-568-1313).

Antiques: New Orleans's
Best Hunting Grounds

In the South, New Orleans is the place to go for antiques. The fascination New Orleanians have for period antiques is understandable—it's part of their preoccupation with the past. In addition, with many 19th-century homes still occupied, there is a continued need for the types of furnishings that complement their graceful high-ceilinged parlors and rooms. In the early 19th century, the French-educated creole aristocrats filled their elegant homes with furniture, objets d'art, and tapestries bought in France. During the 1830s to 1850s, with the arrival of the Anglo-Saxons, there was an influx of 19th-century English furniture. When the plantation culture fell apart after the Civil War, most of what was left of the furnishings from all over the South wound up in New Orleans. Today, there are over 200 antiques shops and auction houses, as well as over 30 restoration and reproduction concerns that service the industry. The range of the kinds of antiques that one can find here is extraordinary—everything from an 18th-century French ormolu clock to antique Oriental rugs to an American art glass pitcher from the turn of the century. The city's antiques shops are concentrated in two areas: Royal and Chartres Streets between Iberville and St. Philip Streets in the French Quarter contain most of the finer merchandise from England, France, and the Orient; the other district is Uptown on Magazine Street, beginning approximately at Jackson Avenue and extending almost to *Audubon Park*. The offerings here are eclectic—some shops specialize in local or regional furniture valued more for its nostalgic qualities; others limit their inventory to luxurious 19th-century English or 18th-century French pieces. Many of the French Quarter shops display only a part of their inventory and maintain large warehouses in other parts of the city. The biggest bargains, however, are found at the auction houses, where excellent pieces often go for a fraction of what they could fetch in New York or on the West Coast. What follows is the tip of the iceberg.

FRENCH QUARTER *Henry Stern Antiques* (329-31 Royal St.; phone: 504-522-8687) is a long-established dealer in fine English furniture and paintings from the late 18th and early 19th centuries. *Lucullus* (610 Chartres St.; phone: 504-528-9620) is delightfully crowded with French and English dining room furniture, crystal, porcelain, and decorative objects relating to food and wine. A browser's paradise, *M.S. Rau Inc.* (630 Royal St.; phone: 504-523-5660) has two large floors packed to the rafters with everything from art glass to antique music boxes, and more crystal and porcelain than you may have thought existed. For connoisseurs of English and French furniture there's *Waldhorn Co. Inc.* (343 Royal St.; phone: 504-581-6379). *Hayes Antiques*

(828 Chartres St.; phone: 504-529-4221) is a quaint shop filled with a remarkably good selection of early-20th-century bibelots, prints, and photographs.

MAGAZINE STREET *Stan Levy Imports* (1028 Louisiana Ave. near Magazine St.; phone: 504-899-6384) is a good source of European pieces as well as Southern armoires, 19th-century Louisiana furniture, and objects from the region of more recent vintage; the items are affordable, too. More modest treasures are found at *Bep's Antiques* (2051 Magazine St.; phone: 504-525-7726), where you just might discover that indispensible objet d'art among the hundreds of old bottles, homey Victorian washstands, and charming little side tables. *Jon Antiques* (4605 Magazine St.; phone: 504-899-4482) has an especially good selection of English and French porcelains, as well as furniture, from the 18th and 19th centuries. *Ditto 19th Century Antiques* (4838 Magazine St.; phone: 504-891-4845) specializes in clocks, cut-glass, and above-average bric-a-brac.

AUCTION HOUSES One indication of the great bargains to be had at New Orleans auction houses is the large number of local and national antiques and art dealers present. Auctions are usually held on Saturdays, and illustrated catalogues are published for the major ones. The principal houses are *Morton M. Goldberg Auction Galleries Inc.* (547 Baronne St.; phone: 504-592-2300); *Neal Auction Galleries Inc.* (4139 Magazine St.; phone: 504-899-5329); and *New Orleans Auction House* (801 Magazine St.; phone: 504-566-1849).

A Shutterbug's New Orleans

Its remarkable architecture, ever-changing moods, and festive character make New Orleans a photographer's dream town. Think of the possibilities: brilliantly colored *Mardi Gras* floats lumbering through the streets, surrounded by thousands of masked revelers clamoring for trinkets from the float riders; an early misty morning on Jackson Square, when the old buildings appear in an almost ethereal light; a lush, tranquil courtyard shaded by sweet olive, banana, and magnolia trees; old sternwheelers churning along the Mississippi River; street musicians strumming and tooting under iron-lace balconies.

With backdrops like these, even a beginner can achieve remarkable results with a surprisingly basic set of lenses and filters. Equipment is, in fact, only as valuable as the imagination that puts it into use.

LANDSCAPES, RIVERSCAPES, AND CITYSCAPES An especially good vantage point from which to photograph the French Quarter is one of its taller buildings or whatever elevation you can find. To capture Jackson Square's beautiful proportions, position yourself on the Moon Walk pavilion near the river or the *Jax Brewery* terraces. The rooftop restaurant of the *Omni Royal Orleans* hotel on St. Louis Street is ideal for photographing Chartres Street's activity, as well as for a bird's-eye view of the Quarter's old buildings, which from here are silhouetted against the river. Panoramic views of the Quarter are especially good from the 11th-floor lobby of the *Westin–Canal Place* hotel on Iberville Street near the river. The Garden District and the city's public parks are the best places to capture New Orleans's natural aspects— its lush vegetation, majestic oaks, and profusion of flowers.

Although a standard 50mm to 55mm lens may work well in some landscape situations, most will benefit from a 20mm to 28mm wide-angle. Panoramic views taken of Jackson Square fit beautifully into a wide-angle format, allowing not only the overview, but the opportunity to include other points of interest in the foreground.

To isolate specific elements of any scene, use your telephoto lens. This is the best way to photograph the *Presbytère* or focus in on *Rex* sitting atop his float. The successful use of a telephoto means developing your eye for detail.

PEOPLE As with taking pictures of people anywhere, there are going to be times in New Orleans when a camera is an intrusion. Consider your own reaction under similar circumstances, and you have an idea of what would make others comfortable enough to be willing subjects. People are often sensitive to having a camera pointed suddenly at them, and a polite request, while getting you a share of refusals, will also provide a chance to shoot some wonderful portraits that capture the spirit of the city as surely as the scenery does. For candid shots, an excellent lens is a zoom telephoto in the 70mm to 210mm range; it allows you to remain unobtrusive while the telephoto lens draws the subject closer. And for portraits, a telephoto lens can be effectively used as close as five to seven feet.

For authenticity and variety, select a place likely to produce interesting subjects. A *Carnival* parade is obviously ideal. But look for other places where people gather—the *Community Flea Market* in the *French Market,* at the sidewalk artists' easels on Jackson Square, at the *Audubon Zoo*'s exhibits (especially good for photographing children). Street musicians and performers are always around to add a human element to a shot of a historic building or a quaint piece of French Quarter architecture. Seek out vignettes—a cluster of tuxedoed waiters taking a break on the sidewalk outside *Antoine's,* perhaps, or a gardener at work among the shrubbery and flowers in the garden behind *St. Louis Cathedral.* In portraiture, there are several factors to keep in mind. Morning or afternoon light will add richness to skin tones. To avoid the harsh facial shadows cast by direct sunlight, shoot in the shade or in an area where the light is diffused.

SUNSETS New Orleans's urban density challenges any photographer's ingenuity when it comes to capturing sunsets. So does its geographic position, which puts the western horizon opposite the most photogenic parts of town. The best bet is to find a vantage point that provides a wide-angle western view. Tall buildings are the obvious places.

When shooting sunsets, keep in mind that the brightness will distort meter readings. When composing a shot directly into the sun, frame the picture in the viewfinder so that only half of the sun is included. Read the meter, set, and shoot. Whenever there is this kind of unusual lighting, shoot a few frames in half-step increments, both over and under the meter reading. Bracketing, as this is called, can provide a range of images, the best of which may well be other than the one shot at the meter's recommended setting.

Use any lens for sunsets. A wide-angle is good when the sky is filled with color-streaked clouds, when the sun is partially hidden, or when you're close to an object that silhouettes dramatically against the sky. Telephoto lenses also produce wonderful silhouettes, either with the sun as a backdrop or against the palette of a brilliant sunset sky. Bracket again here. For the best silhouettes, wait 10 to 15 minutes after sunset. Unless using a very fast film, a tripod is recommended.

Orange, magenta, and split-filters are often used to accentuate a sunset's picture potential. Orange will help turn even a gray sky into something approaching a photogenic finale to the day and can provide particularly beautiful shots linking the sky with the sun reflected on the water. If the sunset is already bold in hue, however, the orange may overwhelm the natural colors—as will a red filter—but will nonetheless produce dramatic, highly unrealistic results.

NIGHT If you think that picture possibilities end at sunset, you're presuming that night photography is the exclusive domain of the professional. If you've got a tripod, all you'll need is a cable release to attach to your camera to assure a steady exposure (which is often timed in minutes rather than fractions of a second).

For situations such as nighttime celebrations on the Mississippi River, a strobe does the trick; but beware: Flash units are often used improperly. You can't take a view of the skyline with a flash. It may reach out as far as 30 feet, but that's it. On the other hand, a flash used too close to a subject may result in overexposure, resulting in a "blown out" effect. With most cameras, strobes will work with a maximum shutter speed of 1/125 or 1/250 of a second. If you set the exposure properly and shoot within range, you should come up with pretty sharp results.

A SHORT PHOTOGRAPHIC TOUR
Here are some of the Big Easy's best views.

ROYAL STREET With its iron-lace balconies and creole architecture, its antiques shops, restaurants, and street performers, this is the quintessential street to capture New Orleans's romantic spirit. To shoot antiques-shop windows, you'll need a polarizing filter to eliminate reflections, but no special equipment is needed to capture the picturesque architecture and street musicians. Royal Street's iron lace is the finest in the city. The building at 700

Royal Street is a superb example of the craft, a photogenic structure with ironwork framed by a profusion of baskets of fern. The three-tiered balcony of the *LaBranche House* (at the corner of Royal and St. Peter Streets), with its unusual gray ironwork, is perhaps the most photographed in the entire Quarter. Farther down Royal (at No. 1100) are rows of connected balconies extending on one side of the street almost to the end of the block. Across the street, in the middle of the block at 1118-1132 Royal, is *Gallier House,* with its strikingly original balcony painted in bright "Paris green."

JACKSON SQUARE Walk up Decatur Street to the broad pavilion that separates the square from the Mississippi River, and from any angle you'll get a good shot. First, there is Jackson Square itself, its beautifully symmetrical buildings and *St. Louis Cathedral* forming a backdrop for the equestrian statue of Andrew Jackson. Flanking the cathedral are the *Cabildo* and *Presbytère,* and the red brick *Pontalba Apartments.* As you're facing the cathedral, to the right is the *Café du Monde,* marking the beginning of the picturesque *French Market.* To the left are the landing docks for the steamboat *Natchez* and several other excursion boats. These are framed by the skyscrapers of the business district and the twin bridges that span the river. Then there's the river itself, with cargo ships, tugboats, barges, and excursion craft usually plowing by.

NATURE AND PARKS Mild winters, a long growing season, and a profusion of evergreens make New Orleans's lush landscape ideal for nature photographers. Flowers of one kind or another are always in bloom. In the fall, look for geraniums and chrysanthemums hanging along balcony rails in the French Quarter. In late winter and early spring, azaleas, gardenias, and camellias accent the elegant homes in the Garden District and along St. Charles Avenue. Trees and shrubbery—aspidistra, sweet olive, magnolia, and oak—are always around to lend their color, too. The best places to look for them are in the public parks, especially *City Park,* filled with moss-draped oaks dating back hundreds of years. *Longue Vue Gardens* is a rich source of flowering plants year-round, and any number of courtyards are decorated with bromeliads, jasmine, and ivy.

MARDI GRAS Parades are not the only source of great photos during New Orleans's *Carnival* season. On *Fat Tuesday* itself, the French Quarter becomes a candid photographer's paradise. Thousands of people fill the streets, many of them in costumes exotic enough to rival the parade floats themselves for spectacle. Marching bands appear from nowhere, their members always garbed in glittery attire, and revelers fill the balconies, many of them more than happy to perform for the camera. Shutterbugs in search of the truly bizarre should head for the corner of St. Ann and Burgundy Streets, the site of an annual costume contest that attracts the most outrageous getups of all. The limits of taste are repeatedly challenged as gawdiness and bawdiness rule the day.

Directions

Introduction

The streets and neighborhoods of New Orleans are ideal for walkers. This curiously intimate, sensual city begs to be seen up close; for it is only in this way that the visitor can fully absorb its sights and sounds in all their glorious details. Among the city's great assets for the pedestrian are its manageable scale, its profusion of trees and green spaces, its quiet, elegant neighborhoods, and the laid-back friendliness of its population.

There is probably no more congenial place to stroll than the French Quarter, to view its fascinating architecture with an impromptu band of street musicians providing the background music. New Orleans also offers walks down oak-shaded avenues lined with stately old mansions of classical proportions, and promenades along the mighty Mississippi as it rushes past its banks toward the Gulf of Mexico.

New Orleanians are proud of all of the city's attractions, so feel free to ask advice from anyone who looks like a local, whether you're searching for a street address, a landmark, or a good place for gumbo. It's more than likely that he or she will oblige with a minute or two of native expertise.

But New Orleans does hold one challenge for visitors: When directions are the point of discussion, it becomes a city of contradictions. The points of the compass mean little or nothing in light of the crescent-shape street plan of the older parts of town. Instead, directions are determined by geographical features: One is Canal Street, which connects the city's two natural boundaries—the Mississippi River to the south and Lake Pontchartrain to the north. For most of the 19th century, Canal Street divided the original creole city (what is now essentially the French Quarter) from the "American Sector," where later citizens of other origins settled. Today, everything on the French Quarter (or eastern) side of Canal is "downtown," and everything on the "American" (or western) side of Canal is "uptown."

The other two directional points used by the natives are "riverside" (south) and "lake" (north). These are necessary because of the crescent formed by the Mississipi at New Orleans as it flows toward the Gulf of Mexico. Uptown streets are laid out in curves roughly paralleling the bend of the river, making a compass useless in navigating one's way from one street to another. For example, the city's rather prosperous neighborhood known as Uptown is not north of the Canal Street dividing line, as its name implies, but actually south of it. So when you're asking directions, don't be surprised to hear such explanations as "Magazine Street is on the river side of St. Charles Avenue." Likewise, you may be told that a certain address is on the "uptown-lake corner" of the street.

Matters are further muddied by the fact that, because of its twisting route, the Mississippi at New Orleans actually flows from west to east. Yet the section across the river, south of the city's core, where you will find New

Orleans communities like Algiers, is known as the West Bank. The rationale behind this is that if the Mississippi flowed in a straight line, the communities across from the city proper would be west of the river. Confused? Don't despair: Read on, then follow our lead and all will be well.

In 1718, Jean-Baptiste le Moyne, Sieur de Bienville, chose this as the site for the new French royal colony of La Nouvelle Orleans mainly because it was the highest point on the riverbank. Most of the French Quarter is at mean sea level—in other words, zero elevation. The remainder of the modern city remains below sea level, meaning rainwater must be pumped from an elaborate system of subterranean drains into Lake Pontchartrain. It's done with immense mechanical pumps built in the 1890s which still function efficiently.

The boundaries of Bienville's original city (the French Quarter) remain in effect today. They are Iberville Street, one block from Canal and parallel to it; the Mississippi River; Esplanade Avenue; and North Rampart Street, formerly the Rue des Ramparts, where the original town's fortifications were set up. The Quarter covers a rectangle formed by 72 city blocks. The rest of the city flowed from this central core—today's Central Business District, southwest of the Quarter, followed by the Warehouse, Garden, and then the Uptown and University sections. The Lakefront and Mid City areas lie north of the riverside neighborhoods, in the direction of Lake Pontchartrain; the Faubourg Marigny, originally a 19th-century suburb established by "free persons of color" and now an interesting, multicultural neighborhood (see *Drive 1: Esplanade Avenue–City Park*), is just east of the French Quarter.

The oldest street names reflect the city's history, religious traditions, and folklore. The French Creoles referred to the French Quarter as the Vieux Carré (meaning, roughly, "old squared-off area"). Because French royal families were in power at the time of city's founding, streets were given such names as Royale (from which the final "e" has since been dropped), Dauphine, Toulouse, Bourbon, and Du Maine (now contracted to "Dumaine"). Later, in other parts of town, the religious traditions of the mostly Catholic population were also echoed in the names of such streets as Conception, Ascension, Annunciation, and Piety. Almost a score of streets honor the Catholic saints, or the illustrious personages of the same name—St. Louis, St. Peter, St. Ann, and St. Philip in the original colony, and St. Roch, St. Charles, St. Andrew, and St. Mary, among others, in later eras. In some neighborhoods, Greek mythology was the inspiration—Thalia, Erato, Homer, Coliseum, and Olympia are all New Orleans street names. As the city expanded, literary figures were honored, too—among them Dante, Shakespeare, Milton, and Poe.

The following chapters outline nine excursions through New Orleans's colorfully named streets and distinctive districts as well as to some interesting spots in outlying areas. The first is a ride on the St. Charles Avenue streetcar, which provides a special perspective on the city. Next there are six walking tours: an exploration of the historic French Quarter, a stroll along majestic Royal Street, and journeys through literary New Orleans as well as to the riverfront, the art-filled Warehouse District, and last but certainly not least, the splendid Garden District. Finally, we offer two driving tours. *Drive 1: Esplanade Avenue–City Park* meanders through and then out of town, and *Drive 2: New Orleans Plantations* wanders even farther afield to a place magically frozen in time.

Some bits of information you'll likely need to get around comfortably: Outsiders still stumble over the pronunciation of many street names. Those who use their best college French will invariably miss the mark. For example, in New Orleans, Chartres is pronounced "*Char*-ters." The "gun" in Burgundy is stressed ("Bur-*gun*-dy"). Say "*Eye*-berville" when asking for directions to Iberville Street, and "Or-*leens*" when searching for Orleans Street. The biggest challenge of all may be Tchoupitoulas, pronounced "Chop-uh-*too*-luss." Also, the median dividing an avenue is called the "neutral ground," and a sidewalk is occasionally referred to as a "banquette" (pronounced "*bank*-et"), an old French word designating the banked walkways beside the roadbeds. Practice makes perfect.

Regardless of what they call their streets, one thing is certain: New Orleanians are notoriously bad drivers. Many of the streets are one-way, a fact sometimes ignored by certain of the local citizenry. When driving in the French Quarter, it's a good idea to approach corners slowly. Drivers on the Quarter streets between Canal and Esplanade have the right-of-way. On intersecting streets that extend from the river to North Rampart Street, stop signs are posted at each corner, but they are occasionally ignored or unseen by those unfamiliar with the Quarter's traffic system.

Aggravating the situation are missing traffic signs, as well as street signs that have been removed or turned around. In some parts of town, streets are identified by tiles embedded in the pavement cement at street corners. On some French Quarter buildings, elaborately colored tiles identify the street names used during the Spanish colonial period; as some of the names are no longer used, these are another possible source of confusion.

A word of advice: As in most major American cities, street crime is a fact of life in New Orleans. Visitors should take the same precautions they would take in any big city. This is especially true along the quieter side streets of the lower French Quarter near Esplanade Avenue, as well as the mostly residential blocks near North Rampart Street. The city's old cemeteries are best visited in groups, the larger the better, and only during the daytime.

That said, stop for a beignet and a café au lait, and then travel with us through a luxurious, lovely, laid-back, lusty, lilting day in the life of the Big Easy. We promise you, you won't forget it.

The St. Charles Streetcar

The St. Charles Avenue streetcar, part of the oldest continuously operating municipal railway system in America, leisurely makes its way through one of the most beautiful urban residential areas in the country. The quaint, yet efficient, old coaches begin their journey of a little over three miles at Canal Street in the heart of the Central Business District, gently lurching their way uptown, bells clanging, until they eventually reach the grassy median of oak-shaded St. Charles Avenue, a very tony thoroughfare.

Along the way, windows on both sides of the car afford views of elegant old mansions, as well as some of New Orleans's most noteworthy churches, its two largest universities, plantation-style houses, and numerous public buildings that are both architecturally and historically significant. For most of the trip, hundreds of oaks, most of them 100 years old or more, form a leafy tunnel along the 50 blocks of St. Charles Avenue.

The St. Charles streetcars aren't trolleys (a groups of connected cars pulled by some kind of locomotive), nor are they cable cars (which in San Francisco are mechanically operated with an elaborate system of underground pull-cables). Rather, they are powered electrically by overhead cables. The 35 olive-green and russet cars operating today were built in 1923 and 1924 by the Perley A. Thomas Car Company, based in High Point, North Carolina. Over the years, they have undergone extensive renovations without succumbing to excessive modernization. New mahogany window sashes have replaced the old ones; the roofs, once canvas-topped, now are lined with metal. Exact-change fare boxes and metal automatic doors were installed just over a decade ago to allow for one conductor, rather than the previous two, to operate the coach. But the seats are still made of hard, smooth, varnished wood, and there is no climate control system.

New Orleanians use the streetcars often, so they're likely to be jammed with local commuters traveling to and from work in the Central Business District or with students shuttling to and from school. The cars rarely exceed speeds of 15 or 20 miles an hour, so there's usually ample time for looking around at all the sights. Traffic signals and autos blocking the median as they await a chance to cross also provide some time to appreciate particular buildings or curiosities.

The commentary that follows assumes you will board either at the corner of Carondelet and Canal Streets or at the corner of St. Charles Avenue and Common Street. Each description of a point of interest indicates whether it is on the right side or the left side when the coach is traveling *uptown*— that is, away from Canal Street and toward Carrollton. Our route ends at the intersection of St. Carrollton Avenue.

This streetcar excursion can be used as an introduction to New Orleans as a whole, since you'll be passing by many of the key points of interest

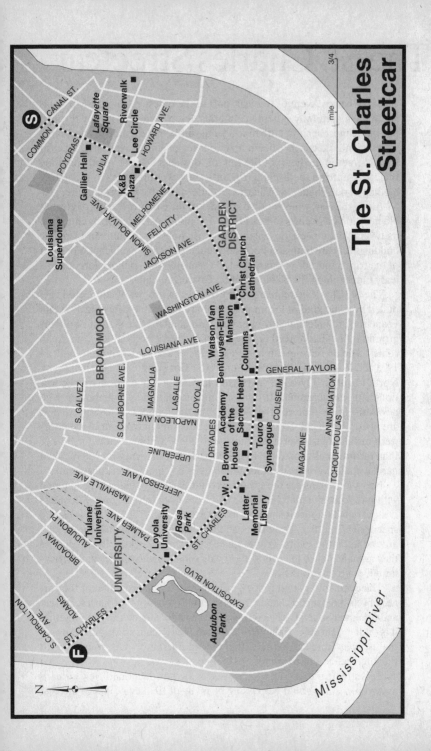

The St. Charles Streetcar

described in the individual walks in this section and in *Special Places* in THE CITY. As you ride, note those attractions that especially intrigue you and plan to return later for a closer look. (The fare for the streetcar is $1; dollar bills are accepted.)

The first major intersection after Canal and Carondelet Streets is Poydras Street, in the heart of the business district. On the left, notice the elaborate entrance to the *Riverwalk Mall,* a few blocks away on the Mississippi Riverfront (also see *Walk 4: The Riverfront (and Farmer's Market)*). On the right, the *Louisiana Superdome* is visible between the office towers.

One block past Poydras Street on the right is *Gallier Hall* (543 St. Charles Ave.; phone: 504-565-7457), a monument-like Greek Revival temple named in honor of its designer, celebrated architect James Gallier Sr. It functioned as the *City Hall* from 1853 until the 1950s; today, it is used for some of the city's official events (also see *Special Places* in THE CITY). Directly across from *Gallier Hall* on the left is Lafayette Square, a lush, lovely green space with the first of the many large oak trees that line the route. At the edge of the square, near the street, is a white granite pedestal with a life-size bust of 19th-century philanthropist John McDonough. He was a major benefactor of New Orleans public schools, and many of them still bear his name. The next four blocks of St. Charles Avenue contain a hodgepodge of old and new commercial buildings, forming one of the boundaries of the Warehouse District, an area of late-19th-century structures now being rehabilitated into apartment complexes, restaurants, galleries, and shops (also see *Walk 5: The Warehouse District*).

The streetcar now turns right at Lee Circle. On the left, at the corner of Lee Circle and Howard Avenue, is the *Howard Memorial Library.* Dating from 1889, this fortress-like red stone building was designed by Henry Hobson Richardson, a Louisiana native who became one of the most respected American architects of the late 19th century. The building, no longer a library, is now the headquarters of a private foundation and is not open to the public.

The streetcar next edges around Lee Circle, at the center of which, surrounded by a grassy mound of turf, is the *Lee Monument.* Supported by a 60-foot-high fluted column is a statue of Confederate General Robert E. Lee, arms folded as he gazes south (where else?).

At the end of this half circle, the ride continues toward *K&B Plaza* on the right. This is one of the first truly modern New Orleans office buildings, designed by the New York–based architectural firm Skidmore Owings Merrill. On the pavilion surrounding the structure and in the ground-floor lobby are the works of major contemporary artists, part of the corporate art collection of the K&B regional drugstore chain (also see *Special Places* in THE CITY).

For the next dozen-odd blocks, the streetcar travels through the Lower Garden District, which 100 years ago was a tony neighborhood of graceful, galleried Greek Revival mansions. They now contain shops, restaurants, bars, and other businesses.

Watch for the canopied *Pontchartrain* hotel on the right, between St. Andrew and Josephine Streets. This small, elegant, white hostelry contains the famous *Caribbean Room* restaurant (see *Eating Out* in THE CITY). Across the street from the *Pontchartrain* is the former *Restaurant de la Tour Eiffel,* a large, raised structure of geometric ironwork built in 1987 and inspired by the design of Paris's Eiffel Tower. (The restaurant closed in 1990, and is now used by the *Pontchartrain* hotel for special events.)

One block past the *Pontchartrain,* the far corner of Jackson Avenue marks the start of the Garden District. Filled with handsome 19th-century houses and lavish gardens, the neighborhood extends five blocks to the left (toward the Mississippi River) from St. Charles Avenue to Magazine Street and about another 13 blocks straight ahead to Louisiana Avenue. The streetcar stop at St. Charles and Jackson is a good starting point for a walking tour of the district (see *Walk 6: The Garden District*); afterwards you can return to St. Charles Avenue and reboard the streetcar (it will cost you another fare) at any of several convenient stops.

On the right, eight blocks past Jackson Avenue, look for the late-Gothic-style *Christ Church Cathedral,* which dominates the 2900 block of St. Charles. Since its construction in 1887, the church has been the seat of the Episcopal Church in New Orleans. The complex of buildings owes its design to New York architect Lawrence Valk, who used traditional English elements for the interior.

The *Watson Van Benthuysen–Elms Mansion,* at the corner of Seventh Street on the right (3029 St. Charles Ave.; phone: 504-895-5493), is the only one of the St. Charles mansions open to the public. The owners occasionally will permit tours of the house, by reservation only; there is an admission charge. The immense stone house, set on a grassy mound, was built in 1869 by Van Benthuysen, who was responsible for expanding the streetcar system beyond First Street and who also served as the treasurer of the Confederate States of America. Each of the principal rooms is decorated in the style of a different period. The dining room, with Jacobean appointments, contains the original chandelier brought from Paris. In the Louis XVI drawing room are mirrors and consoles, also imported from France. A sitting room done in the French Empire style still has the house's original lavish wall covering. And the staircase—hand-carved, spiral, and free-standing—is a remarkable feat of engineering and design.

Eight blocks up, between Peniston and General Taylor Streets on the right, is the *Columns* hotel, built in 1883 as the home of Simon Hersheim, the well-to-do owner of a large cigar factory on Magazine Street. The building, set far back from the street, is notable for the massive pairs of white columns flanking its large verandah. French director Louis Malle filmed part of *Pretty Baby,* his movie about life in a Storyville bordello, in its elaborate Victorian interior.

Two blocks beyond the *Columns,* on the corner of Constantinople Street and St. Charles Avenue on the left, is the *Sully Mansion,* a brick-and-wood house that is now a bed and breakfast establishment. It was built in 1890 in Queen Anne style by architect Thomas Sully for his family. His 25-year career, from 1880 to 1905, was enormously productive, as he designed some 35 homes along the avenue; alas, many of his creations are no longer standing.

Three blocks farther on the left, at the corner of General Pershing Street and St. Charles Avenue, is *Touro Synagogue,* seat of one of the city's most important Reform Jewish congregations. Distinctly Middle Eastern in its use of geometric motifs, this 1909 building was named for Judah P. Touro, the son of a Rhode Island rabbi who came to the city as a young man and became one of its most generous philanthropists.

Napoleon Avenue is the next large intersection; a block past Napoleon on the right is the *Academy of the Sacred Heart* (4521 St. Charles Ave.), a Catholic girls' school. The impressive building, with its wraparound balconies and layers of shuttered and arched windows, is set on beautifully manicured lawns. Several of the streets near Napoleon Avenue were named for sites where the French emperor led his army into battle, such as Jena, Milan, and Constantinople. (General Pershing Street had been called Berlin Street, but the name was changed after World War I.)

Two streets past the school, at the corner of Bordeaux Street on the right, is *W. P. Brown House* (4717 St. Charles Ave.), the city's most majestic example of Romanesque Revival architecture. Designed by a disciple of Henry Hobson Richardson, this awesome residence was built from 1902 to 1905 and cost $250,000 (a princely sum in that era). The mass of ivy-covered stone rests on one of the best-maintained lawns in town. Brown, a rags-to-riches entrepreneur, began his career as a clerk in a Mississippi country store and wound up cornering the cotton market. He had the house constructed as a wedding gift to his bride.

Two more blocks up on the right, set back from the corner of Robert Street, is the *Orleans Club* (5005 St. Charles Ave.; phone: 504-895-8655). A private social and cultural club for women since 1925, the mansion (not open to the public) contains a library and reading room and meeting and lecture rooms. Note the lacy, intricate ironwork on the columns, rails, balconies, and fence.

On the next block on the left is the *Latter Memorial Library* (5120 St. Charles Ave.; phone: 504-596-2625). Constructed in 1907 as a private home and occupied by a long list of affluent New Orleanians, it was donated to the city in 1948. The downstairs rooms, outfitted with several period pieces, make for opulent reading areas. The library is open daily; there's no admission charge.

The next major intersection, two blocks up, is Jefferson Avenue. The starkly modern *Jewish Community Center* is on the left and *Danneel Park,* a small playground, is on the right. Movie buffs are likely to recognize the stately building two blocks farther along, on the far right corner of Arabella Street: It is a replica of Tara, Scarlett O'Hara's homestead as depicted in the film version of *Gone with the Wind.* Copied in the 1940s from MGM Studios' movie set, the whitewashed brick exterior has the classic, clean lines, square columns, and graceful entryway of the Hollywood original. (Also see *Special Places* in THE CITY.)

One block past "Tara," at the corner of *Rosa Park* on the right, is one of the most imposing and elaborate mansions on the avenue (5809 St. Charles Ave.). It is one of the few remaining creations of architect Thomas Sully, whose 1896 two-story colonial-revival design includes double and triple columns, garlanded friezes, and fanciful finials. Notice the curvilinear dormers in the huge attic. Another Sully house is two blocks farther up on the left, at No. 6000. The house is distinctive for its swan's neck pediments, casement windows, and portico entrance designed with swags and garlands—all earmarks of the colonial-revival style Sully helped to popularize in New Orleans.

After another three blocks, the *Round Table Club* (6330 St. Charles Ave.) can be seen at the corner of Exposition Boulevard on the left. The club is the male version of the *Orleans Club* you passed several blocks back. Organized in 1898 by a group of men interested in literature, science, and art, the private club contains reading rooms, a billiard parlor, and a library.

Across the street on the right is the campus of *Loyola University,* a Catholic institution operated by the Society of Jesus. The red brick buildings facing St. Charles are in the Tudor-Gothic style. Today, the 14-acre campus has an enrollment of about 5,000. It was founded in 1911, evolving from *Loyola Academy,* a prep school established on the site in 1904.

Right next to *Loyola* is *Tulane University,* a private, non-sectarian institution that began in 1834 as the *Medical College of Louisiana,* became the *University of Louisiana* in 1847, and in 1883 adopted its present name following a bequest by philanthropist Paul Tulane. The neo-Romanesque buildings facing St. Charles were constructed from Bedford stone in 1894. The campus covers some 93 acres, and the university has an enrollment of about 10,000 students.

Across the avenue from *Tulane* on the left is *Audubon Park,* with picnic grounds, a bridle path, lagoons, a golf course, and a major zoo, occupying 340 acres extending to the Mississippi River. The park combines a former sugarcane plantation and part of the estate belonging to the city's first mayor, Etienne De Boré, who invented a way to granulate sugar in 1794. Purchased by the city in 1871 and dubbed *"New City Park,"* the site later was renamed in honor of 19th-century naturalist and artist John James Audubon, who spent several years studying and painting Louisiana flora and fauna. From 1884 through 1885, the *World's Industrial and Cotton Exposition* was held here to commemorate the 100th anniversary of the first shipment of cotton from Louisiana to a foreign port. Today the park is divided into three sections. The first fronts St. Charles Avenue and is a huge playground for golfers, horseback riders, tennis players, joggers, and bikers. Its green spaces are dotted with lagoons where ducks gather daily for handouts, and there is a beautiful tropical plant conservatory, unfortunately not open to the public. The second section is the *Audubon Zoo* (6500 Magazine St.; phone: 504-861-2537), fronting Magazine Street, between the park and the Mississippi River. One of the country's finest, the 55-acre zoo has more than 1,500 species in re-creations of their natural habitats. The third sector is the riverside area between the zoo and the Mississippi, which has a tranquil and scenic walkway along the river. If you want to head back to town from here, the *John James Audubon* riverboat operates a shuttle between the zoo and the *Aquarium of the Americas* and can take you back to the foot of Canal Street (also see *River Tours* and *Special Places* in THE CITY).

Just past *Audubon Park* on the right is Audubon Place, a private street guarded by twin stone gatehouses. It dates back to the early 20th century, when a Texas real estate magnate developed this parcel of land now shared by 28 homes.

A block away is the Broadway intersection, and two blocks farther up, on the corner of Millaudon Street on the left, is a curiously Moorish building set at the end of a neat, well-maintained formal garden. This was formerly the site of *Dominican College* (7214 St. Charles Ave.), a liberal arts institution for young women that was founded in 1860 by a group of Irish nuns. The college closed in the 1970s, and the 1872 building is now owned by *Loyola University,* which uses it as a dormitory and for administrative offices.

Past this point, the blocks along the avenue once were part of the town of Carrollton, an independent municipality until 1874. Carrollton was first a village, and later became a resort and railroad terminus. Although it was annexed to New Orleans more than a century ago, it still has its own unique character, with quiet, cozy side streets and modest houses, neighborhood bars, and bakeries.

St. Charles Avenue ends at the intersection of Carrollton Avenue, and while the streetcar makes a right turn on its tracks and continues along the median for several more blocks, the first stop after the turn is a good place to get off and take a breather. The grassy hill ahead of you is the river levee, a perfect vantage point for viewing the rolling Mississippi where it bends— a geographic phenomenon that gave this section of Carrollton the name Riverbend. This makes an ideal place to enjoy a picnic spread, but if you didn't bring one, the *Camellia Grill* across the street offers a tasty menu of casual fare (626 S. Carrollton Ave.; phone: 504-866-9573). Pull up a stool for some old-fashioned, gracious counter service and your choice of first-rate hamburgers, club sandwiches, pecan pie, or "freezes" (icy, frothy drinks that can be made either with or without ice cream)—a refreshing way to end your streetcar introduction to the Big Easy.

The French Quarter

0 |—— mile ——| 1/4

BARRACKS

Thierry House ■

GOV. NICHOLLS

Lalaurie House ■   ■ Clay House   French Quarter Maisonettes

Gallier House ■   Soniat ■ House   ■ Ursuline Convent

URSULINES

Beauregard-Keyes House

ST. PHILIP

Lafitte's Blacksmith Shop ■

DUMAINE

Cornstalk House ■

■ Madame John's Legacy

MADISON

ST. ANN

Bourbon Orleans ■   Presbytere   St. Louis Cathedral
PÈRE ANTOINE

ORLEANS   ■ 🅂 Jackson Square   Pontalba Apartments

PIRATES

St. Anthony's Garden   ■ Labranche House   ■ Cabildo

ST. PETER

Maison LeMonnier ■ 🅕

WILKINSON

TOULOUSE

DAUPHINE   BOURBON ST.   ROYAL   CHARTRES   DECATUR   N

ST. LOUIS

CONTI

N PETERS

BIENVILLE

Walk 1:
The French Quarter

New Orleans's French Quarter—or Vieux Carré, as it is sometimes still called—has one of the most impressive concentrations of 18th- and 19th-century buildings in North America—and that's only a small part of its charm.

Unlike colonial Williamsburg, Virginia, the French Quarter is not a manicured quasi-museum. Unlike Washington, DC's Mall, it is not a collection of austere public buildings. Rather, it remains a vibrant, constantly evolving, and integral part of the city it inhabits. Behind the façades of its buildings, some of them almost 200 years old, are myriad distinctive restaurants, elegant residences, churches, shops, striptease shows, museums, jazz clubs, libraries, hotels—in other words, every component, and then some, of a modern American city. Although a popular tourist destination, it is clearly also a place where people live and work. Neatly dressed residents go to and from their offices amid sightseers and street performers, itinerant musicians in town for a gig, shopkeepers, daintily dressed Southern matrons doing their marketing, and sidewalk artists displaying their work.

Occupying a 90-square-block area in the heart of the modern city of New Orleans, the Quarter is diffused with a sense of history. Legends from its quirky, colorful past could—and do—fill volumes. To this day, it resounds with the exotic earthiness of its French, Spanish, and African origins, even as dozens of T-shirt shops, tacky souvenir emporia, and glitzy malls increasingly threaten the unique atmosphere of its streets and alleys.

The French Quarter manages somehow to remain the least "American" of America's urban neighborhoods. The Quarter's essential atmosphere owes more to the Mediterranean than it does to the Gulf of Mexico. Its quaintly distinctive architecture, constructed on a nearly ideal human scale, partly accounts for that, as does the sense of mystery conveyed by its shuttered windows, hidden interior patios, and aromatic gardens.

Once you've escaped the rank commercialism of Bourbon Street and the waterfront from Canal Street to Jackson Square, you can easily succumb to the seduction of the Vieux Carré's streets. They are tailor-made for strolling, with many stretches of sidewalk sheltered from the frequent showers and the tropical sun by overhead balconies. Royal and Bourbon Streets are daytime pedestrian malls, and three sides of Jackson Square are permanently closed to automobile traffic.

Depending on your penchant for lingering, a walking tour of the French Quarter's interior can be done in either a half or a full day. Our route begins at Jackson Square and its environs and continues away from the river. For a comprehensive look at all the French Quarter has to offer, this tour should be supplemented with three others: *Walk 2: Royal Street; Walk 3: A Literary Tour of New Orleans;* and the French Quarter sections of *Walk 4: The Riverfront (and Farmer's Market).*

The first task is to get your bearings. The official boundaries of the rectangularly shaped French Quarter district are Iberville Street, parallel to and one block from Canal Street; the Mississippi River; Esplanade Avenue, the divided boulevard beginning at the river; and North Rampart Street, site of the early colony's fortifications. They enclose 12 blocks between Iberville and Esplanade and approximately five blocks from the river to Rampart Street. This walk begins at the Quarter's focal point: *St. Louis Cathedral,* on Chartres Street at Jackson Square between St. Peter and St. Ann Streets. While the present cathedral was built in 1794, with a new façade added between 1849 and 1851, there has been a church of some kind at this site on Jackson Square since the city's first settlement in the early 18th century. This beautiful Spanish-style structure remains the paramount symbol of the city's traditionally strong ties to Roman Catholicism. (For additional details, see *Special Places* in THE CITY.)

To the left of the cathedral is the *Cabildo.* Built by the Spaniards in 1795, it served as the seat of the colonial governments of both Spain and France (*cabildo* was the Spanish term for "council"). In 1803, in the room at the front of the second floor, the Louisiana Purchase was signed, transferring the entire Louisiana Territory (stretching from the Gulf of Mexico to the Canadian border) from France to the United States. The *Presbytère,* the *Cabildo*'s twin to the right of the cathedral, was originally the seat of the French and Spanish colony's church government, although it functioned primarily as a courthouse.

Today the *Cabildo* and the *Presbytère* house the most important historical collections of the *Louisiana State Museum* (phone: 504-568-6968). The *Cabildo*'s permanent collection contains such curiosities as a bronze casting of Napoleon Bonaparte's death mask and mementos of the pirate Jean Lafitte. Inside the *Presbytère* are permanent and temporary exhibitions relating to the arts, crafts, documents, and costumes of New Orleans and Louisiana. Both are closed Mondays; admission charge (also see *Special Places* in THE CITY).

St. Louis Cathedral faces Jackson Square, laid out in 1721 as the Place d'Armes, a parade ground used for military drills and church and government functions. In 1848, still a dusty parade ground, it was rechristened to honor General Andrew Jackson's 1815 victory over the British at the Battle of New Orleans during the War of 1812. The battle took place six miles from the square, downriver in the town of Chalmette. The statue of Jackson on his rearing horse, a casting of which appears in Washington, DC's Lafayette Square, was erected in 1856. The work of American sculptor Clark Mills, it's believed to be the first equestrian statue to have the horse with more than one hoof off the ground. Jackson Square divides the lower, more residential section of the quarter, beginning at St. Ann Street, from the upper, more commercial, section, extending from St. Peter Street up to Iberville.

The square's symmetry is completed with the two, three-story brick buildings flanking it along St. Peter and the opposite street, St. Ann. They are the *Pontalba Apartments,* completed in 1850 from plans by Henry Howard, who designed them at the behest of Spanish Baroness Micaela Almonester y Pontalba, daughter of Don Andrés Almonester y Roxas, the richest citizen to inhabit the Spanish colony a half century earlier.

The baroness was intent on stopping the shift of waterfront activity from the old district to the American sector on the other side of Canal Street. Toward that end, she had these twin buildings constructed, each extending a full block, with upper-level luxury apartments and street-level shops and offices. At the center of each cast-iron balcony rail, the baroness's monogram, with the intertwined letters A and P, is visible. Today, the upper building on St. Peter Street is owned and administered by the city government, and the lower one on St. Ann Street by the state government in Baton Rouge. The apartments are private residences, as they have been for almost 150 years. (Also see *Special Places* in THE CITY.)

After a look at the confectioneries, bakery, restaurants, and shops here, return to the corner of Chartres and St. Ann Streets and continue along Chartres, walking away from the cathedral. A half block away on the right is the one-block-long Madison Street, which offers a fine perspective of the corridor of handsome old residences leading to a view of the colonnades of the *French Market* on Decatur Street.

Continuing along Chartres leads to the mostly residential Lower Quarter, considerably quieter and less traveled than the blocks on the other side of Jackson Square. Stroll and admire the occasional glimpse of a courtyard, visible through the wide, gated carriageways, and the balconies, casting curious shadows across the narrow street.

Continue on Chartres past the cross street, Dumaine, to 920 Chartres, on the right side, with a walkway leading to a two-story outbuilding edged with giant banana plants. Across the street at 921 Chartres is the *Contesta Apartments Building,* with an especially large courtyard framed by a pair of arches at the end of the stone carriageway. On the sidewalk in front of the gate is a relic of the horse-and-buggy era, a row of alphabet tiles spelling out "Stalls for Rent."

Proceed past the intersection of St. Philip and Chartres Streets to Ursulines Street. On the near left corner is a modest masonry cottage in the classic French-creole style, with an outbuilding at the rear. In the antebellum city, almost every house of any substance in the Old City was equipped with such auxiliary structures, which functioned as slave quarters; always narrow, simple homes with brick ground floors and wooden upper ones, they usually also contained kitchens and storage rooms. Today they are popular with couples and single residents as modest-sized homes. Visible from the corner of Ursulines and Chartres Streets are two of the Quarter's most important buildings—the *Beauregard-Keyes House and Garden* to the left and the old *Ursuline Convent* to the right.

Before entering the *Beauregard-Keyes House* (1113 Chartres St.; phone: 504-523-7257), take a peek through the grate at the beautifully landscaped, formal garden. Joseph Le Carpentier, a professional auctioneer, had it built in 1826 in the neoclassical style then beginning to appear in the old city. The site is on a portion of the three city blocks he purchased from the Ursuline nuns living across the street. Le Carpentier lived here with his daughter and her husband, attorney Aliens Morphy. (Although the house bears the name of the Confederate General Pierre Gustave Toutant Beauregard, he lived here for only two years in the 1860s.) During the 1940s and 1950s, it was owned by novelist Frances Parkinson Keyes, one of the many writers who chose the city as her creative home. The most famous of Keyes's romantic novels is *Dinner at Antoine's,* a reference to the historic restaurant a few blocks away at 713 St. Louis Street. The house has been painstakingly restored and contains many of the antique rugs and furniture owned by Mrs. Keyes, as well as her fascinating collection of dolls. The house is closed Sundays; admission charge (also see *Special Places* in THE CITY).

Just across the street is the cream-colored masonry wall surrounding the old *Ursuline Convent* (1100 Chartres St.; phone: 504-529-3040), one of the oldest buildings in the Mississippi Valley. Much of the present structure dates from 1749; the architecture of the two stories and attic that can be viewed from the outside reflect influences of the Louis XV style.

The convent was home to the Sisters of St. Ursula, who arrived in New Orleans from France in 1727. Isolated from the bustling center of the French colony, the Ursulines managed a military hospital and established an orphanage, and schools for the children of the colonists, as well as for the slaves and Native Americans. At different times during the 19th century, the convent building served other functions. It housed a Catholic school for boys in 1831, then the Louisiana Legislature from 1831 to 1834. From the late 1830s to 1899, it was the official residence of the Archbishop of New Orleans. Today it houses the archdiocesan archives. The convent is open for tours only; closed Mondays. There's an admission charge (see *Special Places* in THE CITY).

The small church at the left of the convent wall is *Our Lady of Victory,* one of the oldest Catholic churches in New Orleans. It was originally the convent chapel. At the turn of the century, long after the Ursulines moved their headquarters, it became *St. Mary's,* the parish church of the Italian immigrants who settled in the French Quarter during the late 19th and early 20th centuries. Notice the ornamentation of raised cement work on the flat façade of stuccoed brick. On the frieze above the church's door frame, a pair of angels in flight carry a chalice between them. Under the cross on the gable, the papal coat of arms stands out in relief.

Next door, with a carriageway flanked by two charming iron horse heads, is the *French Quarter Maisonettes* (1130 Chartres St.), one of the oldest guesthouses operating in the district. Through the carriageway gate, there's a very pleasant courtyard. Just across the street is *Soniat House* (1133 Chartres St.), originally an 1829 townhouse built by Joseph Soniat du Fossat, a wealthy aristocratic planter. The townhouse, as well as the adjacent building on the right, was used as a guesthouse until the early 1980s, when it became a hotel with rooms decorated in period antiques and rugs. (For additional details on the *French Quarter Maisonettes* and *Soniat House,* see *Checking In* in THE CITY.)

Continue on Chartres to the corner of Gov. Nicholls Street. To the right is a row of five nearly identical Greek Revival buildings. In the mid-19th century, they were designed by J. N. B. de Pouilly, the architect of *St. Louis Cathedral,* as luxurious duplex houses.

Turn left and walk down Gov. Nicholls Street, one of the Quarter's most pleasant thoroughfares, with many small trees lining the sidewalk for several blocks. In the middle of the 600 block on the left is the handsomely proportioned *Clay House* (618-620 Gov. Nicholls St.), built as a residence in about 1828 by John Clay, brother of Henry Clay, the 19th-century American statesman. Although the house is not open to the public, the exterior is well worth a look. At each end of the long brick wall to the left of the house is a door pierced with peepholes. Peer through both of them for views of the spectacularly lush garden. At the garden's rear is a two-story balconied building, added after 1871; in the 1890s it was used as a schoolhouse.

Proceed down Gov. Nicholls to the next corner, Royal Street. The building on the near left corner (1140 Royal St.) is the infamous *Lalaurie House,* also known as "The Haunted House." According to the oft-quoted legend, Delphine Lalaurie, who acquired the house from her father in 1831, was one of the town's most prominent hostesses. When a fire broke out one night in 1834, firemen and neighbors discovered in the attic seven starved, tortured slaves in chains. Word of the atrocity quickly spread, and an infuriated mob sacked the house. Delphine and her husband, Dr. Louis Lalaurie, escaped in a carriage. The couple fled to Mandeville across Lake Pontchartrain, then to Mobile, Alabama, and finally to Paris. Local folklore says that the slaves' ghosts still haunt the house's numerous private apartments and account for occasional disturbing noises such as groans, screams, the savage hissing of whips, and the clanking of chains.

From here, make a short detour across Royal Street to the 700 block of Gov. Nicholls Street. In the middle of the block on the left, at 716 Governor Nicholls, is a two-story apartment house known as the *Spanish Stables.* In the 19th century, it served as a mews for the carriage horses of the neighborhood. Look through the wide central gate for a view of the excellently maintained garden at the center of the quadrangle.

Across the street at No. 721, behind a brick wall, is the *Thierry House,* built in 1814 for Jean-Baptiste Thierry, editor of the *Courrier de la Louisiane,* an early French-language daily newspaper. Though relatively modest in scale, the house is the earliest remaining example of the Greek Revival style that ultimately influenced much of Louisiana's architecture. Henry Latrobe, who designed the house at the tender age of 19, later became a nationally prominent architect of the early 19th century. The small, pillared portico leading to the entry of the house was inspired by the temples of ancient Greece.

Backtrack to the corner of Royal and Gov. Nicholls and turn right down Royal. In the center of the block, on the left side, is the immediately recognizable bright-green balcony of the *Gallier House* (1118-1132 Royal St.; phone: 504-523-6722), a charming example of the French Quarter's elegant Victorian manses and now open for public view. Before entering, be sure to look across Royal Street at the stunning vista of iron-lace balconies running the length of the block, one of the most impressive in the entire district.

Gallier House was built in 1857 by the respected architect James Gallier Jr. for his own family. He followed the fashion of the day by using trompe l'oeil techniques to create the impression of exterior granite blocks on the plastered brick façade and the look of marble and beautifully grained wood in the interior. The color of the balcony, known as "Paris green," was meant to simulate the patina of oxidized copper or bronze. Tours of the elegant house and garden, with a restored cistern, are given every hour or so, and end with coffee on the balcony. The house is closed Sundays; admission charge (also see *Museums and Historic Houses* in THE CITY).

If you're ready for a break at this point, you're in luck. From *Gallier House,* turn left and continue along Royal to the corner of Ursulines and turn left again. A short distance down the block is the *Croissant d'Or,* an excellent French bakery offering croissants, French pastries, and, at lunch, sandwiches, soups, and salads. If the weather is pleasant, you can enjoy your snack in a picturesque little courtyard, complete with a fountain and chattering birds (also see *Eating Out* in THE CITY).

Turn right when leaving the bakery and return to Royal Street. Turn left and proceed one block to St. Philip Street. Take a right on St. Philip Street and walk the block to Bourbon Street. At the far left corner of Bourbon and St. Philip is *Lafitte's Blacksmith Shop* (941 Bourbon St.; phone: 504-523-0066). Now a popular bar and lounge, this building, dating from 1772, has the oldest record of ownership of any private building in the city. Although the story has never been documented, local legend says it once was a smithy where the Lafitte brothers posed as blacksmiths while plundering cargo vessels near the mouth of the Mississippi River. They supposedly used the shop as a transfer point for stolen goods. Jean Lafitte and his band assisted General Andrew Jackson in defeating the British at the Battle of New Orleans and thus are known as the "hero pirates" of New

Orleans. Visible behind the building's broken plaster are soft bricks and posts (known as *briquets-entre-poteaux*), a typical construction method of the time.

Retrace your steps back to Royal Street and turn right. Continue on the right side of Royal to the *Cornstalk House* hotel at 915 Royal. The tall, cast-iron fence with the pattern of intertwining stalks and ears of corn, erected circa 1850, is one of only a few in the city. It was cast in Philadelphia by the Wood & Perot Foundry and delivered to New Orleans by ship. The dark-green and yellow paint is a modern addition; black was the original color of all the iron fences of the period (also see *Checking In* in THE CITY).

Across the street on the near left corner of Royal and Dumaine Streets are the connecting *Miltenberger Houses* (900-910 Royal St.), built in 1838 by the widow Miltenberger for her three sons. Her great-granddaughter, Alice Heine, was one of New Orleans's social heroines (and the grandniece of Heinrich Heine, the German poet). In 1874, at the age of 16, Heine became a duchess by marrying the French Duc de Richelieu. After the duke's death in 1879, she went to Paris, where she met Albert, Prince of Monaco (the present Prince Rainier's great-grandfather). They hit it off royally, and she married him in 1889, becoming the Princess of Monaco.

At the corner of Royal and Dumaine Streets, turn left and walk a few yards. At No. 632, on the right side, is a simple, raised-frame cottage painted a neutral color. Dating from 1726, this unassuming building is the oldest house in the Quarter, and one of the oldest in the Mississippi Valley. Its first owner was Jean Pascal, a sea captain from France's Provence region, who was given the site by La Compagnie des Indes, which controlled the French colony. The brick and stucco structure, a fine example of the West Indies plantation architectural style, was one of the few to survive the two fires that nearly demolished the entire city in the late 18th century. It was the model for the house called *"Madame John's Legacy"* in the 19th-century novel *Tite Poulette* by Creole author George W. Cable, and it is still commonly known by that name (also see *Special Places* in THE CITY).

Return to Royal Street, turn left, and walk one block to St. Ann Street. At the corner, linger for a moment to enjoy the profusion of ironwork balconies. This is one of the most frequently photographed sites in all the interior Quarter, since it captures much of its architectural spirit. Look right along St. Ann Street for a view of the arched entrance to *Louis Armstrong Park,* developed in the 1970s to honor the city's illustrious jazz musician. Used primarily for local festivals, there are lagoons, bridges, and walkways throughout the park.

Continue down Royal Street for about a half block to the little garden at the rear of *St. Louis Cathedral,* bounded on one side by Père Antoine Alley and on the other by Pirates Alley, both running alongside the church and leading to Jackson Square. The little garden is one of the loveliest green spaces in the French Quarter. Although officially named *Cathedral Garden,* locals call it *St. Anthony's Garden* in memory of Antonio de Sedella, who came to New Orleans in 1779 and was affectionately known by the cathedral's creole parishioners as Père Antoine.

Orleans Street is almost directly behind the garden. Walk down Orleans to the middle of the block; on the right is the *Bourbon Orleans* hotel (717 Orleans St.). In 1817, it debuted as the famed *Orleans Ballroom* (also known as the *Quadroon Ballroom*), where young Creole bachelors would come to meet and dance with elegantly dressed young women of European and African descent, chaperoned by the Sisters of the Holy Family, an order of black nuns. The nuns acquired the site in 1881 and used it as a motherhouse and a school until 1964, when they sold the property to the developers of the hotel. The *Bourbon Orleans* was created by John Davis, who would later operate the *Orleans Theater* and establish the first operatic performances in America in what was the old *French Opera House* (destroyed by fire in the 1920s) on the corner of Bourbon and Toulouse Streets. The famed ballroom, at the center of the second floor, is now a meeting room for local businesspeople (also see *Checking In* in THE CITY).

Return to Royal Street; turn right and walk one block to the corner of St. Peter Street. On this corner, at the left, are two of the French Quarter's most remarkable buildings. The one on the near corner of Royal and St. Peter Streets is *LaBranche House* (700 Royal St.), with its triple tier of oak leaves and acorn-patterned cast-iron balconies; it is now a mixed-use office and residential building. Across from *LaBranche House* is *Maison LeMonnier* (640 Royal St.), a three-story structure that is frequently referred to by locals as the "First Skyscraper," since it was easily the district's tallest building when it was erected in 1811 by Dr. Yves LeMonnier and a pharmacist, François Grandchamps. The doctor had a study on the third floor, and his monogram, "YLM," is still visible on the wrought-iron balconies. Today, it contains time-share and hotel apartments.

By this time, it may be time for lunch or dinner; if you need some refreshment, the *Royal Café* (700 Royal St.; phone: 504-528-9086) is right on the corner of Royal and St. Peter Streets. The breakfast, brunch, lunch, and dinner menus offer variations on many traditional creole dishes, and the view off the bustling street corner from the balcony offers some of the best street theater in town.

Walk 2: Royal Street

If the French Quarter has a Main Street, it is neither raw and boisterous Bourbon nor glitzy Decatur, but rather Royal Street.

Royal Street is to New Orleans what Fifth Avenue is to New York; though both streets may be less glamorous than in their heyday, they reflect the soul of their respective cities. Royal boasts the French Quarter's most remarkable concentration of commercial and residential creole architecture, as well as some of the district's best restaurants and shops.

The focus of this walking tour is on the shops, restaurants, and ambience found along the five blocks of Royal between Iberville and St. Peter Streets, the core of the street's commercial life. It can be taken as an adjunct to the more comprehensive French Quarter walking tour, which includes the blocks of Royal beyond St. Peter and focuses on historical and cultural landmarks (see *Walk 1: The French Quarter*).

Royal Street has been a daytime pedestrian mall for almost two decades, making it ideal for strolling, appreciating its elegant façades and fascinating antiques-shop windows, and people watching.

When the streets of the French Quarter were laid out in 1722, the arterial thoroughfare behind the little church (which later became *St. Louis Cathedral*) was named Royal-Bourbon, in honor of France's ruling family. Soon the name was changed to La Rue Royale (perhaps as a hedge against any future changes in the seat of power).

Today, the great majority of the street's balconied townhouses, modest creole-style masonry cottages, and imposing public buildings reflect the architecture of the early 19th century. This area of the city was largely destroyed by two devastating fires—one in 1788, the other in 1794; only a few of the French colonial buildings survived. Since the neighborhood was rebuilt during the Spanish domination of New Orleans, the damaged structures were replaced by Spanish colonial houses—two basic elements of which are the "iron lace" balconies and interior courtyards that set the standard for the city's architecture for years to come. Supposedly, one of the reasons the Spaniards built in this style was to protect themselves and their families from intruders from the streets. Closed and shuttered on street level, the houses had inner courtyards that functioned as naturally air conditioned gathering places for friends and family. Many of the courtyards were connected with each other through a system of passageways, so residents could visit others on the block without ever having to step outside.

None of the Quarter's other streets can compare with Royal for examples of intricately patterned iron balconies. The eight-block corridor between St. Louis and Gov. Nicholls Streets is a virtual museum of elegant creole ironwork. The balconies were constructed with one of two types of ironwork: either hand-wrought into patterns and designs or cast in molds. While

Royal Street

0 mile 1/8

MADISON

ST. ANN

St. Anthony's Garden

PÈRE ANTOINE

Jackson Square

ORLEANS

PIRATES

■ St. Louis Cathedral

ST. PETER

F

■ Labranche House

WILKINSON

■ M. S. Rau Inc.

Old Town Praline Shop ■

TOULOUSE

■ Dansk Factory Outlet

Historic New Orleans Collection ■

Gerald D. Katz Antiques ■

ST. LOUIS

Brennan's ■

Moss Antiques ■

Manheim Galleries ■

Raymond Weill Co. ■

ROYAL

CONTI

■ Old Bank of Louisiana

EXCHANGE ALLEY

CHARTRES

A Gallery for Fine Photography ■

Royal Antiques ■

BOURBON ST.

BIENVILLE

Rothschild's ■

■ Dixon and Dixon

Brass Monkey ■

■ Diane Genre Oriental Art and Antiques

Hanson Art Galleries ■

French Antique Shop ■

IBERVILLE

N

S

wrought-iron work was introduced to New Orleans in the 1790s, its exorbitant expense curtailed its use. When the less expensive cast iron was introduced about 1830, it was an instant success and balconies were often added to existing structures. A good example of the results of such additions is the splendid *LaBranche House* at the corner of Royal and St. Peter Streets. The house—actually a series of connected townhouses—was built in 1840, but its wraparound galleries framed in cast iron were added after 1850 (also see below).

After the 1803 annexation of the Louisiana Territory "Americanized" New Orleans, the city grew wealthier, and so did its Royal Street shops. Although the emporia were cramped and cluttered, their merchandise was often comparable to items from such cosmopolitan capitals as London and Paris. The many French and English antiques dealers found on Royal Street today are the successors to those dealers who began setting up shop in the early 1800s, when the street was the center of the city's furniture trade. By the 1850s, Royal's profusion of such places prompted the *Daily Picayune* to observe that "Royal is hardly large enough for the daily growing furniture business."

But as the 19th century drew to a close, the street began to earn its share of criticism. Detractors painted Royal as being plagued with peddlers who flocked to the city during the cooler seasons and made nuisances of themselves, blocking traffic with their overflowing carts. By the 1880s, George W. Cable, one of the creole city's literary giants, described the neighborhood as "a region of architectural decrepitude where an ancient and foreign-seeming domestic life in second stories overhangs the ruins of a former commercial prosperity, and upon everything has settled a long Sabbath of decay."

But the street continued to prosper despite its critics, and its European veneer lent it an air of class and Old World respectability that it still retains. The architectural scale and style of its buildings are one reason for this; another is that the majority of its shops have escaped the rubber-stamp, shopping-mall mentality that would have turned it into just another commerical strip. Royal Street is still the place to find New Orleans's finest French and English antiques shops; several of its galleries sell high-quality works by distinguished local and national artists; and a few of the restaurants on or near Royal are among the city's best. In some cases, the businesses on this street have been run by the same family for generations.

If you want to have lunch before beginning, one good restaurant is at Royal Street's very gateway, at the corner of Iberville: *Mr. B's Bistro.* This bustling, laid-back dining room offers creole cooking as well as contemporary treatments of fish and other fare, cleverly created soups and salads, and first-rate desserts (also see *Eating Out* in THE CITY).

This walk begins at the corner of Royal and Iberville Streets, where the *French Antique Shop* (225 Royal St.; phone: 504-524-9861) will please window shoppers, browsers, and buyers. The Granet family's glittery emporium of exquisitely crafted 18th- and 19th-century French furniture and objets d'art specializes in chandeliers of ormolu, brass, and other fine metals. While the prices are not inexpensive, the lustrous wood cabinets and tables are the stuff of dreams.

The contrast in mood couldn't be sharper between the *French Antique Shop* and *Hanson Art Galleries* (229 Royal St.; phone: 504-566-0816), a few doors down. This shop is a showplace for the contemporary painting, graphics, and sculpture of such popular artists as Peter Max, Erté, and Leroy Neiman, as well as New Orleans native Adrian Deckbar.

A few steps farther is *Diane Genre Oriental Art and Antiques* (233 Royal St.; phone: 504-525-7270), an uncluttered showroom spotlighting beautifully crafted antique Chinese and Japanese lacquerwork, ornate vases, antique woodblock prints, and fine Oriental textiles. Next door is the *Brass Monkey* (235 Royal St.; phone: 504-561-0688), which offers an array of antique walking sticks; one would make the perfect accessory for a leisurely stroll like this. You'll also find a huge variety of French and English bibelots, vases, and other decorative objects.

The next stop is for more serious antiques collectors. *Dixon and Dixon of Royal* (237 Royal St.; phone: 504-524-0282) offers 10,000 square feet filled with 17th-, 18th-, and 19th-century antiques, estate jewelry, rugs, and a striking selection of old European oil paintings. *Rothschild's* (at 241 and 321 Royal St.; phone for both: 504-523-5816) is the place to look for antique silver, estate and contemporary precious jewelry, chandeliers, porcelain, and furniture.

Continue to the 300 block of Royal, which is chockablock with more antiques shops. *Royal Antiques* (307-309 Royal St.; phone: 504-524-7033) has 17,000 square feet of showrooms filled with English and French country antique furniture, chandeliers, mirrors, porcelain, and jewelry.

For photography buffs, a feast awaits next door at *A Gallery for Fine Photography* (322 Royal St.; phone: 504-568-1313). The two floors of exhibition space hold a treasury of photographs spanning more than a century, including the finest original prints of such masters as Ansel Adams, Edward Curtis, Yousuf Karsh, and Henri Cartier-Bresson, along with a collection of great photography books. You'll also find many excellent shots of New Orleans musicians, street scenes, and portraits by the city's best photographers.

Farther down the street, *Waldhorn Antiques* (343 Royal St.; phone: 504-581-6379), opened in 1880 by Moise Waldhorn, specializes in antique silver, important old European jewelry, and fine 18th- and 19th-century English furniture. The building was erected circa 1800 during the Spanish colonial period and had been the headquarters for three different banks before *Waldhorn* occupied it. The fourth generation of Waldhorns now runs the business.

Set back from the sidewalk, the imposing stucco building on the opposite side of Royal Street was the *Old Bank of Louisiana;* constructed in 1826, its columned portico was added in the 1840s. The design of the surrounding iron fence and gates were based on those at Lansdowne House in London. The building has served several functions in modern times—an *American Legion* hall, headquarters of the *Greater New Orleans Tourist Commission,* and, today, a district police station.

The antiques shop across Conti and Royal Streets is *Manheim Galleries* (409 Royal St.; phone: 504-568-1901), founded at this site in 1919 by Bernard Manheim. Constructed in 1820 as the Louisiana State Bank, its design was the final work of Benjamin Henry Latrobe, a major American architect of the period. Some aspects of the building recall his design of the Bank of Pennsylvania in Philadelphia. The gallery's specialties are Oriental porcelain, antique European furniture, and the realistic porcelain birds of Edward Boehm.

Nearby is *Raymond Weill Co.* (407 Royal St.; phone: 504-581-7373), one of the country's premier stamp dealers. Some of the most unusual and rare stamps in the world are here, bought at auction by the Weill brothers, Raymond and Roger, for hundreds of thousands of dollars.

Next door is *Moss Antiques* (411 Royal St.; phone: 504-522-3981), with a good selection of small silver items such as dresser bottles, pie servers, fish sets, and fruit knives, as well as large and small pieces of furniture.

If you've not had breakfast or lunch, *Brennan's* restaurant (417 Royal St.) offers delectable food in a stunning atmosphere. Poached eggs in exquisite sauces are the specialty here, along with gumbo, trout, crab, and veal dishes. The old-fashioned rooms and large, lush patio are elegant and handsome (also see *Eating Out* in THE CITY).

The ornate, white marble building that occupies the entire block across the street from *Brennan's* was built in 1907 to house the Louisiana Supreme Court. To make room for the large edifice, the state demolished the entire block, including General Andrew Jackson's Royal Street headquarters during the Battle of New Orleans and the original site of Antoine Alciatore's 1840s boardinghouse, which preceded *Antoine's* restaurant. Used in recent decades by a branch of the state *Wildlife and Fisheries Department,* the Beaux Arts–style white marble building has just been restored to its original design and function.

From the corner of Royal and St. Louis Streets, continue along Royal to the 500 block. On the left, not far from the corner of St. Louis and Royal, is *Gerald D. Katz Antiques* (505 Royal St.; phone: 504-524-5050), one of the city's largest dealers in antique American and European jewelry.

Farther along is the *Merieult House* (533 Royal St.; phone: 504-523-4662) and the adjacent *Williams Residence* (same phone), both part of the *Historic New Orleans Collection.* Both were bought in 1938 by the late General and Mrs. L. Kemper Williams, who lived in the *Williams Residence* through the 1940s and installed their superb collection of historical materials relating to New Orleans, the lower Mississippi Valley, and the Gulf Coast at *Merieult House,* the first of the properties you will see. The granite pilasters of *Merieult*

House are typical of the simple French architectural style prevalent in 1792, when it was built for Jean-François Merieult. This is one of the few buildings in the area that escaped the second of the devastating 18th-century fires that destroyed most French colonial buildings in the Quarter. Today, the collection includes research libraries, exhibition spaces, and, immediately next door, the Williamses' preserved former living quarters (tours available), the *Williams Residence*. *Merieult House* and the *Williams Residence* are closed Sundays and Mondays; there's a charge for tours (also see *Museums and Historic Houses* in THE CITY.)

At the corner of Royal and Toulouse Streets is the *Dansk Factory Outlet* (541 Royal St.; phone: 504-522-0482), an excellent source of practical and decorative kitchen equipment, dishes and glassware, all at discount prices. Some great bargains can be found here, but inspect everything carefully before buying, since some items are factory seconds or have design flaws.

Crossing Toulouse Street, and staying on the left, continue on Royal to the *Old Town Praline Shop* (627 Royal St.; phone: 504-525-1413). Locals consider the creole pecan-praline candies sold here to be the real thing—crunchy, buttery, and fresh. They can be eaten on the premises, packaged to go, or shipped anywhere in the world. (Also see *Quintessential New Orleans* in DIVERSIONS.)

A couple of doors down, at 627 Royal, is *Patti's Court,* a modest, early-1790s building believed to be the second-oldest on the street; the original structure dates from 1777, but was destroyed by fire and replaced by the current one. But it is famous for more than its age. In 1860, it became the temporary home of the visiting 17-year-old diva Adelina Patti, who appeared in the title role of Bellini's opera *Lucia di Lammermoor* in the old *French Opera House.* (The opera house stood at the corner of Bourbon and Toulouse Streets a couple of blocks away before being destroyed by fire in 1920.) Otherwise, it was the base of operations for the Cavelier family, which ran a mercantile business; the buiding is not open to the public.

Directly across from the Patti house is one of the city's most fascinating antiques shops, *M. S. Rau Inc.* (630 Royal St.; phone: 504-523-5660). It has two floors overflowing with glassware, porcelain, garden ornaments, chandeliers, antique furniture, and a charming collection of huge, mechanical music boxes. This family institution was founded in 1912 by Mendel Rau and his wife, Fanny. Their sons, Joseph and Elias, took over shortly after Mrs. Rau's death in 1989. The Raus' emphasis on cut glass is believed to have helped revive a worldwide interest in the American Brilliant Period, which began about 1880 and lasted until 1910. For an excellent overhead view of Royal Street, climb the rear stairs to the second floor and walk to the balcony (the doors are usually open).

On leaving *M. S. Rau,* walk the few yards to the corner of Royal and St. Peter Streets. On the right is the *LaBranche House,* dating from 1840 and perhaps the most photographed building in the French Quarter because of its three tiers of spectacular iron-lace balconies. The quaint pattern of the ironwork, with entwined oak leaves and acorns, is considered one of the finest in the district; it is a private building housing offices and apartments.

Across from the *LaBranche House* on Royal is the *A&P Food Store* (701 Royal St.; phone: 504-523-1353), an oft-overlooked source of creole cookery ingredients. Many savory souvenirs—New Orleans coffee and chicory, all sorts of spices and sauces indigenous to the area, and myriad other creole foodstuffs—can be found here.

At this point, you are a block away from the sights and bustle of Jackson Square, an ideal place either to begin another tour or to just sit back, relax, and watch New Orleans go by.

A Literary Tour

URSULINES

0 — mile — 1/4

ST. PHILIP

DUMAINE

Madame John's Legacy

MADISON

French Market

ST. ANN

St. Anthony's Garden

F

Presbytere

St. Louis Cathedral

Jackson Square

Pontalba Apartments

Bourbon Orleans

ORLEANS

PÈRE ANTOINE

PIRATES

La Librairie d'Arcadie

Faulkner House

Cabildo

ST. PETER

Le Petit Théâtre du Vieux Carré

WILKINSON

Maison de Ville

TOULOUSE

Antoine's

Napoleon House Bar

ST. LOUIS

Hermann - Grima House

Broussard's

CONTI

S

Second City Criminal Court Building

N. PETERS

DAUPHINE

BOURBON ST.

Eighth District Police Station

BIENVILLE

Old Absinthe House

EXCHANGE ALLEY

CHARTRES

DECATUR

ROYAL

Galatoire's

IBERVILLE

Maison Blanche

N

CANAL ST.

Walk 3: A Literary Tour of New Orleans

New Orleans's mystique has long lured writers, and the French Quarter has been both a haven to and a source of inspiration for large numbers of them. Some have lived and worked here, others merely have passed through. Many, like Tennessee Williams, came and went frequently, and lived in a variety of places in the city he called his "spiritual home."

Truman Capote, who wrote his first novel, *Other Voices, Other Rooms,* in New Orleans, described his impressions of the city this way: "New Orleans streets have long, lonesome perspectives; in empty hours their atmosphere is like Chirico, and things innocent, ordinarily (a face behind the slanted light of shutters, nuns moving in the distance, a fat dark arm lolling lop-sidedly out some window, a lonely black boy squatting in an alley, blowing soap bubbles and watching sadly as they rise to burst), acquire qualities of violence. . . . New Orleans is a secret place."

Capote was not alone in his fascination with the city. In the 1920s, a group of writers and artists often would gather in the home of Jackson Square resident (and Ohio expatriate) Sherwood Anderson, best known for *Winesburg, Ohio,* a collection of short stories. The French Quarter became the American counterpart to Paris's Left Bank; according to one of Anderson's friends, cartoonist Bill Spratling, "there were casual parties with wonderful conversation and with plenty of grand, or later to be grand, people. . . . Carl Van Doren and Carl Sandburg and John Dos Passos and many others were there from time to time and there was a constant stimulation of ideas."

One of those "later to be grand" people was a skinny young man from Oxford, Mississippi, who would eventually win the Nobel Prize and forever change the face of American literature—William Faulkner. In a foreword to a friend's privately published collection of caricatures, Faulkner wrote that the French Quarter "has a kind of ease, a kind of awareness of the unimportance of things that outlanders like myself . . . were taught to believe were important." Perhaps the mystique of the French Quarter and the city itself is best described by one of Tennessee Williams's most famous creations, the tragic Blanche DuBois, who remarks, "Don't you just love these long, rainy afternoons in New Orleans when an hour isn't just an hour—but a little piece of eternity dropped into your hands?"

Many of the landmarks on this literary walking tour are noteworthy for reasons other than their literary significance (see *Walk 1: The French Quarter* for additional information). And though some of the sites are not extant, you can imagine such literary legends as Williams, Faulkner, and Gertrude Stein crisscrossing the Quarter, absorbing its earthy, often raucous, charm.

The French Quarter is where at least two famous pen names were born. As a riverboat captain, Samuel Langhorne Clemens stopped here between 1857 and 1861, contributing occasionally to the *Crescent,* a local literary journal in which Clemens's nom de plume, Mark Twain, first appeared. By 1882, his name now known nationwide, Clemens returned to New Orleans to write *Life on the Mississippi,* which includes ten chapters filled with his impressions of the city.

Later, in 1896, William Sidney Porter was writing for the *Item,* a local newspaper, when he ventured into a bar one night and mentioned he was scouting for a pen name for his short stories. As legend has it, a customer called to the bartender, "Oh, Henry, another of the same." We don't know if the fellow got his drink, but Porter got the message and signed the name "O. Henry" on his work thereafter. The expert weaver of tales had moved to New Orleans, where he wrote five stories, after a stint in a Texas prison.

Begin this literary stroll where a piece of Tennessee Williams folklore was spawned: the old, now-abandoned *Second City Criminal Court Building* (410 Chartres St. at the corner of Conti, next to *K-Paul's* restaurant). Williams was hauled into court one night as a witness against his landlady, who was accused of pouring water on a boisterous tenant hosting a noisy party. Trying to be as diplomatic as possible, Williams told the court, "I think it highly unlikely that a lady would do such a thing." The woman was fined $50 anyway, and she confronted Williams later about what she believed to be his damaging testimony. "Any fool could tell I'm not a lady," she chastised. A similar scene turns up in Williams's 1978 play, *Vieux Carré.*

A half block down Chartres, toward Jackson Square, at the corner of St. Louis Street is the *Napoleon House Bar* (500 Chartres St.; phone: 504-524-9752). The exiled French emperor was invited to reside here by the mayor of New Orleans, but never set foot in the place. Nonetheless, its patio has been a favorite meeting place for writers. The main bar, laden with yellowed prints and dusty busts of its namesake, is a good place to pull up a chair and soak up some of the genuine tavern-like ambience. If hunger strikes, try a *muffuletta,* the lusty Italian sandwich made with thick, crusty bread, ham, salami, and mozzarella cheese, and a briny salad of olives and pimientos.

Looming across Chartres Street from *Napoleon House* is the *Omni Royal Orleans* hotel (621 St. Louis St.), a favorite lodging place for writers during the 1960s and 1970s. Williams often stayed here on his many visits to the city, as did Lillian Hellman and Truman Capote. Though Williams was hardly a starving artist (his estate was valued at $10 million when he died), he is said to have complained bitterly about the cost of the room when he visited the then *Royal Orleans* in 1969. But that didn't deter the hotel from naming a corner suite for him and decorating it with photographs taken during the author's many sojourns into the French Quarter. (For additional details about the hotel, see *Checking In* in THE CITY.)

From *Napoleon House,* cross Chartres and walk one block to Royal Street. Cross Royal to *Antoine's* (713 St. Louis St.; phone: 504-581-4422). Founded in 1840, the legendary French-creole restaurant has hosted hundreds of prominent authors, American and foreign. When William Faulkner was awarded the Legion of Honor, the highest decoration bestowed by the French government, he came to New Orleans to receive the medal at the French Consulate, then celebrated with a meal in one of the labyrinth of ancient rooms at *Antoine's*. Frances Parkinson Keyes, a popular novelist of the 1940s, paid the restaurant the ultimate literary compliment, naming one of her romantic tales *Dinner at Antoine's*. (Also see *Eating Out* in THE CITY.)

After leaving *Antoine's*, turn left and return to Royal Street; then turn right and walk one block to Conti Street. The imposing building on the corner of Royal and Conti surrounded by the railed black iron fence is now New Orleans's *Eighth District Police Station*, formerly the *Vieux Carré District Station;* earlier, the building housed the *Old Bank of Louisiana*. In the 1920s, the building had yet another use: The city's artistic community held their lavish costume balls here. At the time, William Faulkner lived in a small apartment a few blocks away, on Pirates Alley across from *St. Louis Cathedral*. He attended several of the balls, despite his shy, reclusive habits. A couple of decades later, Tennessee Williams was known to haunt the antiques shops along this stretch of Royal. Once, when he was making a purchase, a merchant asked him if he was the Tennessee Williams who wrote plays. He replied that he was the Tennessee Williams who wrote checks.

Continue up Royal, walking toward Canal Street for two blocks to Iberville Street. Turn right at Iberville and walk a block and a half. On the left side of Iberville was the rear entrance to the now-defunct *D. H. Holmes* department store, referred to in John Kennedy Toole's Pulitzer Prize–winning novel, *A Confederacy of Dunces*. At the store's main entrance, around the corner on Canal Street, was the famous clock that was a favorite meeting place of New Orleanians, including Toole's hapless hero, Ignatius J. Reilly. A half block farther down Iberville is the rear of the *Maison Blanche* department store, referred to by name in two of Williams's plays—*Summer and Smoke* and *Sweet Bird of Youth*.

Return to Bourbon and turn left, remaining on the left side. In the middle of the block is *Galatoire's* (209 Bourbon St.), a setting that inspired Eudora Welty's short story "No Place for You, My Love" and contemporary author Sheila Bosworth's novel *Almost Innocent*. In addition, it was to this restaurant that Stella and Blanche repair for a meal, leaving Stanley at home with a plate of cold food, in Williams's *A Streetcar Named Desire* (also see *Eating Out* in THE CITY). Across the street, the *Old Absinthe House* (240 Bourbon St.; phone: 504-523-5181) hosted an impressive list of writers over the years, among them Walt Whitman and Oscar Wilde (not together!). Passing through town on a lecture tour in 1883, Wilde is said to have quipped that when Southerners were complimented on their cities, they would always reply ruefully, "You should have seen it before the war." Today, the *Old Absinthe House* is occupied by *Tony Moran's*, an Italian restaurant on the second floor, and a lively bar and lounge at street level. The bar's patrons are mostly visitors to the city who leave their business cards stapled to the walls.

Walk up Bourbon and turn left on Conti to *Broussard's* restaurant (819 Conti St.; phone: 504-581-3866). Now a pricey, crystal-laden eatery serving rich French creole dishes like crabmeat ravigote and flounder with crabmeat filling, this was an unpretentious creole bistro in the 1920s when William Faulkner endowed it with some notoriety as the only restaurant mentioned by name in *Mosquitoes,* an early novel set in New Orleans.

Backtrack to Bourbon and Conti Streets, turn left, and walk one block down Bourbon (heading toward Esplanade); then turn left at St. Louis Street and walk to No. 820. This is the *Hermann-Grima House* (also see *Museums and Historic Houses* in THE CITY), which served as the model for the family home in the romantic novel *Feast of All Saints* by contemporary author Anne Rice, a native of New Orleans. Returning once again to Bourbon, turn left. The handsome, but now seedy, building at 515 Bourbon is where the Greek-born American author and journalist Lafcadio Hearn lived in the 1880s. Hearn, working as a journalist at the time, wrote numerous articles on New Orleans life, and compiled the first creole cookbook before traveling to Japan to write about that country's culture and lifestyle.

Continue down Bourbon to the next block, walking toward Esplanade Avenue. At 623 Bourbon is a stately townhouse sandwiched among the bars and nightclubs that fill much of Bourbon Street today. Behind the front door at 623, however, is a glamorous home with a lush courtyard; Thornton Wilder, author of *Our Town,* spent several months writing here in the 1940s. Continue down Bourbon to Toulouse and turn right. At 727 Toulouse is *Maison de Ville,* a small, quiet, and pricey hotel where Tennessee Williams occasionally stayed and labored over his typewriter. Williams always reserved room No. 9, where he reportedly worked for about five hours a day. On one particularly productive day, when he was scheduled to check out, he kept a honeymooning couple waiting in the lobby for several hours until he had finished his work (also see *Checking In* in THE CITY).

A few doors farther down Toulouse, walking toward Royal Street, is No. 719, home of the late Lord Bradford. Bradford, the former night city editor of *The Times-Picayune* newspaper, became one of Faulkner's patrons when he published the writer's early *New Orleans Sketches.* Bradford had other noteworthy literary connections—novelists Sinclair Lewis and John Steinbeck were guests at his apartment, and his grandson, Richard Bradford, wrote the critically acclaimed novel *Red Sky at Morning.*

Across the street (at 722 Toulouse St.) are the administrative offices of the *Historic New Orleans Collection* (also see *Special Places* in THE CITY). During the 1940s, the structure was an apartment building; Tennessee Williams lived on the third floor (his former apartment is identifiable by the dormer window, barely visible above the roofline).

Walk a few more doors down Toulouse. At the intersection of Royal and Toulouse Streets (741 Royal St.) is a 16-room, creole-style townhouse, which in the 1930s and 1940s was rented for $16 a month by the late Lyle Saxon, important for his lyrical depictions of New Orleans. His best-known works are *Father Mississippi, Fabulous New Orleans,* and *Children of Strangers.* Saxon is said to have employed an especially talented cook, who rustled up lunches and suppers at which the author entertained fellow writers.

Continue one block farther along Toulouse to the corner of Chartres. *Victor's Café,* a literary hangout until its demise in the 1960s, stood on the near left corner. In the 1920s, it was a favorite neighborhood dining spot for Faulkner and fellow Quarterite Sherwood Anderson. About 20 years later, a hypochondriacal Tennessee Williams was hard at work on a play that he first called *The Poker Night,* but later changed to *A Streetcar Named Desire.* In his memoirs, he credits *Victor's* as an integral part of the creative process: "I would work from early morning to late afternoon, and then, spent from the rigors of creation, I would go around the corner to a bar called Victor's and revive myself with a marvelous drink called a Brandy Alexander, which was a specialty of the bar."

Turn left at the corner and continue on Chartres for a block toward Jackson Square. At the near left corner of Chartres and St. Peter Streets, where the square begins, is *Le Petit Théâtre du Vieux Carré,* a community theater founded in the 1920s that continues to present two seasons of amateur performances each year (also see *Theater* in THE CITY). The theater entrance is on St. Peter Street. One of the many stories surrounding "Little Theater," as it's locally known, concerns novelist Sinclair Lewis. In the 1940s Lewis visited the city with a woman he introduced as his niece and convinced the theater's management to cast her in a starring role—and in exchange, he would write the script. The reviews of the resultant travesty were far more complimentary to Lewis's writing than to his "niece's" acting.

Return to Chartres and walk the few steps to *La Marquise Pastry Shop* (635 Chartres St.; phone: 504-524-0420), a coffee-and-dessert spot with excellent croissants, pastries, and other snacks, as well as good coffees and teas. Should you decide to stop in for a refreshment, you'll be in what once was a private home where Faulkner and Anderson often visited friends, inspiring Anderson's short story "A Meeting South."

Afterward, return to St. Peter Street and Jackson Square. On the square, you may see a bizarre vending cart in the shape of a huge hot dog. This is one of the "Lucky Dog" carts, known to readers of John Kennedy Toole's *A Confederacy of Dunces* as "Paradise Vendors." Facing the square at St. Peter and Chartres, to the right are the *Upper Pontalba Apartments,* extending the full block from Chartres to Decatur Streets. Apartment 540-B on the second floor is where Anderson and his wife lived in the 1920s while he produced two impressionistic essays, "A New Testament" and "More Testament." The Andersons were known among New Orleans writers for their hospitality as well as their parties, often offering shelter to literary types who were down on their luck and needed a place to stay. Faulkner was one of them.

Jackson Square itself has a certain literary cachet. Tennessee Williams's poem "Morning on Bourbon Street" mentions the equestrian statue of General Andrew Jackson, and Blanche DuBois, the ill-fated romantic in *A Streetcar Named Desire,* refers to the sound of *St. Louis Cathedral*'s bells as the only truly clear thing in life. In Lillian Hellman's autobiographical *An Unfinished Woman,* she recalls running away at the age of 14 from her aunts' home uptown to the French Quarter and hiding in the cathedral. In his novel *Mosquitoes,* Faulkner compared peering through the iron fence surrounding the square with gazing through an aquarium.

With the cathedral at your left, continue along Chartres, across St. Ann Street and one block to Madison Street. At the corner of Chartres and Madison is the *Librairie Book Shop* (823 Chartres St.; phone: 504-525-4837), which stocks a large selection of used books, especially hardcover fiction and reference volumes. It is owned by Gary Beckham, who also runs *Beckham's Book Shop* in the French Quarter (228 Decatur St.; phone: 504-522-9875), one of the largest used-book emporia in the city. After you've finished browsing, walk down Madison for a short block toward the *French Market,* to Decatur Street. Truman Capote fondly reminisced about the famous market in "A Voice from a Cloud," an autobiographical essay: "I would walk through the humid, balconied streets, past St. Louis Cathedral and go on to the French Market, a square crammed in the early morning with the trucks of vegetable farmers, Gulf Coast fishermen, meat vendors, and flower growers. It smelled of earth, of herbs and exotic, gingery scents, and it rang, clanged, clogged the ears with the sounds of vivacious trading. I loved it." On the near left corner of Madison and Decatur Streets is *Tujague's* bar and restaurant (823 Decatur St.; phone: 504-525-8676); in a former life it was *Madame Begué's,* an O. Henry favorite and the most celebrated New Orleans eating and drinking establishment at the turn of the century.

Walk back down Madison to Chartres Street; turn right, and continue one block to Dumaine Street. Turn left on Dumaine and walk the few steps to No. 615. During the 1940s and 1950s William March Campbell, a shipping executive who wrote under the pen name William March, lived here and produced such respected novels as *Company K* and *The Bad Seed.* (The latter was adapted with great success for Broadway and Hollywood.) Across the street (632 Dumaine St.) is *Madame John's Legacy,* one of New Orleans's most legendary buildings, both in historical and literary terms (though it's not open to the public). Dating from the mid-18th century, this is one of the oldest structures in the Mississippi Valley and the model for the main character's house in George W. Cable's 19th-century novel, *Tite Poulette.* In the book, Cable masterfully depicted the everyday life of the Creoles in New Orleans in the late 1800s (also see *Special Places* in THE CITY).

From *Madame John's Legacy,* walk a half block to Royal Street. Turn left on Royal and continue to the intersection of Royal and Orleans Streets. Turn right onto Orleans; in the middle of this block is *La Librairie d'Arcadie*

(714 Orleans St.; phone: 504-523-4138), a bookshop specializing in French-language books and fine antique prints and engravings. Just across the street is the *Bourbon Orleans* hotel (717 Orleans St.), which until the mid-20th century was a convent. The *Quadroon Ballroom* on the second floor figures in Faulkner's *Absalom, Absalom* (also see *Checking In* in THE CITY). At the corner of Orleans and Royal (at 719 Royal St.) is yet another building in which Tennessee Williams lived, this one in the early 1940s following his theatrical success with *The Glass Menagerie.* Much of his later play *Camino Real* also was written here. He often told friends how much he enjoyed the view of the verdant garden behind *St. Louis Cathedral* from his balcony.

Now turn right onto Royal, walk one block to St. Peter, and turn left toward Jackson Square. What is now the *Gumbo Shop,* a busy, tourist-infested bistro specializing in re-heated gumbo shipped in frozen blocks from the Uptown district, was once the home of Oliver LaFarge, a New Orleans writer whose novel *Laughing Boy* won a Pulitzer Prize in 1930. Nearby, on the same side of the street (632 St. Peter St.), is where Williams lived while working on two of his most successful plays, *A Streetcar Named Desire* and *Summer and Smoke.* Williams often said that of all the Quarter places in which he lived, this was his favorite. He once wrote, "What I liked most about it was a long refectory table under a skylight which provided me with ideal conditions for working in the mornings. I know of no city where it is better to have a skylight than New Orleans." Until the 1950s, streetcars rumbled along tracks in the French Quarter, and since Royal Street was on the *Desire* line, the playwright no doubt heard the dull clang of the streetcar's bell as it passed under his window.

The final stop on this literary stroll is one of the most important. Across from the *Gumbo Shop* is a short alley that runs parallel to the 600 block of St. Peter. Walk the few steps through it to Pirates Alley, which runs along the side of *St. Louis Cathedral;* on your immediate left is *Faulkner House* (624 Pirates Alley; phone: 504-581-3262). This elegantly appointed, beau-tifully organized bookshop, specializing in the works of Southern writers and rare volumes of all sorts, was William Faulkner's first permanent home in New Orleans. The author was working on one of his early novels, *Soldier's Pay;* today you can buy a copy of that book on the spot where much of it was composed.

A good place to end this tour is at the charming *Coffee, Tea, or . . .* (630 St. Ann St.; phone: 504-522-0830). From the *Faulkner House,* walk through Pirates Alley to Chartres, turn left, walk past the *Cabildo* and the *Presbytère* to St. Ann Street, and turn left again. The shop offers coffees, several kinds of teas, croissants, pastries, cookies, and homemade soups. If the weather is pleasant, you can enjoy your snack in the quiet, diminutive Spanish court-yard out back, where, amid the banana plants and flowering shrubs, you sit back and read about the exploits of Stanley Kowalski and Blanche DuBois, Amanda Wingfield, Regina Fox, or any of the other characters created in the imaginations of New Orleans writers.

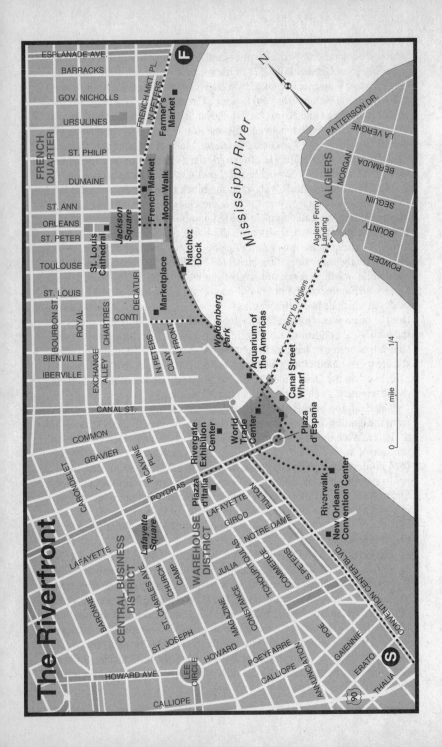

Walk 4: The Riverfront (and Farmer's Market)

More than any other factor, it is the mighty Mississippi, that rambling, 2,350-mile-long river, subject of songs and sonnets, renowned the world over, that shaped New Orleans's destiny and its character from that day in 1718 when the city was founded. River commerce and international shipping always have been a mainstay of New Orleans's economy. Without the river, the city's piquant creole cuisine might never have existed, for it was the Mississippi that brought about the confluence of French, Spanish, African, and Caribbean cultures that created this distinctive cooking style. Were it not for the river, jazz might have remained little more than a local curiosity, since the earliest jazz performers first began carrying their syncopated message to the world on riverboats shuttling between New Orleans and Chicago.

The sustenance New Orleans draws from the Mississippi is even more basic: The river has always been the source of the city's drinking water, and as long as it "keeps on rollin'," New Orleanians will never go thirsty. It is said that once you've tasted New Orleans's river water (it's purified before it's potable), you'll keep coming back for more.

Much of the city's growth, especially before the advent of air travel, has been due principally to its position near the mouth of the Mississippi River, which is about 100 miles south of New Orleans at the Gulf of Mexico. It began with the flatboats that plied the waters between New Orleans and the American heartland, carrying every sort of cargo, both human and otherwise. Then came the big, legendary steamboats of the late 19th and early 20th centuries, laden with hundreds of tons of cotton, grain, merchandise, and foodstuffs on trips between New Orleans and the Midwest. This was the era when the city's port was the terminus of the immense transportation network formed by the Mississippi and its many tributaries. Today every manner of vessel can be spotted gliding on the muddy water, lugging grain, coal, petroleum products, sand, gravel, salt, sulfur, and chemicals. The Mississippi has the third-largest drainage basin in the world, exceeded in size only by the watersheds of the Amazon and Nile Rivers. More than 300 rivers empty into it, with waters from as far east as New York and as far west as Montana flowing into the lower river.

There is a certain Latin fatalism that New Orleanians have had about the river for the past three centuries—it has been a frequent blessing and an occasional curse. All but a small part of New Orleans's soggy landmass is at or below sea level. One result is flooding in the spring, when the mid-continent's snows to the north melt into the tributaries, funneling billions of gallons of new water into the Mississippi. The floods were an annual event until the late 1920s, when immense mounds of earth, called levees, were raised along both of the river's banks to hold back the swelling waters.

Mark Twain, the Mississippi River's biographer, summed up his subject as "not a commonplace river, but on the contrary . . . in all ways remarkable." More than 100 years later, Twain's description still holds; in fact, the river is more vital to the city's landscape and character today than it was in his day.

For most of New Orleans's existence, city dwellers were cut off from the river because of a barrier of connected wharves and warehouses that extended from one end of town to the other. But in the 1970s, New Orleans port officials began removing the outdated, deteriorating sheds and pilings from the banks at either side of Canal Street. Grass-roots support for a series of parks and other public "people" spaces to replace the wharves and pilings took hold. The result was a strip of open riverbank stretching about 30 blocks along the French Quarter, Canal Street, and the Warehouse District.

The Mississippi Riverfront, as it's now called, is a prime source of entertainment as well as enterprise, and a perfect area for a leisurely stroll. A convenient starting point is in the Warehouse District at the corner of Convention Center Boulevard (which parallels the river) and Thalia Street. At this point you are standing almost directly under the pair of river bridges known as the Crescent City Connection, the principal links between New Orleans's east and west banks. As you face the water, you will see the older span (formerly called the Greater New Orleans Bridge) on the right; completed in 1958, it was the first bridge connecting central New Orleans to Algiers, the only section of the West Bank within the city limits. The Crescent City Connection's second, wider span, parallel with the first, was completed in 1988. At night, this newer bridge's superstructure is outlined in lights, adding considerable sparkle to the nocturnal waterfront views.

With the river to the right, proceed down Convention Center Boulevard to the mammoth *Ernest N. Morial Convention Center,* which has undergone two expansions since it opened shortly after the *1984 World's Fair.* Although the fair ended in bankruptcy, it is credited with helping to resuscitate many of the warehouses and small factory buildings along the New Orleans waterfront (in the early 1900s the area bustled with small port-related industries and offices). The convention center is the country's third-largest, with 700,000 square feet of contiguous exhibition space, 43 large meeting rooms, and a 35,000-square-foot ballroom. Nearby, many of the multistory buildings that once housed light industrial operations have been converted into posh, contemporary apartment complexes.

At the end of Convention Center Boulevard, turn right and take the canopied path leading to yet another result of the *World's Fair*—the *Riverwalk* shopping mall, with two levels of upscale shops, cafés, restaurants, and fast-food stands extending a quarter mile along the riverbank. Originally the

International Pavilion of the *1984 World's Fair, Riverwalk* was developed in 1986 as a mall by the Rouse Company, designers and developers of several similar projects in other American cities. Many of *Riverwalk's* upper-level eateries have tables with sweeping views of the Mississippi, and there are railed pedestrian walkways that offer close-up views of cargo vessels, tugs, and excursion boats skimming along the river.

Outside the mall's main exit is the Plaza d'España, an open area with an expanse of geometric red, white, and black Spanish tiles and a large circular fountain. A jazz or rock group will more than likely be tooting and plucking away at the open-air bandstand. If your own whistle needs whetting at this point, there's a good selection of drinks, plus sandwiches and hot food, at *LeMoyne's Landing* (on the plaza near the Algiers ferry landing; phone: 504-524-4809); you can sit at the bar inside or at one of the tables outside. At the river's edge, you can usually see a docked paddle wheeler, an excursion boat, or some other pleasure craft pulling up to load or unload passengers. (For information on sightseeing boats, see *River Tours* in THE CITY.)

From here you can take an optional but worthwhile detour to another interesting open space, the Piazza d'Italia. Go to the *New Orleans Hilton* hotel's main entrance, just behind *Riverwalk*, at the end of Poydras Street. Walk four short blocks along Poydras; on the left corner of Poydras and Tchoupitoulas Streets is a striking, contemporary tower, a postmodern interpretation of the ancient campaniles (freestanding church bell towers) so visible in the ancient squares of many Italian towns. Tucked behind it to the left is Piazza d'Italia, built with money raised by New Orleans's large Italian-American community. The tower and the whimsical postmodern rendition of a Roman ruin were created in 1979 by the nationally recognized architect Charles Moore, in cooperation with the local architectural firm of August Perez and Associates. There is a fountain and Roman arches with a humorous frieze of Roman-style masks that depict some of the modern-day local citizens who had a hand in building the piazza (one of those depicted is Moore himself). Note that the shape of the fountain's pool is that of the Italian peninsula. Unfortunately, the piazza and its fountain have not been well maintained—it was to be the focal point of a real estate development that did not materialize. Retrace your steps to the Plaza d'España.

From the central fountain in the Plaza d'España, walk diagonally to the right down a slight incline to Canal Street. Before you is the large, modern *Rivergate* exhibition center, once used for conventions and trade shows and now slated for possible renovation or demolition before being reincarnated as a casino; at presstime, its fate was still uncertain (see *Nightclubs and Nightlife* in THE CITY).

For a pleasant interlude, take a ride on the ferry to Algiers, which departs from the end of Canal Street; it's one of the most fun free things to do in the whole city. The ferry operates daily from 6 AM to 9 PM, and the refreshing, interesting excursion across the mighty Mississippi takes between 10 and 20 minutes round trip, depending on the river traffic. The large, pleasant outdoor observation deck on the ferryboat's pedestrian level provides a panoramic view of the busy riverfront, beginning at the left with the twin river bridges, then *Riverwalk Mall* and Plaza d'España, the high-rise buildings on and around Canal Street, the *Aquarium of the Americas, Woldenberg Park,* Jackson Square, and part of the *French Market.* When the ferry docks at Algiers Point, you can either stay aboard or disembark and head for the river levee (to the left as you leave the ferry house). The grassy levee in Algiers is another good spot for a grand vista of the city's riverfront profile.

On returning to the east bank, just after exiting the ferry house at Canal Street, look to the immediate left. The sleek, angular high-rise building across from the *Rivergate Exhibition Center* is the *World Trade Center* (2 Canal St.). Enter the lobby and take the elevator 33 floors up to the *Top of the Mart* restaurant (phone: 504-522-9795), a plush, comfortable, glass-enclosed lounge that makes a complete revolution every 90 minutes. Have a snack and take in the spectacular bird's-eye views of the city, the Mississippi, and miles and miles beyond.

Leave the *World Trade Center* by way of its lobby and walk right, past the Canal Street ferry and across the traffic intersection, to the fascinating *Aquarium of the Americas* (1 Canal St.; phone: 504-861-2537). Notice the row of playful abstract sculptures in tropical colors as you pass. The aquarium's strikingly contemporary building, completed in 1990, houses 10,000 specimens of fish, birds, and reptiles, displayed in their natural habitats in more than a dozen major exhibits. The aquarium is open daily; there's an admission charge. (For more information, see *Special Places* in THE CITY.)

After leaving the aquarium, walk to the left along the river to *Woldenberg Park,* a large, grassy, tree-filled oasis with comfortable benches. The herringbone brick path leads past handsome outdoor sculptures by some of New Orleans's leading contemporary artists. If you're lucky, you'll happen on a band playing on the little bandstand, or one of the frequent ethnic food-and-crafts festivals held in the park on weekends.

At the end of *Woldenberg Park,* turn left (away from the river) and walk the short distance to North Peters Street. This will put you at the *Marketplace,* an extensive two-story complex of shops and restaurants, including *Tower Records* (408 N. Peters St.; phone: 504-529-4411), with the most colossal collection of compact discs and cassettes outside of New York City; *Bookstar* (414 N. Peters St.; phone: 504-523-6411), its two floors filled with thousands of recently published volumes in every category; and the *Hard Rock Café* (440 N. Peters St.; phone: 504-529-5617), with the chain's trademark rock-music memorabilia, high-decibel speakers, and menu of hamburgers, chili, and other all-American fare.

Starting at the *Marketplace,* North Peters Street briefly merges with Decatur Street (the missing part having been obliterated by old rail lines), and then re-emerges again as North Peters at the *French Market.* Walk to the waterfront just behind the large parking lot to the landing dock of the *Natchez,* a sternwheeler built in the 1920s with a steam engine that functions excellently to this day. The engine's steam drives not only the boat's paddle wheel but also the authentic old calliope on the top deck; its toots and squawks often can be heard for blocks. The *Natchez* makes two daily excursions up and down the river, each about two hours long (for more information, see *River Tours* in THE CITY).

Just beyond the *Natchez* dock, at Decatur and Toulouse Streets, is *Jackson Brewery,* a shopping and restaurant complex composed of two connected five-story buildings—the *Millhouse,* completed in 1988, and the *Brewhouse,* opened in 1985, which replaced the original old *Jax Brewery.* Inside is a profusion of gift and souvenir shops, confectioneries, bookstores, restaurants, and an eclectic assortment of other retail outlets.

The Moon Walk begins where the *Jackson Brewery* ends (at the corner of Decatur and St. Peter Streets, just across the extension of St. Peter leading to the river). No, it has nothing to do with space suits and rocket boosters (or Michael Jackson, for that matter); the Moon Walk gets its name from Moon Landrieu, New Orleans's mayor from 1970 to 1978, who spearheaded the development of the French Quarter as a tourist attraction. Across Decatur Street from Jackson Square, the river levee is pleasantly landscaped, with a row of rustic lampposts that are lit at night and wide, wooden stairs that lead right to the muddy water of the Mississippi. From the Moon Walk, look across the river to the left. That nearly hairpin turn in the river is Algiers Landing, the deepest spot—recorded at 192 feet—in the Mississippi (the river's average depth from source to mouth is about 12 feet).

Walk down the Moon Walk's shoreside steps and cross the railroad tracks to the large pavilion overlooking Jackson Square. The view from here is splendid. At center stage is *St. Louis Cathedral,* fronted by the lush garden of the square itself. Flanking it are the handsome, stuccoed *Cabildo* and *Presbytère,* and forming the square's other two sides are the elegant, red brick *Pontalba Apartments,* built in the 1850s by a Spanish noblewoman and often described as the first true apartment buildings in the United States. (For additional details on these structures, see *Special Places* in THE CITY.)

Facing the square, take the pavilion steps to the right to the *Café du Monde* (813 Decatur St.; phone: 504-581-2914), the gateway to the *French Market* and a delightful spot to relax with New Orleans–style café au lait (chicory-flavored coffee with hot milk) and the puffs of fried, sugar-topped fritters known as beignets (pronounced ben-*yays*). If the weather is pleasant, wait for a table on the terrace and enjoy one of the city's most picturesque spots, with its view of Jackson Square and Decatur Street's never-ending bustle.

Housed in a building once known as the *Butcher's Market,* the café marks the beginning of the *French Market,* the colonnaded arcade that stretches along the riverfront for several more blocks. A farmer's market for more than two centuries (even before the first Europeans arrived, the Choctaws and other local Indians traded on this site), it was long the "belly" of New Orleans, lined with stalls crammed with not only fruits, vegetables, poultry, fish, herbs, game, and other meat, but also such nonedible merchandise as clothing and hardware.

Documents of the early 1800s describe Indians selling freshly butchered rabbits at the market, women hawking rice cakes, river boatmen stocking up for the trip back home, and an endless parade of merchants dealing in dry goods, trinkets, poultry, and pralines. While the French were content to have their market outdoors on the levee, the Spanish built the first structures to provide sanitary conditions for marketing meat. Over the years the buildings and merchandise have changed, but much of the heady atmosphere of exchange remains. The *French Market* is open daily (also see *Special Places* in THE CITY).

Farther down Decatur Street is a hodgepodge of boutiques selling homemade quilts, creole foodstuffs, toys, pralines, and ice cream, all still part of the *French Market.*

Walk along the river one block away from Jackson Square to Decatur and Dumaine Streets; here is the *Bazaar,* where clothes, fabrics, cooking utensils, and every sort of household goods were once sold. It is one of several riverfront structures designed in mid-1800s by New Orleans architect Joseph Abeilard, one of the scores of "freemen of color" who, as professionals and craftsmen, contributed greatly to the French Quarter's architecture. The *Bazaar* was destroyed by a hurricane in the 1930s, and was rebuilt shortly afterward with money from the federal Public Works Administration. Today, it houses a number of specialty shops selling apparel and accessories. Behind the *Bazaar,* in the *French Market,* is *Bella Luna* (near the corner of Decatur and Dumaine Sts.), a contemporary-creole and Italian restaurant with stunning, second-floor views of the river. This might be a good spot to stop for lunch or dinner, depending on the hour. The kitchen specializes in such traditional dishes as fettuccine with cream, gumbo, and bread pudding, as well as mesquite-smoked gulf fish and shrimp (also see *Eating Out* in THE CITY).

Go back to the river and continue walking straight ahead (downriver) to the 1000 block of Decatur Street, intersecting Ursulines Street, to the old *Vegetable Market.* At the turn of the century, the market was jammed with Sicilan-American fruit and vegetable vendors. Today, beneath the colonnaded arches are cafés, restaurants, and crafts shops. On a typical weekend, street musicians and performers usually add their glides and strums to the scene.

With the river to the right, continue across Gov. Nicholls Street to the *Farmer's Market,* a large, roofed shed built in 1936 to allow retailers, wholesalers, and farmers from nearby parishes to sell fruits, vegetables, herbs, and spices. The market, which is open 24 hours a day, still holds a wide assortment of produce—notably tomatoes, sweet potatoes, mirlitons (the pale-green, pear-shape squash known in Mexico as *chayote*), pumpkins, watermelons, and in the early summer, sticks of raw sugarcane (whittle off the tough peel, cut the hard pulp into strips, and chew). But don't look for real bargains here.

The *Farmer's Market* leads right into the *Community Flea Market,* where scores of tables overflow from the sheltered walkway onto the open space known as *French Market Place.* Weekends are the best times to scavenge among the dozens of stalls, piled high with everything from T-shirts and used jeans to handmade furniture and antique-glass butter dishes. Filling the air is the scent of piquant spices and fresh shrimp, gulf fish, and crabs wafting from the shops along this arcade, which specialize in all sorts of local and regional foodstuffs. The massive, terra-cotta–colored building in the background is the *Old US Mint,* home of the *New Orleans Jazz Collection and Mardi Gras Museum* (400 Esplanade Ave.; phone: 504-568-6968). The museum is closed Mondays; admission charge (also see *Special Places* in THE CITY).

We've saved the best of this walking tour for last: a fascinating ride back to the center of town along the riverfront on one of the vintage streetcars known as the *Ladies in Red.* Facing the river at the intersection of Esplanade and North Peters Street, walk the few yards to the streetcar tracks and the car stop, where you can board the streetcar for $1. The cars travel a delightful 1.9-mile rail route all the way to Julia Street in the Warehouse District, with many convenient stops along the way. The ride amounts to a series of second looks at many of the New Orleans riverfront's stunningly diverse sights.

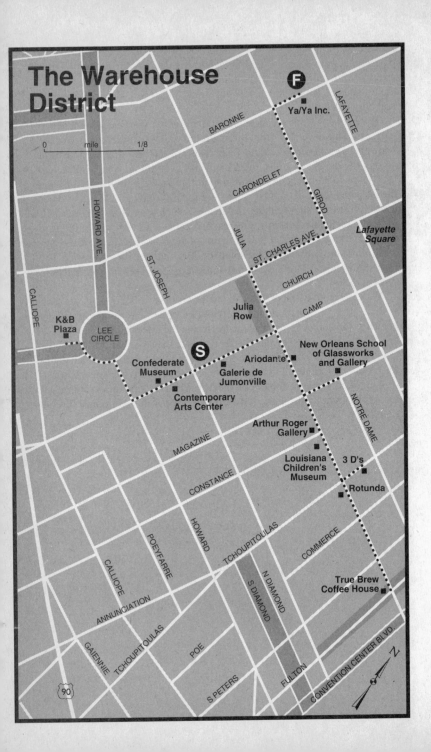

The Warehouse District

F

Ya/Ya Inc.

0   mile   1/8

LAFAYETTE

BARONNE

CARONDELET

GIROD

JULIA

HOWARD AVE.

ST. JOSEPH

ST. CHARLES AVE.

Lafayette Square

CHURCH

CAMP

CALLIOPE

K&B Plaza

LEE CIRCLE

Julia Row

S

Confederate Museum

Galerie de Jumonville

Ariodante

New Orleans School of Glassworks and Gallery

Contemporary Arts Center

NOTRE DAME

MAGAZINE

Arthur Roger Gallery

Louisiana Children's Museum

3 D's

CONSTANCE

Rotunda

HOWARD

POEYFARRE

TCHOUPITOULAS

COMMERCE

CALLIOPE

N DIAMOND

S DIAMOND

True Brew Coffee House

ANNUNCIATION

GAIENNIE

TCHOUPITOULAS

POE

FULTON

CONVENTION CENTER BLVD.

90

S PETERS

N

Walk 5:
The Warehouse District

In their preoccupation with New Orleans's history and traditions, most people find it easy to forget that the city also has a modern, innovative, artistic side. The Warehouse District, a part of town near the Mississippi Riverfront that once bustled with the business and commerce of a flourishing port, has been completely refurbished and redesigned; it is now the home of the city's avant-garde.

Less than 15 years ago, this area was known mostly for its skid row and the abandoned buildings that bore mute testimony to a bygone era of shipping. But then the *1984 World's Fair* came to town, and the city rediscovered that the dozens of old office buildings, wholesalers' warehouses, small factories, and assorted other structures were a hidden, underdeveloped treasure. Now the district has evolved into the New Orleans equivalent of New York's Soho.

There are more than 100 art galleries throughout New Orleans, but most of those with fine regional or national reputations are clustered around the Julia Street area in the Warehouse District. The handsome, excellently proportioned rooms in these buildings are ideal for showcasing paintings, sculpture, ceramics, glass, and photographs. At any particular time, one Warehouse District gallery might display the shockingly original mixed-media work of an up-and-coming local artist while its neighbor features the subtle, abstract-expressionist oils of a nationally recognized painter.

The emphasis of this walking tour through 12 square blocks of the Warehouse District will be on its function as a center for the city's contemporary art scene. But appreciation for its artistic contributions should not eclipse the historical and architectectural value of its buildings. Anyone who wants to get a deeper understanding of the area's renovation and architectural significance need look no farther than the *Preservation Resource Center (PRC;* 604 Julia St.; phone: 504-581-7032). A nonprofit advocacy group seeking to preserve and restore the landmarks of the Warehouse District and other historic neighborhoods, the *PRC* was responsible for *Julia Row's* rejuvenation. Given the least bit of prodding, an enthusiastic *PRC* member will be happy to give you a fistful of brochures and a crash course in local architecture.

The most suitable place to begin an artistic tour of the district is the *Contemporary Arts Center (CAC),* just off Lee Circle (900 Camp St.; phone: 504-523-1216). Energetic and enterprising, the *CAC* spearheaded the development of the Warehouse District, and its spirit is echoed throughout the thriving art scene here. Founded in 1976, it's a quasi-clubhouse for artists and the center of the city's lively cultural community, acting as a showplace for the work of up-and-coming local painters, sculptors, musicians, playwrights, and actors whose talents might otherwise be overlooked. It is housed in a renovated 1920s-vintage brick building that was the former headquarters of the local *Katz & Besthoff* drugstore chain. Each year, more than 200 exhibitions and other events in the visual arts, cinema, video, children's education, theater, dance, performance art, and music take place in this bilevel, 6,500-square-foot space. There are also two theaters, classrooms, and a screening room for films and videos. The *CAC* is closed Mondays and Tuesdays; there is an admission charge (also see *The New Orleans Art Scene* in DIVERSIONS).

The contrast between the boldly avant-garde *Contemporary Arts Center* and the traditional *Confederate Museum* just across the street (929 Camp St.; phone: 504-523-4522) couldn't be more striking. Entering this late-Romanesque stone edifice with its cavernous interior of dark, reddish cypress is like journeying back in time about 150 years. Images of the Civil War (some diehard rebels still refer to it as "The War of Northern Aggression") are evoked by tattered flags and battle standards, ungainly rifles and cannonballs, and reams of yellowed documents. Established in 1891, the museum houses such historic items as the uniform, sword, hats, and epaulets of Confederate General Pierre Gustave Toutant Beauregard, the New Orleanian who began the Civil War by ordering the first shot to be fired at Fort Sumter, South Carolina. He was one of the museum's founding fathers. One section is devoted to clothing and books that belonged to Jefferson Davis, president of the short-lived Confederate States of America. If you like, you can take a piece of the Confederacy home with you; a small gift shop features such souvenirs as Confederate banknotes circa 1864, books, and limited-edition prints of war scenes by artists of the period. The museum is closed Sundays; admission charge.

Outside, more Confederate memorabilia—on a somewhat larger scale—awaits. From the *Confederate Museum,* take a right and walk a half block to the corner of Howard Avenue. Turn right on Howard and continue one block to Lee Circle, a lovely knoll of green space that surrounds a 3½-ton, 16½-foot bronze statue of Confederate General Robert E. Lee, gazing southward. The memorial was dedicated in 1884, with many of Lee's family and friends present.

Continue left for about a quarter of the circle to the broad expanse of St. Charles Avenue. You might see the *St. Charles* streetcar pass as you cross St. Charles to *K&B Plaza* (1055 St. Charles Ave.; phone: 504-586-1234), a thoroughly modern office building ringed by an especially fine collection of 20th-century sculpture. Inside the lobby (closed weekends) are more outstanding examples of modern sculpture and painting, part of the K&B drugstore chain's corporate art collection (also see *Special Places* in THE CITY).

After leaving *K&B Plaza,* recross St. Charles Avenue, go right for a quarter of Lee Circle until you get back to Howard Avenue; turn right and walk on Howard for one block to Camp Street; turn left, and walk along Camp, crossing St. Joseph. On the way, pop into the *Galerie de Jumonville* (866 Camp St.; phone: 504-524-0082), one of the newest of the Warehouse District's galleries. It's on the ground floor of one of the nine connected townhouses that form Gasquet Row, constructed between 1838 and 1843.

Walk another block on Camp to Julia Street and turn right. You are now at the hub of the Julia Street gallery scene. Within the next four blocks of Julia are almost a dozen of the city's finest art galleries, ensconced in several renovated 19th-century shopfronts, offices, and former private homes. *Galerie Simonne Stern* (518 Julia St.; phone: 504-529-1118) specializes in fine contemporary paintings (most notably abstract expressionism), sculpture, photography, and master prints. Represented are artists with local, national, or international reputations. Continue on Julia to the *Arthur Roger Gallery* (432 Julia St.; phone: 504-522-1990), which boasts the most lavish exhibit spaces in New Orleans. Previous shows have focused on such artists as New York photographer Herb Ritts, New Orleans figure painter George Dureau, and Louisiana landscapist Elmore Morgan. On the next corner, at Julia and Constance Streets, is the *Louisiana Children's Museum* (428 Julia St.; phone: 504-523-1357), a lively place where children can romp through a series of ingenious educational installations, including a working mini-supermarket and an authentic TV studio. The museum is closed Mondays; there's an admission charge (also see *Museums and Historic Houses* in THE CITY).

From the museum, continue another block on the same side of the street and in the same direction to the *Downtown Gallery* (420 Julia St.; phone: 504-524-1988), which spotlights many Louisiana-born masters who worked between 1900 and 1950, along with samples of Art Deco, Art Nouveau, and Primitivism. A few steps away is the *Sylvia Schmidt Gallery* (400-A Julia St.; phone: 504-522-2000), which concentrates on works of contemporary realism and abstract expressionism.

On the next block of Julia, intersecting with Tchoupitoulas Street, is the *Rotunda,* a former grocery warehouse and an excellent example of the innovative refurbishing of the Warehouse District. If you're hungry for lunch, you couldn't have picked a better time, since the *Rotunda* houses *Emeril's* (800 Tchoupitoulas St.), one of the city's most popular restaurants. Owner-chef Emeril Lagasse is a widely acknowledged master at blending the traditional flavors of creole cooking with new American ingredients—crab and corn in puff pastry with creole corn sauce, for example, or spicy, New Orleans–style barbecued shrimp (also see *Eating Out* in THE CITY).

The *Rotunda* also is home to a trio of art galleries, just around the corner from *Emeril's* on Julia Street. *LeMieux Galleries* (332 Julia St.; phone: 504-565-5354) showcases "Third Coast" artists (natives of various towns along Louisiana's gulf coastline). Next door, *Still-Zinsel Contemporary Fine Art* (328 Julia St.; phone: 504-588-9999) has more contemporary paintings, sculpture, and photography, along with drawings and paintings on paper.

The *Gasperi Gallery* (320 Julia St.; phone: 504-524-9373) displays a colorful variety of Southern primitive and folk art.

For those looking for a short break (or to put a finishing touch on lunch), a good cup of coffee is only a few steps away. Continue on Julia Street toward the river for two blocks, to the corner of Fulton Street. Here, *True Brew Coffee House* (200 Julia St.; phone: 504-524-8441) serves cappuccino, espresso, mochaccino (hot chocolate with a shot of espresso and topped with whipped cream), and *café crème*, a frothy concoction in hot or frozen versions combining eight ounces of milk, a hazelnut fudge-coffee concentrate, and brown sugar. As you would expect from any self-respecting coffeehouse in an art district, *True Brew* is frequented by artists, actors, and writers, but it's also popular with doctors, lawyers, and office workers who infiltrate from the adjacent business district. Wall space is reserved for local artists' creations, and the intimate 60-seat theater on the premises often features works by local playwrights.

Once sufficiently recaffeinated, cross to the other side of Julia and turn left. Just a block beyond South Peters Street, on the corner of Commerce Street, is *Christopher Maier Furniture Design* (329 Julia St.; phone: 504-586-9079). This is a working studio and showroom for Maier's classically proportioned, custom-designed wood furniture, influenced by Greco-Roman forms and shapes, and featuring inlay work and exotic materials.

Walk on the right side of Julia Street for a block and a half to the corner of Tchoupitoulas Street. Turn right onto Tchoupitoulas and walk the half block to No. 746, site of the *Julia Place* apartment building and *3 D's* restaurant (phone: 504-566-7255). In the Warehouse District's industrial days, this building was a factory that produced burlap bags for the tons of coffee beans that passed through the port daily. The restaurant, with its slightly arched windows and dramatic, black slate floors, offers such dishes as hot artichoke dip and a "suburban pâté" of chicken breast. Like other Warehouse District dining spots, *3 D's* doubles as gallery space, with revolving shows of local artists and occasional poetry readings.

From *3 D's,* return to Julia, turn right, and walk a half block to *Ariodante* (535 Julia St.; phone: 504-524-3233), where you can browse among one-of-a-kind furniture, glass, ceramics, jewelry, and decorative objects created by a variety of artisans. From the gallery, continue a half block along Julia to Magazine Street, cross Magazine, and turn right. A half block up Magazine is the *New Orleans School of Glassworks and Gallery* (727 Magazine St.; phone: 504-529-7277). In the rear studio, among the white-hot kilns, you can watch teachers and students shaping and blowing blobs of molten glass into beautiful vases, sculptures, and bibelots.

Walk the half block back to Julia, turn right, and proceed to Camp Street. A few steps from the corner is *Wyndy Morehead Fine Arts* (603 Julia St.; phone: 504-568-9754), where an eclectic assortment of artwork is showcased against the dark gray walls. A hidden courtyard in the back doubles as a sculpture garden. Outside this gallery is a perfect vantage point from which to admire *Julia Row,* the beautiful brick structure across the street. This series of 13 connected brick townhouses in the Greek Revival style was called "The 13 Sisters" when they were built in 1832 by a company speculating in real estate. Each unit contains commercial space on the ground floor and apartments on the two balconied upper floors. In the mid-1800s, these were among the most fashionable addresses in town for newly arrived non-creole immigrants (Creoles had claimed the French Quarter as their own). The houses, which offered such architectural novelties as ornamented doorways and high ceilings, were efficiently designed with elegantly proportioned rooms. But by the turn of the century, the neighborhood had begun to deteriorate, and it remained rather seedy until its revival in the early 1980s.

Continue along Julia to St. Charles Avenue, turn right, walk one long block to Girod Street, then turn left on Girod. Baronne Street intersects Girod two blocks later; turn right and head for No. 636. A pair of galleries on the street level is worth a visit. Inside the door and to the right is *Marguerite Oestreicher Fine Art,* which features figurative artwork; to the left and up a few steps, *Bronwen White* specializes in contemporary painting from Great Britain, Scandinavia, and Latin America (phone: 504-581-9253 for both galleries). A few doors down, *Estudio Gallery* (630 Baronne St.; phone: 504-524-7982 or 504-947-9651) is the working studio and exhibition space of local artists Zella Funck and Martin LaBorde. A visitor might find the couple hard at work on a silkscreen or other printmaking project. Next door, *Ya/Ya Inc.* (628-630 Baronne St.; phone: 504-529-3306) is the showplace of artist Jana K. Napoli and her young, inner-city protégés, who are becoming well known for creating colorful, whimsically painted furniture.

From here, it's easy to continue your explorations in other parts of the city. To get to the French Quarter, turn right from *Ya/Ya Inc.* and walk five and a half blocks to Canal and Baronne Streets; to reach the riverfront area, walk a block and a half to the right to Poydras Street, then turn right and continue six blocks to the river.

The Garden District

0 —— mile —— 1/8

BARONNE

CARONDELET

ST. CHARLES AVE.

S

Rink Shopping Center

Louise S. McGehee School

PRYTANIA

Lafayette Cemetery †

Toby - Westfeldt House

COLISEUM

F Commander's Palace

CHESTNUT

PHILIP

Warwick Mansion

WASHINGTON AVE.

CAMP

Forsyth - Payne Residence

6TH

4TH

3RD

2ND

1ST

MAGAZINE

N

CONSTANCE

Walk 6:
The Garden District

Some years, spring comes to New Orleans as early as the end of February, when the city's numerous trees, flowering plants, and shrubs begin to bloom. Early spring is the best time to appreciate the natural pleasures of the city's Garden District, a lushly verdant residential oasis less than a mile from the urban center. If the previous winter was mild (as often happens), azaleas spring onto the scene in February and March, their bright pinks and fuchsias blanketing much of the area surrounding the Garden District's graceful old houses. Camellias, in pure whites, delicate pinks, and soft reds, show up at about the same time. By mid-March, the air becomes fairly saturated with the perfumes given off by the blossoming shrubs and trees—luscious-smelling gardenia, jasmine, sweet olive, wax ligustrum, roses, and ginger, plus the pungent scent of magnolia blossoms. Many of the district's bushes and trees were planted more than 150 years ago, after being brought from France, the Caribbean, or the huge sugarcane, cotton, and indigo plantations that once lined the Mississippi River's banks north of the city.

The mid-19th century was the Garden District's golden age, when one stately house after another, in a profusion of romantic architectural styles, sprouted among the hundreds of oak trees lining the then-makeshift thoroughfares. In the antebellum period of the 1840s and 1850s, New Orleans was a culturally divided city, with the creole descendants of French, African, and Spanish colonists ensconced in the Vieux Carré and the newly arrived American entrepreneurs (mostly Scottish, Irish, and English merchants, manufacturers, shippers, and planters) settling uptown, in the sections beyond what is now Canal Street. The factors dividing the two groups were language (French was still the lingua franca of the Creoles) and religion (the Protestantism practiced by most of the American newcomers was virtually unknown in the older, Roman Catholic part of town). Therefore, not long after their arrival, the more prosperous of the new citizenry set about developing their own genteel, close-knit community, in a section not far from the uptown riverfront, then known as Lafayette City.

That sense of separateness lingers even today. Strolling through the Garden District makes you feel as though you've entered another country—and traveled through the past to another era as well. The boundaries of this self-contained, aristocratic little world are not officially defined, but the term "Garden District" is commonly understood to embrace the 65 square blocks within the rectangle formed by St. Charles Avenue, Jackson Avenue, Magazine Street, and Louisiana Avenue.

The elegantly proportioned houses of the district, mostly imposing mansions of whitewashed cypress or stuccoed brick in soft, neutral tones, represent a cavalcade of mid- to late-19th-century architectural styles—principally Greek Revival, Second Empire, Italianate, and "Victorian Ornamental." Collectively, the buildings share a number of distinctive characteristics: Large front verandahs (also called "galleries") stretch from one end of the houses to the other; massive or delicate columns extend from the gallery floors to ornate friezes; and delicate, frilly ironwork usually frames the galleries.

The first owners spared little expense in the design and construction of their homes, which were built to withstand the ravages of the heat and dampness of the city's nine-month-long summers. Some of the houses were built in the old Louisiana style, with the main floor set upon a high masonry foundation, an architectural feature designed to protect the dwellings from the frequent floods that predated the construction of retaining levees along the Mississippi River. Inside, there are as many as 20 or 30 rooms; hand-painted murals decorate some of the ceilings, and many of the mansions have sweeping staircases with hand-carved mahogany banisters and newel posts. The finest Italian marble was used to construct the mantels, and the fabrics, furniture, and rugs were almost always European imports. An indication of the quality of their construction is the pristine condition many of the homes are in today. Most have been carefully preserved; some are even inhabited by descendants of the original owners.

Some of the Garden District mansions, however, have not survived the onslaught of time. They were either neglected and allowed to deteriorate or sold and converted into apartment or commercial buildings. Those that survived intact are still private residences, so none are open for public inspection. However, the beauty and history of their architecture can be appreciated quite well even from a distance.

The best starting point for a walking tour of the Garden District is the corner of St. Charles Avenue and First Street—two blocks past Jackson Avenue if you're traveling on the St. Charles streetcar from the Central Business District. This tour can be combined with *The St. Charles Streetcar,* our first DIRECTIONS tour.

From St. Charles, walk one block toward the river to Prytania Street, where, on the near left corner of First and Prytania Streets, is the *Louise S. McGehee School* (2343 Prytania St.). Once one of the Garden District's residential showplaces, it's now a girls' private elementary and high school. Designed in the "Free Renaissance" style of the early 1870s by James Freret, a prominent local architect, it features a wide front porch with wraparound railings separated by pairs of fluted Corinthian columns. The house is remarkable for its fully finished basement, an element rarely used in New Orleans, since the water table lies just a few feet belowground.

Across Prytania Street is the *Toby-Westfeldt House* (2340 Prytania St.), perhaps the most admired of the Garden District's structures; surrounded by an unpretentious white picket fence, its simple, austere lines are not unlike the plantation houses upriver from the city (see *Drive 2: New Orleans Plantations*). The house is believed to be the oldest in the district, built around 1838 by Thomas Toby, a native Philadelphian and manager of the large plantation that once surrounded the house. Its popular name is "Toby's Corner," a holdover from its earliest days when the corner was the terminus of the city bus line. The house underwent extensive improvements in 1855, but its basic design and character remain intact.

Continue down First Street to the 1300 block, considered by many to be the most beautiful strip in the neighborhood. Walk a block and a half past the intersection of First and Coliseum Streets to the home at 1331 First, dating from 1869 and distinguished by its monumental floor-to-ceiling windows, fine stucco work, dental molding, side projections, and lavish ironwork. Although No. 1315, the house across the street, may be somewhat less magnificent, its sweeping, inviting entrance is also noteworthy. This is also one of the few Garden District homes that retains its original accessory buildings, lush garden, and stately oaks.

Continuing down the next block of First, examine the decorative fence at No. 1239, distinctive for its woven iron wire, a patented process in which the iron rods were pulled, rather than cast or wrought. Designed in 1857 by architect James Calrow, a temporary resident of New Orleans whose work is well represented throughout the Garden District, the house was built at a cost of $13,000. At 1236 First is another fine house built in the Greek Revival style, completed in 1847. Inside, the home is embellished with black marble mantels and elaborate plaster ceiling medallions from which hang period crystal chandeliers.

On the next block of First, past the intersection of Camp Street, is the *Payne-Strachan House,* one of the district's most important historical sites. In 1889 Jefferson Davis, former President of the Confederate States of America, died in the left rear first-floor guestroom while visiting a friend, Judge Charles Erasmus Fenner. The two-story building, constructed of cement-covered brick, has the clean, simple lines of the Greek Revival style, with wide front galleries extending across both floors, supported by six Ionic columns. Built from 1849 to 1850, the house was commissioned by J. N. Payne, the judge's father-in-law.

Return to the corner of First and Camp and turn left on Camp. A few yards away is the *Warwick Mansion* (2427 Camp St.). Originally a residence, it later served as a private school for children of the Garden District's affluent citizens. Continue one block along Camp to Third Street. Turn right on Third, to No. 1206. Inside this house, erected before the Civil War and designed in an eclectic mix of architectural styles, Confederate General John B. Hood and two members of his family died in 1879; they were victims of the devastating yellow-fever epidemic of 1878. Across the street, at 1213 Third, is one of the city's best examples of the 19th-century "Italianate Villa" school of architecture. The style—typified by curved façades and porches, slightly arched windows with rounded lintels, and elaborate friezes lining the roof—was popular on the East Coast at the time, but was not commonly used in New Orleans. The original owner was Archibald Montgomery, a Dublin native who employed another Irishman, Henry Howard, to design the residence for him.

Continue down Third Street for one block to 1331 Third, a house of special interest to art buffs because of its association with French Impressionist painter Edgar Degas. It was built for Michael Musson, a successful cotton merchant who also was the city's postmaster. Musson's sister (who was Degas's mother) was born in New Orleans, and when the painter visited here, he stayed with other relatives who lived on Esplanade Avenue near the French Quarter. Degas's letters home reflect his positive impressions of the pretty creole women, the buildings of painted wood (an extreme rarity in France), and the steamboats on the river. During one visit to the city, Degas painted a scene at the New Orleans Cotton Exchange; the painting today hangs in the municipal museum at Pau, in the French Pyrenees.

From here, continue down Third, past Coliseum Street, to the monumental structure at 1415 Third, one of the largest houses in the Garden District. Among its striking features are the sweeping curved portico and upper gallery that extends the full width of the façade, lofty Ionic columns, ornate dental moldings, and the center parapet above the roof line. Built in 1865 for Walter G. Robinson, a genteel Virginian, the home is said to have had the city's first indoor plumbing. The elaborate ceiling frescoes in the large parlor and dining room are the work of Domenico Canova. The building next door (1417 Third St.) is a noteworthy example of the "carriage house," a New Orleans version of the small, quaint stables for carriage horses found in the narrow alleys of London.

Continue along Third Street in the same direction and turn left onto Prytania Street. No. 2605 is the only example of the Gothic Revival style in the Garden District—and one of the few in the entire city. Both the main house and its matching guest cottage are made of stuccoed brick. Notice that the pointed arches above the windows and doors are repeated in the balcony's ironwork motif.

Backtrack across Third Street to No. 2520 Prytania, built in 1853; its asymmetrical design is a blend of the Greek Revival and Italianate architectural styles. The balcony is distinguished by its delicate finial ornaments and is supported by cast-iron lower railings. On the same block, at No. 2504, is a home built in 1859 and currently owned by the *Women's Opera Guild.* While the interior is decorated in Victorian style, the exterior is a hybrid of Italianate and Greek Revival. Across the street is No. 2507, an early-1850s building that was inhabited by Joseph H. Maddox, owner of the *New Orleans Daily Crescent,* an important newspaper of the period. The fireplace in this house is decorated with original hand-painted tiles that depict a bayou scene.

Continue along Prytania to Second Street; turn right and continue to Coliseum Street. At the corner, note the house at 1410 Second, with its Corinthian columns and stucco façade. Like most of New Orleans's 19th-century homes with brick exteriors, this one was painted or stuccoed and then repainted to resemble stone.

Turn right on Coliseum, and walk a block and a half to 2627 Coliseum Street, where the gingerbread-like trim and elaborate ironwork lend a storybook aspect to the red brick mansion, built during the post–Civil War Reconstruction period. It was originally inhabited by James Eustis, an American ambassador to France.

Proceed down Coliseum Street to Fourth Street and turn right. In front of the Italianate Villa–style house at 1448 Fourth Street is a cast-iron fence with a cornstalk motif, similar to the celebrated one surrounding *Cornstalk House* in the 900 block of Royal Street (see *Walk 1: The French Quarter*). Dominating the 1400 block of Fourth Street, this lavishly landscaped mansion is a prime example of how much money was freely spent in constructing these elaborate Garden District houses. History places the cost of construction at $23,750, no small sum in 1859, when the two-story structure was built. Surrounded by giant magnolias, elms, and palms, as well as prodigious shrubbery, it features verandahs with wrought-iron railings lining three sides of the exterior. Inside, there are 15 large, high-ceilinged rooms; the double parlor's measurements are a palatial 43 feet by 26 feet.

Continue down Fourth Street and turn left at Prytania. Walk one block along Prytania and turn left onto Washington Avenue. To the right, this block of Washington forms a boundary of *Lafayette Cemetery,* which was laid out in 1833 by the original residents of Lafayette City, a precursor of the Garden District. Like other New Orleans cemeteries, Lafayette is filled with aboveground tombs and mausoleums resembling stone and marble cottages, each used as the final resting place for generations of the same family. The cemetery gates usually are open, but strolling around the tombs is not always safe; do not enter unless there are at least four or five in your group, and do not attempt to enter at night.

Now that your architectural appetite has been satisfied, you may be hungry for food and drink. Two dining options are just a few steps away from here. For a snack of fresh pastries accompanied by any one of several varieties of coffees and teas, try *La Tazza,* a little café in the *Rink Shopping Center* on the corner of Washington and Prytania (2727 Prytania St.; phone: 504-891-6968). If you want to indulge in a lavish lunch or dinner, however, you couldn't do much better than *Commander's Palace,* on the opposite corner at Washington Avenue and Coliseum Street. This establishment is consistently ranked among New Orleans's most creative creole restaurants. Reservations are advised (unless business is extremely slow) and men are required to wear jackets at all times (also see *Eating Out* in THE CITY).

To return downtown by streetcar, walk two and a half blocks along Washington Avenue to St. Charles and board the streetcar on the Garden District side of the median. To go uptown toward Carrollton Street, the stop is on the Washington Avenue side of the median. Another option is to call a taxi from a public telephone at the *Rink Shopping Center;* the fastest and most reliable service is *United Cabs* (phone: 504-522-9771).

Drive 1: Esplanade Avenue–City Park

Readers of old maps and documents are often surprised to learn that in the past Esplanade Avenue, the tree-lined boulevard that forms one of the French Quarter's boundary lines, was often referred to as Esplanade Ridge. Granted, in the topography of New Orleans (most of which is below sea level), a hill is defined as any mound of earth taller than a very tall man, and a "ridge" is nothing more than a strip of sloping terrain. But even so, the founding fathers' "Esplanade Ridge" was a slight exaggeration; it is unlikely that you will sense the very slight elevation that gave this avenue its name.

Parallel to central Canal Street, Esplanade Avenue (or Ridge, if you will) begins at the Mississippi River, and for 10 blocks forms an approximate dividing line between the French Quarter and the Faubourg Marigny "suburb" (the French *faubourg* means "false city") to the east, a neighborhood largely built up by "free persons of color" in the 19th century. Some of its original residents came straight from abroad to settle here, and others were freed US slaves. The wealthiest earned their livelihoods as merchants and artisans. Then, as now, there were many residents of mixed race and ancestry.

Today the Faubourg provides authentic local color in contrast to the French Quarter, which in recent years has been heavily groomed for mass tourism. The Faubourg Marigny's restaurants and nightclubs (many on Frenchmen Street) are genuinely funky, and there is a noticeable lack of neon and T-shirt shops. In other words, real people live and go out here. The mix of ethnicities and economic classes—there are poor, middle-class, and well-to-do sub-sections—makes the Faubourg Marigny a contemporary microcosm of New Orleans rather than a prettified relic. Beyond Faubourg Marigny, Esplanade Avenue continues another mile or so northwest toward Lake Pontchartrain, ending at Bayou St. John and the entrance to *City Park*.

In the very earliest decades of New Orleans's existence, Esplanade had no name; it was little more than a strip of terrain between the colonial town now known as the French Quarter and the plantations and small farms of Faubourg Marigny. It did, however, mark the beginning of the trade route from the center of town to Bayou St. John, which connects with Lake Pontchartrain, a coastal bay along the Gulf of Mexico.

During the city's boom era of the 1830s, Esplanade became a very desirable residential area, known as La Promenade Publique. Well-to-do French Creoles built stately frame houses amid lavish gardens, with oak, magno-

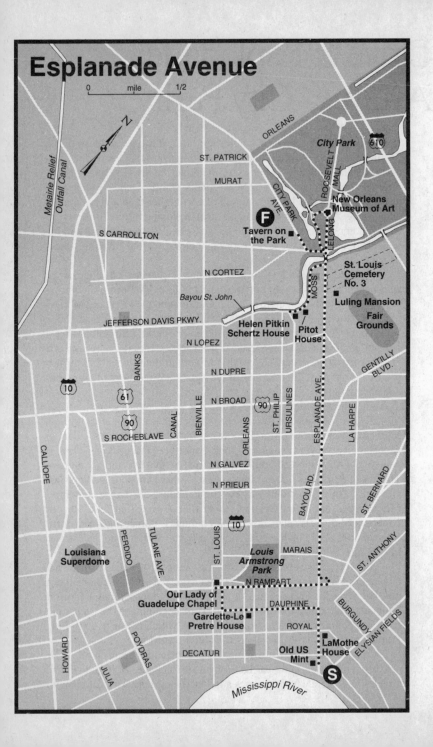

Esplanade Avenue

0 mile 1/2

N

Metairie Relief Outfall Canal

ORLEANS

City Park

610

ST. PATRICK

MURAT

CITY PARK AVE.

ROOSEVELT MALL

New Orleans Museum of Art

S CARROLLTON

F

Tavern on the Park

LELONG

N CORTEZ

MOSS

St. Louis Cemetery No. 3

Bayou St. John

Luling Mansion

JEFFERSON DAVIS PKWY.

Helen Pitkin Schertz House

Pitot House

Fair Grounds

N LOPEZ

N DUPRE

GENTILLY BLVD.

BANKS

N BROAD

90

ST. PHILIP

URSULINES

ESPLANADE AVE.

LA HARPE

10

61

BIENVILLE

CANAL

ORLEANS

90

S ROCHEBLAVE

N GALVEZ

N PRIEUR

BAYOU RD.

ST. BERNARD

CALLIOPE

10

ST. LOUIS

Louis Armstrong Park

MARAIS

ST. ANTHONY

Louisiana Superdome

PERDIDO

TULANE AVE.

N RAMPART

Our Lady of Guadelupe Chapel

DAUPHINE

BURGUNDY

ELYSIAN FIELDS

Gardette-Le Pretre House

ROYAL

HOWARD

POYDRAS

JULIA

DECATUR

Old US Mint

LaMothe House

S

Mississippi River

lia, elm, and palm trees. Although most of the houses survive today, in various states of repair and disrepair, a few have been restored to the elegant single-family dwellings they once were. And happily, giant oaks and flowering shrubs still line the curbs and the broad, grassy medians.

Taking in Esplanade's sights on foot is pleasant, though somewhat more strenuous than our other walks; going by car allows for an extended look beyond the avenue, along tranquil Bayou St. John, whose banks are lined with numerous old raised cottages, as well as bosky *City Park.* One of the last stops on this tour, *City Park* is an ideal spot for a picnic lunch.

The logical starting point is at Esplanade and the Mississippi River, in front of the *Old US Mint* (400 Esplanade Ave.; phone: 504-568-6968). The huge Federalist-style granite structure occupies the entire block bounded by Esplanade Avenue and Barracks, North Peters, and Decatur Streets (the main entrance is on Esplanade Avenue). The oldest federal mint building still standing, it produced silver dollars and other US coins, as well as Confederate currency, from 1838 to 1909. Today, it is the home of the *New Orleans Jazz Collection* and *Mardi Gras Museum,* featuring such jazz artifacts as Louis Armstrong's first trumpet, and numerous *Mardi Gras* costumes. There's also a historical research library on the premises. The museum is closed Mondays; there's an admission charge. The library is open by appointment only on Wednesdays through Fridays (also see *Special Places* in THE CITY).

On leaving the *Old US Mint,* cross Decatur Street at the Esplanade intersection traffic signal and travel one block up, away from the river, to the corner of Chartres Street. On the near right corner, at 524 Esplanade, is what may be the boulevard's oldest remaining structure. This two-story residence, with an oversize attic, was built in 1810 for Gaspar Cusachs, a local historian, who embellished the ceilings with florid paintings and intricate moldings and medallions. Unfortunately, the house is closed to the public, but you might catch sight of some of the rooms shown in the 1989 film *Blaze,* the movie biography of former Louisiana Governor Earl K. Long.

Continue up one more block—pausing to note *LaMothe House* at 621 Esplanade, a 150-year-old double townhouse that's now a hotel (see *Checking In* in THE CITY)—to 704 Esplanade, the towering stucco building with the large side courtyard on the far right corner. Built in 1856 by John Gauche, a wealthy Creole, it's one of the largest and most flamboyant of all the residences on the avenue. The intricate iron balconies that extend around three sides of the building are said to have been cast in Saarbrücken, Germany, from a design by the German Renaissance engraver Albrecht Dürer.

Continue two blocks up Esplanade to Dauphine Street, turn left, and drive seven blocks to Orleans Street. The lofty structure on the far left corner (716 Dauphine St.) is the *Gardette–Le Pretre House,* dating from 1836. In June 1861, Confederate General Pierre G. T. Beauregard is said to have sent here part of the captured flagstaff from his victory at Fort Sumter,

South Carolina; it was presented to the Orleans Guards, who were part of the local militia.

Continue up Dauphine Street for three more blocks to St. Louis Street, then turn right on St. Louis for two blocks to the divided thoroughfare, North Rampart Street. Turn left and go one block to Conti Street. At the corner of Conti and North Rampart Streets is *Our Lady of Guadalupe Chapel* (411 N. Rampart St.), built in 1826 to serve as a "burial chapel" for the nearby *St. Louis Cemetery Number One* and *Number Two.* Funerals were frequent at that time, since the city was gripped by a virulent yellow-fever epidemic, which eventually took thousands of lives. The chapel was used exclusively for funerals until 1860, since it was believed that using the main cathedral would unnecessarily expose the general population to the highly contagious disease, transmitted by the mosquitoes that infested the city from spring to fall. To the right of the building is the grotto-like, and rather bizarre, *Shrine of St. Jude,* "the patron saint of lost causes." The shrine's walls are festooned with crutches and other objects signifying cures, as well as little plaques engraved with a simple "Merci," expressions of thanks for favors granted. In the rear of the chapel proper is a statue of St. Expedite, a saint who never existed. The saint was "created" by unknown parishioners who saw only the word "Expedite" on the shipping crate in which the Italian-made statue arrived, and mistook it for his name. To this day, two-line ads regularly appear in the "Personals" column of *The Times-Picayune* classifieds that read, "Thanks to St. Expedite for favors granted."

From *Our Lady of Guadalupe,* make a U-turn on Conti and return via North Rampart Street about eight blocks to Esplanade Avenue. Since no left turns are permitted here, drive one block farther, make a U-turn, and drive one block back to Esplanade; then turn right.

Six blocks up Esplanade Avenue is an intersection with Bayou Road, which once led to Bayou Sauvage. Eight blocks farther, past the traffic signal at North Broad Street, is another diagonal intersection at Grand Route St. John, which is the site of the ancient thoroughfare that once linked Bayou Sauvage to the east and Bayou St. John to the west.

Another five five blocks up Esplanade on the right is Leda Court, a very short street nestled in a lush neighborhood just behind the *Fair Grounds* racetrack. At No. 1438, almost obscured by trees and shrubs, is the splendiferous, neo-Romanesque *Luling Mansion,* one of the great architectural treasures of New Orleans. In 1865, James Gallier Jr., a leading New Orleans architect whose father was also a prominent architect, designed and built the four-story, 22-room mansion from a crude sketch by its owner, Florenz Luling, a cotton merchant exiled from Germany during the Revolution of 1848. The mansion once sat on 80 acres of land, but during the Reconstruction period after the Civil War, Luling's economic difficulties forced him to sell parcels of the estate. In 1880 the house of cement-covered brick, with balconies encircling the three upper floors, became the *Louisiana Jockey Club.* Since the 1920s it has been an apartment house.

Backtrack to Esplanade Avenue and turn left to *St. Louis Cemetery Number Three* (3421 Esplanade Ave.). Installed in 1856, its original gates remain, a relic of the time when the old *Bayou Cemetery* was taken over by the Roman Catholic Archdiocese of New Orleans and given its present, numerical name. Priests and nuns were traditionally entombed here. (Bishops and archbishops were buried beneath the altar of *St. Louis Cathedral* on Jackson Square.) James Gallier Sr., architect of the old *City Hall* (now *Gallier Hall*) in the Central Business District and numerous other major 19th-century public buildings, was buried here with his wife after they lost their lives in a shipwreck in 1866. Other tombs house the remains of Father Adrien Rouquette (1813–87), a poet and missionary to the Choctow Indians, and the black philanthropist Thomy Lafon (1811–93).

One block farther up Esplanade is Moss Street, which runs along the bank of Bayou St. John. The bayou, extending from Lafitte Avenue to Lake Pontchartrain, was a key factor in the selection of New Orleans by Jean-Baptiste Le Moyne, Sieur de Bienville, as the site of the royal French colony in 1718. The local Indians and early settlers used the bayou to move wares to and from the town on the Mississippi River, and its connection to Lake Pontchartrain provided access to the Gulf of Mexico beyond. In the 1790s, the Carondelet Canal was dug near the ramparts at Toulouse Street in the French Quarter to connect Bayou St. John with the town itself. In 1927, the canal was filled in, ending the bayou's commercial function and making it in effect a decorative waterway for the plantation houses and weekend cottages along the banks.

Turn left onto Moss Street and go the dozen-or-so blocks to the *Pitot House,* also known as the *Ducayet House* (1440 Moss St.; phone: 504-482-0312). In the late 1700s, the Ducayets, a well-heeled Spanish colonial family, built this gracefully designed, West Indies–style cottage as a retreat from the busy town. In 1810 it was bought by James Pitot, Mayor of New Orleans from 1804 to 1805. The small house, with its unpretentious columns and wraparound verandah, has been restored and furnished in the style of the early 19th century. It's closed Sundays through Tuesdays; admission charge (also see *Special Places* in THE CITY).

At the end of the next block is the *Helen Pitkin Schertz House* (1300 Moss St.), constructed about 1784, the same time as the *Pitot House.* It was known long ago as the "Spanish Custom House" because of its reputation as a storage place for booty confiscated by the numerous pirates who ran their boats up the bayou. Also done in the West Indies style, the house's broad galleries are supported by Pompeiian brick columns, a design feature that helped promote air circulation throughout the rooms. The galleries and the roof are of wood, while the first floor is of plastered brick. The two dormer windows in the American colonial style were a later addition, as was the rear room. Unfortunately, this house is a private residence and not open to the public.

Backtrack now to Esplanade Avenue, turn left, and cross Bayou St. John. The equestrian statue dominating the circle you see before you is of New

Orleans–born Confederate General Pierre G. T. Beauregard, veteran of the battles of Fort Sumter, Bull Run, and Shiloh. The sculptor is Alexander Doyle, creator of the monumental bronze of Beauregard's commander, Confederate General Robert E. Lee, at Lee Circle in the city's center.

Halfway around the circle is Lelong Avenue, a broad alley that leads to the *New Orleans Museum of Art* (phone: 504-488-2631); it's worth a visit for its superb collections of painting, sculpture, decorative art, and photography that range from pre-Christian Oriental and Mediterranean works to the major contemporary European and American periods. The original neoclassical building, dating from 1912, has been expanded over the years to permit more exhibition and educational space. The museum is closed Mondays; there's an admission charge (also see *Special Places* in THE CITY).

The museum is located in *City Park,* the perfect place to stop and enjoy a picnic. This onetime sugar plantation is one of the largest urban parks in the country, and includes 1,500 acres of picnic grounds, an amusement park, tennis courts, lagoons, flower-filled gardens, and some 22,000 sprawling oaks, some of which are said to be 800 years old. The 8 miles of lagoons, filled with swans and ducks, can best be appreciated by renting one of the self-propelled paddleboats or canoes. The amusement park has a child-scale locomotive that winds through the grounds, a restored 19th-century carousel, and a fantasy village called *Storyland,* inhabited by larger-than-life Mother Goose characters. For the sports-minded, there are four golf courses and 39 tennis courts, along with volleyball courts and baseball fields. For more on *City Park* see *Special Places* in THE CITY.

If you haven't brought a picnic, and want a bite to eat, *Semolina* restaurant (5080 Pontchartrain Blvd.; phone: 504-486-5581) is a good choice, and just a five-minute drive away. To get there, go to the left side of the museum (as you're facing the building), turn right, continue for about 50 yards, and, at the first fork in the road, keep left. Drive along the edge of the lagoon to reach the wide, divided City Park Avenue. (Note the clusters of magnificent oak trees along this stretch. Under their branches, creole gentlemen of the 19th century settled affairs of honor with pistols or swords, giving the trees the name Dueling Oaks.) Turn right onto City Park Avenue and drive several blocks, past *Delgado Community College* and Canal Boulevard. Continue past the traffic signal at Canal Boulevard. City Park Avenue now becomes Metairie Road. Continue one block on Metairie to the traffic signal at Pontchartrain Boulevard. Ahead of you is *Semolina.* To reach the entrance, drive along Metairie Road past the restaurant building and turn left into the rear parking lot. Inside you'll find New Orleans's most popular source of pasta dishes, inspired by some of the world's major cuisines—among them Italian, Cajun, creole, Thai, Indian, and Southwestern American—offered at very reasonable prices in a comfortably casual and colorful atmosphere. Salads and desserts are good, too.

Drive 2: New Orleans Plantations

During much of the 19th century, an elaborate plantation culture flourished along the banks of the Mississippi River. The wealthy families who built the plantations were mostly Creole, descendants of the region's early French and Spanish colonists. The agriculture that attracted them and supported their lavish lifestyles dates back to the early 1700s, when the territory was a French colony. In an effort to further populate the area and develop the swampland, France began recruiting from its prisons and slums, transporting people to the fertile Louisiana territory. When that strategy failed, the country began to offer large tracts of land to anyone who could bring in tenants to work it. The lure worked, but it promoted the slave trade and it benefited only those who were able to accumulate a sufficient number of slaves to do the work.

By the early 19th century, it was technology that ensured the long-term economic future of the aristocratic planter society, even after Louisiana became a part of the United States in 1803. First, a creole planter named Etienne de Boré discovered a method to granulate sugar. Then, Eli Whitney invented the cotton gin, which removed seeds that were tightly entangled within the tough fibers of cotton bolls. And, finally, Robert Fulton designed the steam-driven engine that could help move crops and cargoes up and down the Mississippi. These momentous technological advances spawned a scramble for land along the river—land that had suddenly become valuable.

In the northern half of Louisiana, cotton became king; up to two million acres were used to grow the crop in the 1830s. In the rich, black soil of the southern half of the state, sugarcane was planted on another 250,000 acres. The number of slaves grew accordingly: By 1840, Louisiana's slave population was about 140,000 (about 15% of the total number of slaves in the US at that time). At the outbreak of the Civil War in 1861, an average of 50 slaves lived and worked on each of Louisiana's 1,500 plantations.

The Emancipation Proclamation and the resultant Civil War threw a wrench into the machinery of the South's plantation economy. With the burning and looting that accompanied the military battles, most of the plantations were destroyed. Of the few antebellum plantation houses that survived, many have been painstakingly restored. Some homes were preserved by descendants of the original owners, but most were restored through the contributions of individuals, corporations, and nonprofit foundations. Today, some 20 plantations still stand less than 100 miles upriver from New Orleans. Some are either closed to the public entirely or open only by special appoint-

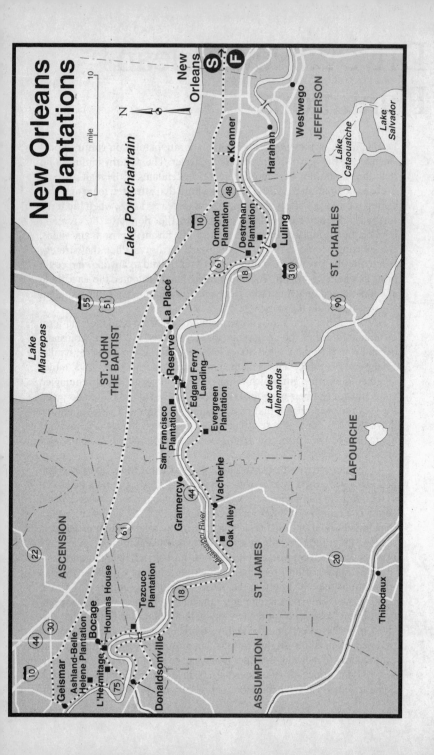

ment, but others offer short guided tours, and a few have been converted into comfortable, even elegant, bed and breakfast establishments.

The plantation designs of the early 19th century were inspired by the tropical architecture of the West Indies. But as the planters prospered, the monumental Greek Revival architectural style, with a large number of variations, became widely used. The houses, designed to accommodate the region's damp, subtropical climate, were also designed to simplify the comings and goings of large numbers of relatives, friends, and workers. They served not only as residences, but also as centers of self-contained communities living, working, and trading on the land. Usually, the houses were built off the ground as a protection from the Mississippi River's frequent spring floods. In order to capture cross breezes, the ground floor of most houses was split into only four large rooms with a minimum of interior walls. Ceilings, windows, and doors were high, and most rooms opened onto porches that could extend around three or all four sides of the building. Steeply sloped roofs carried off the frequent rains and extended out over the porches, known as "galleries," to block heat and glare.

Of the 10 plantations on this driving tour, six offer guided tours lasting about an hour, and two of these serve meals and offer overnight accommodations. The other four are completely private and can be viewed only from the roadside. Although it's possible to visit them all in a single (very busy) day, spending two days touring is a better idea.

This driving tour goes from New Orleans directly to the farthest plantation upriver, then makes stops at the various sites on the return trip to the city.

The trip upriver is a 55-mile drive on Interstate 10 West. More than 10 miles of this drive are on an elevated roadbed cutting through a serenely beautiful coastal marshland. The muddy pools, grassy expanses, and moss-hung cypress trees vibrant with flocks of snowy egrets and other water birds, as well as turtles and other wildlife, make this drive an especially pleasant one. The Bonnet Carré Spillway, a dam-like device stretching about 2 miles through the swampy terrain from the Mississippi River at the left to Lake Pontchartrain at the right, is about 20 miles from the city. The spillway acts like a huge trapdoor, holding back river water from the marshland leading to the lake. When the river swells in the spring to the point of flooding, the spillway's immense bays can be opened, releasing the overflow into the marsh and the brackish lake.

About 35 miles past the spillway, take Exit 177 and turn left on Louisiana Highway 30. After about a mile, follow the sign for *Ashland–Belle Helene Plantation.* At Geismar, located at the junction of Highways 30 and 75, turn left onto Highway 75. This strip, which runs on either side of the river parallel to the levee, is also known as River Road, but its name changes as different state highways merge with it. Throughout this driving tour, you'll be traveling on or near this road; although its name changes, it is easily identifiable because of its position next to the riverbank. At this point of the tour, River Road cuts through part of the state's "chemical corridor" between New Orleans and Baton Rouge, the state capital, with petrochemical plants and refineries silhouetted against the sky in striking counterpoint to the flat sugarcane fields surrounding them.

From the junction of Highways 30 and 75, continue on River Road for 3½ miles to *Ashland–Belle Helene Plantation*. Sadly, the house was closed to the public last year with no plans to re-open, but it is still worth the short drive to view the exterior of this gracious 1842 Greek Revival mansion, which now more than ever silently eulogizes the demise of a bygone era. Even with its architectural bones partly exposed by the peeling stucco, there is much evidence that it may have been the most splendid of all the homes along the Lower Mississippi. Its exterior walls are surrounded by 28 square, massive brick columns soaring 30 feet to the frieze below the roofline. Parts of the plantation's house and grounds have appeared in three movies: *The Beguiled, Mandingo,* and television's "The Autobiography of Miss Jane Pittman." Originally called simply *Ashland,* the plantation was built in 1842 for Duncan Kenner, who practiced law and was a member of the state legislature when he wasn't occupied with his duties as a planter. Kenner also served in the Confederate government in several capacities. Kenner was an inveterate horseman; he maintained his own racetrack on the grounds of the plantation. Its name was changed to *Belle Helene* by a subsequent owner in 1889.

From *Ashland–Belle Helene,* return to the River Road; turn left, then continue for about 7 miles. On the way, look for *L'Hermitage* on the left. It's considered the state's oldest surviving Greek Revival plantation house. Though the house is not open to the public, the calm, simple beauty of its setting, its steeply pitched roof punctuated by two dormer windows, and its handsomely proportioned, galleried façade can be admired from the road. Marius Pons Bringier built it in 1814 as a wedding gift for his son, Michel. Sugarcane was its principal crop, although indigo and tobacco were also cultivated.

Continue downriver 1 mile to *Bocage,* which means "Shady Retreat" in French. This house, built in 1801, was a wedding gift from Bringier to another of his children, his daughter, Françoise, who was 15 years old when she married. Remodeled in the 1840s, this stately, two-story manse is fronted with six wide and two narrow wooden columns. The entablature extending above the roofline partly obscures the gently sloping roof. This house is also closed to the public, but its charms are apparent even from a distance.

A mile farther up River Road is the town of Burnside, and *Houmas House* (phone: 504-473-7841; 504-522-2262 in New Orleans), which sits on one of the prettiest grounds of all the plantation houses in the vicinity. In the 1790s, nearly a half century before the house was built and named for the Indian tribe of the surrounding area, another house sat on this lot. The earlier, smaller one was built by Alexander Latil in early colonial style on land he had purchased from the Houmas. Latil's building was preserved and incorporated into the new plans via a gated, arched carriageway when Colonel John Smith Preston of North Carolina constructed *Houmas House.* Preston had come to Louisiana to assume control of the land, which had become the property of his father-in-law, General Preston Wade, a veteran of the Revolutionary War. Once installed in their new home, the Prestons apparently were homesick for the Eastern shore, since some design elements—such as the belvedere (a glassed-in cupola crowning the roof)—recall the colonial homes of New England and the Carolinas.

In 1858, the plantation was acquired by John Burnside, an Irish immigrant who expanded the sugar acreage to 20,000 and gave his name to the nearby town. Thanks to him, *Houmas House* escaped pillage by Union troops during the Civil War (Burnside claimed neutrality as a British citizen). But the house nevertheless fell into disrepair in later years and languished until 1940, when it was bought by Dr. George B. Crozat of New Orleans and rescued from years of decay.

The spacious grounds are partly shaded by huge, moss-draped oaks. Crepe myrtle trees and a rather formal garden of boxwood hedges add interesting touches to the landscaping. At each side of the house is a small, two-story hexagonal building called a *garçonnière,* which was where the young men of the family (*garçon* is French for "boy") lived before they married.

Inside the house itself, note the exceptionally fine spiral staircase, the collection of 22 large armoires, all made in Louisiana, the original marble mantels, and the beautiful 19th-century English and American antiques. (An additional point of interest is that many of the scenes in *Hush . . . Hush, Sweet Charlotte,* a 1965 movie starring Bette Davis and Olivia de Havilland, were filmed here.) Hour-long guided tours of *Houmas House* are given about every half hour. The house is closed on major holidays.

Drive downriver along River Road about a half mile and turn left on Highway 44. If you want to grab a bite of lunch or a snack at this point, a good restaurant is a short distance away. At the intersection of Highways 44 and 22 (about 1 mile farther), turn left to find the four rudimentary frame cottages that make up *The Cabin* restaurant (phone: 504-473-3007). The buildings were created out of 10 former slave quarters, each about 140 years old, taken from surrounding plantations. The rustic motif extends to the high-ceilinged, hexagonal dining room decorated with antique-looking farm implements. On the menu are sandwiches, crawfish *étouffée,* a gumbo thick with sausage and crawfish, black-eyed peas, red beans and rice, corn bread, and buttermilk pie. The restaurant is closed Monday through Wednesday evenings. (However, you may want to save your appetite for the fancier fare available at *Lafitte's Landing;* see below.)

Next drive about 2 miles downriver on Highway 44 to *Tezcuco Plantation* (phone: 504-562-3929). Framed by beautiful oak and magnolia trees, it was completed in 1855 after five years of meticulous construction. The spacious cottage, a creole variation on the Greek Revival theme, has 25-foot-square front bedrooms and 15-foot ceilings. The plantation was designed and built in the 19th century by its first owner, Benjamin Tureaud, a veteran of the Mexican War. The raised cottage's name is a variation of Lake Texcoco, where, according to legend, a divine eagle carrying a snake in its beak alighted on a cactus. The Aztecs took this as a sign, and built their empire on that spot, the present-day Mexico City.

The house is furnished with period antiques by such prominent Louisiana furniture makers as Mallard and Signoret. The rooms include a warming pantry, an office, a foyer, a parlor, a formal dining room, and three bedrooms. Antique dolls, Art Nouveau pottery, and Civil War memorabilia are also on display. In the carriage house at the rear of the main building is a 23-foot-long torpedo boat used during the Civil War.

Tezcuco Plantation offers both a moderately priced restaurant with a regional menu and 16 pleasantly decorated and comfortable rooms in restored slave cabins; several have a second bedroom. The price of the accommodations (from $55 to $150 per night) includes a tour, breakfast, and a bottle of wine. Guided tours also are given daily every every half hour or so; there's an admission charge. The house is closed on major holidays.

At this point, if you've opted to wait to eat, return to the River Road; turn left, and proceed 1 mile to the Sunshine Bridge across the Mississippi River (there's a $1 toll) to Donaldsonville. The bridge was built in the 1950s during the administration of Governor Jimmie H. Davis, composer of the popular 1930s country-and-western tune, "You Are My Sunshine." Cross the bridge to the west bank of the river and prepare to turn left at the first opportunity, less than an eighth of a mile, at the St. James–Vacherie sign. Continue along the riverbank to the large raised cottage now known as *Lafitte's Landing* (phone: 504-473-1232). The restaurant is housed in an Acadian residence dating from 1797, which was moved in 1978 to its present site from farther inland. The building once served as the headquarters of Viala plantation; legend has it that the notorious pirate Jean Lafitte, who plundered in southern Louisiana's waters during the early 19th century, occasionally used the site as a stopping-off point.

But from this moment on, history takes a back seat to gastronomy. *Lafitte's Landing* is where celebrated Acadian (also known outside Louisiana as "Cajun") chef John Folse first established his national reputation; he continues to supervise the menu when he's not making national TV appearances or traveling to some world capital to preach the gospel of Acadian cuisine. Risks are few when ordering here, but expect boldly seasoned butter sauces on almost everything, from the beautifully sautéed fish to the hearty venison and lamb dishes. The gumbos, crawfish dishes, and jambalaya are exceptionally good, as are the crunchy, meaty soft-shell crab and shrimp dishes. The restaurant is closed Monday evenings, and reservations are advised. Major credit cards are accepted. From *Lafitte's Landing,* return to the entrance at the service road, turn right, and drive the short distance to River Road and turn right.

Follow the River Road for a 15½-mile drive through the heart of Louisiana's sugarcane country, with tall, grassy stalks rising as far as the eye can see on both sides of the road. At a bend in the river just off the road between Lagan and Vacherie is a magnificent stand of oak trees marking the entrance to *Oak Alley* (phone: 504-265-2151; 504-523-4351 in New Orleans). The majestic setting is one of the best among the River Road plantations. While greathouses are normally built first and landscaped later, *Oak Alley*'s classically proportioned, Greek Revival mansion was designed as the finale to the vast, leafy canopy formed by two parallel rows of oaks, 14 on each side. Some of the trees are six feet or more in diameter and 300 or more years old. They are placed 40 feet apart along the grassy, 80-foot-wide path, which narrows slightly as it extends to the house. The trees, valued by the Louisiana Forestry Commission at $2.5 million, are protected during electrical storms by lightning rods. Now they partially obscure the columned façade of the house at the end of the "alley," constructed in 1837 for Jacques T. Roman III and his bride.

Originally christened "Bon Séjour" (which roughly translates as "Pleasant Sojourn"), the mansion received its present name from riverboat travelers awed by the sight of this tunnel of oaks. Spared during the Civil War, *Oak Alley* was more fortunate than its owners, whose financial problems had deteriorated to a point where the plantation was sold at auction in 1866 for $32,000. Afterward, several owners occupied the galleried mansion, its façade now painted a soft pink, and its columns a soothing cream. In 1925 the property was bought by Andrew and Josephine Stewart, who lived here for more than three decades. Today the house has a lived-in look much as it did when the state acquired it from the Stewarts in the 1970s, and tours are still conducted by the family's original service staff every day but *Thanksgiving* and *Christmas*. Admission charge.

Overnight accommodations in the property's five cottages (two small and three large) are available (nightly rates are from $85 to $115). The restaurant's menu contains typical regional fare; the gumbo of chicken and sausage is especially good.

From *Oak Alley,* continue downriver for approximately 10 miles to *Evergreen Plantation,* a private home that is still a working sugarcane plantation. From the short driveway at the fence, the excellently proportioned, Greek Revival house can be seen in all its understated splendor. Set into the sloping roof are three dormer windows, just below the crowning "widow's walk," a name recalling the women who sometimes stood watch there, scanning the river for the sight of a returning husband or other family member. *Evergreen*'s distinctive front stairway, gracefully sweeping from the ground to the second-floor verandah, is a 20th-century addition.

Continue along the River Road another 5½ miles or so back to the river's east bank via the Edgard Ferry, which departs every half hour. You'll need to make a U-turn just past the *St. John the Baptist Catholic Church* onto the paved ramp that leads up to the levee and ferry landing. The 15-minute boat ride is an enjoyable excursion on its own, often punctuated with views of cargo vessels, oil tankers, and barge-pushing tugs.

Once you disembark from the ferry, follow the landing road to the base of the levee and turn left at the stoplight. Proceed upriver along River Road for about 3 miles, to the town of Reserve and the sharp bend in the road dominated by *San Francisco Plantation* (phone: 504-535-2341). The mansion's intricate, almost lacy detail and bright colors are a stunning contrast to the clean, uncluttered design of the Greek Revival houses previously encountered. The outer color scheme is a rainbow of bright blue, peach, and pale green, made even more striking by its profusion of finials, spindles, and friezes. The flamboyant, detailed style is known as "Steamboat Gothic," a reference to both the decorative designs found on turn-of-the-century paddle wheelers and the monumentality of the basic architectural form. Fittingly, a nautical motif is repeated in a few of the three-story home's distinctive features: The two wide galleries resemble twin decks of a ship, and the peak of an observatory above the roofline looks like a crow's nest.

The interior architectural features are based on room plans of the creole houses in New Orleans, unusual for a plantation house: Rooms connect by doorways instead of the hallways found in other plantation houses, for example. Among the visual treats waiting inside are five ceiling frescoes, a floor painted to resemble a colorful rug, *faux-marbre* and *faux-bois* walls and doors (painted to resemble marble and unusually grained wood), as well as scrollwork, fluted pillars, and rococo grillwork in many of the rooms.

Edward B. Marmillion had the house built in 1856. His son, Antoine Valsin Marmillion, furnished it lavishly, then named it "Sans Fruscin," a French phrase loosely translated as "Without a Farthing" (apparently a lighthearted acknowledgment that his urge to outfit the place opulently had left him nearly penniless). With later owners, the name evolved from "Sans Fruscin" to "San Francisco." In the 1970s, Marathon Oil Company, which owns the nearby refinery, purchased the plantation and financed a painstaking restoration of the house, furnishings, and grounds. It's closed on federal holidays; there's an admission charge.

From *San Francisco Plantation,* head downriver to the traffic signal at the ferry landing. Take a left at Highway 53 and continue a little over 1½ miles to US Highway 61 (Airline Highway). At this intersection, turn right and drive just over 15 miles to the traffic signal at Ormond Boulevard. Turn right again and drive 3 miles farther, returning to River Road. Two-tenths of a mile down River Road is *Ormond Plantation,* another private residence that can be appreciated only for its exterior. There is just enough road shoulder to allow for a quick peek at the house's colonial style, typical of the era in which it was built, the late 1790s. The original owner was Pierre Trapagnier, owner of a huge tract between the Mississippi River and Lake Pontchartrain. The house's simplicity is also true to its period, with an unadorned, sloping roof leading to a railed gallery that is divided by seven narrow columns.

Another 3 miles down River Road is a plantation house that scholars claim is the oldest surviving one in the lower Mississippi Valley: *Destrehan Plantation* (phone: 504-764-9315), built in 1787 for Roger Antoine Robin de Logny by Charles Pacquet, a free black man. In return, Pacquet received "one brute Negro," one cow and her calf, 100 bushels of corn in husk, 100 bushels of rice in chaff, and $100 in cash.

The house's design conforms to the West Indies style, which has two stories topped by a highly sloped roof, brick flooring in the ground-level rooms, and seven columns across the front of the structure, dividing the railed verandah. Records show that the symmetrical wings on either side of the building were added some 20 years after the house was built. Another change was the replacement of the original wooden columns in 1840 with massive columns of cemented brick in the classic Doric style.

De Logny's daughter and son-in-law, Jean Noel Destrehan de Beaupre, inherited the home in 1802. Here they reared 14 children and entertained lavishly. Legend has it that among their guests were the pirate Jean Lafitte and the Duc d'Orléans, who in 1830 became France's King Louis-Philippe. The house contains a bathtub of solid marble, believed to have been a gift to Destrehan from Napoleon.

Destrehan de Beaupre's descendants occupied the house until 1910. It subsequently deteriorated badly until the *River Road Historical Society* took control of it in 1972 and began to restore it. It now contains a collection of European and early American antiques and paintings. The house is closed on major holidays; there's an admission charge.

To return to the city from *Destrehan Plantation,* continue downriver on River Road through St. Charles Parish and into Kenner in Jefferson Parish. Turn left on Williams Boulevard and drive 2½ miles to the intersection of Williams Boulevard and I-10. At this junction, turn right and continue about 13 miles into New Orleans.

Index

Index